**WITHDRAWN
UTSA Libraries**

Growing Apart:
The Causes and Consequences
of Global Wage Inequality

RENEWALS 458-4574
DATE DUE

Growing Apart: The Causes and Consequences of Global Wage Inequality

Edited by
Albert Fishlow   Karen Parker

COUNCIL ON FOREIGN RELATIONS PRESS
NEW YORK

The Council on Foreign Relations, Inc., a nonprofit, nonpartisan national organization and think tank founded in 1921, is dedicated to promoting understanding of international affairs through the free and civil exchange of ideas. The Council's members are dedicated to the belief that America's peace and prosperity are firmly linked to that of the world. From this flows the Council's mission: to foster America's understanding of other nations—their peoples, cultures, histories, hopes, quarrels, and ambitions—and thus to serve, our nation through study and debate, private and public.

From time to time books and reports written by members of the Council's research staff or others are published as a "Council on Foreign Relations Book."

THE COUNCIL TAKES NO INSTITUTIONAL POSITION ON POLICY ISSUES AND HAS NO AFFILIATION WITH THE U.S. GOVERNMENT. ALL STATEMENTS OF FACT AND EXPRESSIONS OF OPINION CONTAINED IN ALL ITS PUBLICATIONS ARE THE SOLE RESPONSIBILITY OF THE AUTHOR OR AUTHORS.

Council on Foreign Relations Books are distributed by Brookings Institution Press (1-800-275-1447). For further information on Council publications, please write the Council on Foreign Relations, 58 East 68th Street, New York, NY 10021, or call the Director of Communications at (212) 434-9400. Or visit our website at www.cfr.org.

Copyright © 1999 by the Council on Foreign Relations®, Inc.
All rights reserved.
Printed in the United States of America.

This book may not be reproduced, in whole or in part, in any form (beyond that copying permitted by Sections 107 and 108 of the U.S. Copyright Law and excerpts by reviewers for the public press), without written permission from the publisher. For information, write the Publications Office, Council on Foreign Relations, 58 East 68th Street, New York, NY 10021.

Library of Congress Cataloging-in-Publication Data

Growing apart: the causes and consequences of global wage inequality/edited by Albert Fishlow and Karen Parker.
    p. cm.
Includes bibliographical references and index.
ISBN 0-87609-255-5 (pbk.)
    1. Wages—United States. 2. Wages—Developing countries. 3. Income distribution—United States. 4. Income distribution—Developing countries.
5. International trade.
I. Fishlow, Albert. II. Parker, Karen
HD4975.F52   1999
331.2'1—dc21   99-32627

Contents

Foreword — vii

1. Introduction — 1
   Albert Fishlow and Karen Parker

2. The New Inequality in the United States — 21
   Richard B. Freeman

3. The Causes and Consequences of Changing Income Inequality — 67
   David G. Blanchflower and Matthew J. Slaughter

4. Foreign Direct Investment and Good Jobs/Bad Jobs: The Impact of Outward Investment and Inward Investment on Jobs and Wages — 95
   Theodore H. Moran

5. Increasing Wage Dispersion in U.S. Manufacturing: Plant-Level Evidence on the Role of Trade and Technology — 118
   J. Bradford Jensen and Kenneth R. Troske

6. The Impact of Immigration on the U.S. Labor Market — 149
   Steven A. Camarota and Mark Krikorian

7. What Can We Do? Remedies for Reducing Inequality — 192
   Lisa M. Lynch

Index — 216

About the Authors — 225

Foreword

DESPITE RECENT record growth and employment statistics in the United States, this book appears at the right time. Begun around the last presidential election, when concerns about low American wages and booming international trade first surfaced, it is being published before the next—when the United States must finally reckon with its large and growing external deficit. U.S. attitudes toward globalization will shape the policy debate going into the next election, especially if a slowdown in growth is associated with the rebalancing of global demand.

After the failed efforts by the International Monetary Fund to prevent financial crises in Russia and Brazil, discussion in the United States and abroad has arisen on Asia, the role the lending institution should be playing, and the suitability of the international financial architecture in general. Despite the remarkable resilience in the face of a large external shock, the American public remains skeptical about the trend toward globalization. One small sign of the doubt is the fate of "fast-track" authority in the Congress. It was decisively defeated in October 1998, despite support by a Democratic president and by the Republican majority. Even the North American Free Trade Agreement is now supported by less than a majority of voters, even though it reflects a vast increase in trade for the United States.

Attitudes within the other industrial countries mirror this ambivalence. Look at the recent cases of conflict that have emerged in the World Trade Organization. On one side, there is talk of a new effort to ensure free trade; on the other, bananas became a major issue between the United States and the European Union. Developing countries, afflicted by external shocks and internal financial difficulties, are more doubtful about globalization as well.

The message of this book is that there is no simple link between the forces of globalization and increased wage inequality around the world. Certainly, the global integration of goods and financial markets has facilitated the spread of skill-biased technology and increased the potential returns to investment. These influences, together with higher immigration, may have contributed to increased wage dispersion in the United States. However, it is difficult, if not impossible, to disentangle the influence on wages of expanded foreign investment and trade, more rapid technology diffusion, and changes in labor market structure.

These developments are interrelated and, indeed, mutually reinforcing aspects of a broader process of market integration and innovation.

Even if one could identify "globalization" as the cause of increased wage dispersion, the appropriate solution is not to restrict international commerce. The evidence shows that expanded trade and competition at the global level raises living standards overall, boosting productivity and creating more high-wage jobs. However, ensuring continued public support for a liberal international system will require greater efforts to help workers adapt through better education and measures to alleviate the burden of adjustment on those who cannot easily adapt.

The editors have assembled a first-rate group of authors who are uniquely qualified to address this complex, but crucial, policy challenge.

The Council on Foreign Relations, and the editors, greatly appreciate the contributions made by participants in the study group to this volume. The creative leadership of the group's co-chairs, Jessica Einhorn and John Lipsky, was especially valuable.

Lawrence J. Korb
Maurice R. Greenberg Chair, Director of Studies
Council on Foreign Relations

1

Introduction

ALBERT FISHLOW AND KAREN PARKER

IN THE FALL of 1996, the Council on Foreign Relations convened a study group to examine the nature, causes, and consequences of growing wage disparities in the United States. At that time, the presidential election season was in full swing. The issue of wage inequality had gained considerable salience as a result of presidential contender Patrick Buchanan's rhetoric against immigration, free trade, and other features of the global economy. Indeed, so central was the issue of income distribution to the 1996 campaign that the two leading parties executed a role reversal: The Republican candidates addressed the electorate's concerns about wages and job insecurity in a way they had not done for decades, while the Democratic president took a far more sanguine view of developments in the U.S. labor market.

By the time the study group completed its deliberations, fears of job losses and pay cuts had receded. As a result of a robust seven-year expansion, the U.S. economy was producing jobs at a record pace. Unemployment has fallen close to 4 percent, the lowest level in more than two decades. Labor productivity and wages began to recover from the stagnation of the 1970s and 1980s. Moreover, the incomes of the poorest Americans were growing relatively rapidly—and thus the income gap was beginning to narrow. Yet inflation remained quiescent. In that favorable environment, some participants in the study group questioned the group's guiding premise: that an increasingly unequal wage distribution risked creating a backlash against open trade and investment flows and America's traditionally liberal immigration policy.

The global economy is now emerging from a major global slowdown. The U.S. economy has emerged seemingly unscathed from the biggest global slowdown this decade. Consumption and business investment remain strong, productivity is surging and inflation remains subdued. Indeed, the most notable development of the past decade has been the striking divergence in performance between the United States and other industrial countries. Why, then, should one still be concerned about the issue of wage inequality—and its perceived link to the process of globalization?

The debate over foreign trade, investment, and wages may have been hushed for the time being, but it is certainly not over. The fact that commercial disputes are still so prevalent, despite the strong performance of the U.S. economy, should alert us to the reality that domestic support for free trade is rather shallow. If and when the U.S. economy begins to slow down—under the burden of a huge external deficit and a strong dollar—the concern over competition from abroad will intensify. Indeed, it would not be surprising if globalization were to re-emerge as a political issue in the next presidential election. Discussion has begun on the redesign of the global financial system; less attention has been devoted to the question of how open the global trading system will remain—and how committed the United States is to its maintenance.

Even prior to the global financial crisis of 1997–98, U.S. support for globalization was tenuous. The failure of President Clinton to secure "fast-track" authority to negotiate free trade agreements with Latin America revealed that the decades-old bipartisan consensus in favor of gradual trade liberalization no longer exists. The defeat of fast track was all the more striking given that the legislation was put forward by a Democratic president and supported, albeit halfheartedly, by the Republican leadership of the House and Senate. The initiative failed, moreover, at a time when the U.S. economy was experiencing its best performance in decades, when consumer confidence was at an all-time high, and when American businesses enjoyed a preeminent position in the global market. This watershed event revealed that, in the eyes of many Americans, free trade poses a threat to—rather than an opportunity for—higher U.S. living standards.

The United States is not alone in its ambivalence toward globalization. The election of left-leaning governments in France, Germany, and the United Kingdom, the uneasiness of some Europeans toward the European monetary unit (EMU), and the slow pace of deregulation and liberalization in Japan underscore the tenuous support for integration among our industrial partners. Backing for open trade and capital flows among the denizens of emerging markets—who stand to gain from increased global commerce in labor-intensive manufactures—has also become more tentative. While Asian financial leaders have endorsed the principles of free trade at meetings of the Asia-Pacific Economic Cooperation (APEC) forum—and have begun to liberalize their financial sectors to foreign investment—there also have been calls for greater regulation of global financial flows. Indeed, Malaysia's decision in 1998 to impose capital controls and the subsequent Russian default have led other countries to question the desirability of unfettered capital flows.

Even as the global economy recovers, the nation's trade deficit approaches record levels. The economy will likely slow as a result while unemployment will rise from its low levels. Although the substantial scope for countercyclical monetary and fiscal policy will cushion the slowdown, the halcyon days of falling unemployment and rising wages have passed.

America's trade deficit, which was running at an estimated $145 billion in 1997, will more than double by the end of 1999. Moreover, the sharp reduction in local currency costs that has resulted from the currency devaluations and disinflation in Asia will enhance the incentives for U.S. multinationals to relocate production facilities abroad. The competitive challenges posed by these developments are likely to reignite public concern over job insecurity and slow wage growth. America's leadership role in pressing for open global trade and financial flows could be threatened by a deterioration in domestic public support—at just the time when U.S. leadership is most needed.

The first step toward grappling seriously with these issues is to understand the causes of and remedies for increased wage inequality. This volume draws together the research of a number of distinguished scholars who have focused their attention on this problem. Chapter 2, by Richard Freeman, provides a detailed and comprehensive analysis of recent wage and employment trends in the United States. In Chapter 3, David Blanchflower and Matthew Slaughter examine the phenomenon of rising wage disparities through the lens of the contrasting experiences of other industrial countries. The next three chapters consider possible non-trade explanations for the growing U.S. wage gap. Theodore Moran, in Chapter 4, reviews the literature on foreign direct investment abroad and the wage and employment patterns of American multinationals. In Chapter 5, J. Bradford Jensen and Kenneth Troske exploit new plant-level data on U.S. manufacturing firms to evaluate alternative explanations for rising wage inequality. Steven Camarota and Mark Krikorian assess the impact of immigration on the distribution of U.S. wages in Chapter 6. Lisa Lynch concludes the volume by analyzing, in Chapter 7, the effectiveness of alternative remedies—particularly education and training—in arresting wage declines among low-income Americans.

These researchers find no "smoking gun" in the forces of globalization that can explain why low-income Americans—alone among residents of the major industrial countries—have experienced such a sharp decline in wages, even as workers at the upper end of the income ladder have enjoyed unprecedented gains. However, the chapters do suggest that technological progress, foreign direct investment, and global trade are inextricably linked and may be associated with a rising share of high-wage, skilled workers in the U.S. labor force.

It may never be possible for researchers to identify separately the precise contributions of trade, technology, foreign investment, education, and immigration to changing wage patterns. Indeed, the usefulness of such distinctions probably is limited. Each of these influences appears to be part of a more complicated process in which advanced technology, capital, and managerial know-how spread ever more rapidly throughout the global economy. It is a process that amplifies the potential market for—and thus the rewards for—skill. As a result, relatively small differences in resources or ability, augmented by good strategic planning, can lead to large disparities in outcomes for firms and their workers.

In the following sections, we identify some of the principal findings that emerged from this rich set of chapters. Each chapter addresses a complex set of issues worthy of in-depth analysis and exploration. Careful review will lead readers to appreciate the diversity of facts and interpretations that have evolved from this expanding literature. Through greater understanding of these complex issues, we may be able to identify remedies that are both feasible and appropriate to the challenges at hand. The need is urgent, for the problem of wage inequality threatens not only our economic future, but also the social compact that has helped this country to adapt and excel through a period of extraordinary change.

Principal Conclusions

Stagnant overall wages and increasing wage disparities in the United States constitute a major change in the economic landscape of the last two decades.

From 1900 to 1973, real average hourly earnings rose by about 2 percent per year in the United States. Two percent annual wage growth, when compounded, results in a doubling of income every 35 years, guaranteeing that living standards increase from one generation to the next. By contrast, between 1973 and 1995, the real median earnings of salaried men *fell* by about 0.5 percent per year. While other earnings series show continued gains in real wages in the post-1970 period, they also depict a marked slowdown from historical trends. The real earnings of women rose by 7 percent over the same period, both in absolute terms and relative to men's salaries. However, women's wages also became more unequal.

Total hourly compensation rose modestly between 1973 and 1995— by about 10 to 16 percent. However, these increases largely reflected increased nonwage compensation, especially medical benefits. As a result, the gross domestic product (GDP) per family rose by nearly a quarter, and average family incomes increased by 10 percent, between 1979 and 1994. However, the median family income remained roughly constant; most of the gains were achieved by higher-income households.

Thus it seems that most American families have had to run faster to stay in the same place: Household incomes have been sustained by extended working hours and through increased labor force participation by women. Women's labor force participation rose from about 55 percent in 1985 to 59 percent in 1995. U.S. workers spend more hours on the job than do employees in most other industrialized countries— five to ten full weeks more than their counterparts in Europe.

U.S. families have saved less and borrowed more in order to preserve their living standards. Contrary to popular perception, much of this borrowing has been used to finance consumption of nonessentials, such as travel and entertainment. Installment debt has grown at a rapid pace and is now at record levels. While some of the increase may reflect greater reliance on credit cards for transactions, the steady rise in household debt service, despite lower interest rates, indicates that real borrowing has grown. Household net worth nevertheless has reached record levels, as broader participation in the equity markets and rising stock prices have boosted wealth. However, aggregate measures of household wealth obscure two divergent trends: Equity market participation and the associated income gains remain highly skewed toward higher-income households, while middle- to lower-income families carry a substantial amount of debt. Measures of living standards that rely on consumption data may be misleading, to the extent that the rise in consumer spending—which has now driven the saving rate below zero—is unsustainable.

According to research by Jeffrey Williamson, the surge in wage inequality over the past two decades is comparable to that which occurred in the United States in the early years of this century.[1] However, in that earlier period, average wages continued to rise, so that few workers experienced an absolute decline in their incomes. Nevertheless, the decades that followed saw a surge in isolationist and protectionist sentiment. America's liberal immigration policy was reversed in the 1920s, and the imposition of high tariff barriers and successive rounds of competitive devaluation contributed to a global depression.

There have been growing wage disparities among and within all classes of workers.

Men in the top 10 percent of the wage distribution received 4.75 times the pay of those in the bottom 10 percent in 1995, a 20 percent increase in the multiple since 1979. For women, the 90/10 pay gap increased by 47 percent.

Much of the rise in inequality has resulted from declining wages of low-income workers. While the incomes of those in the top 20 percent of the wage distribution remained broadly stable between 1979 and 1995, workers in the lowest quintile suffered a marked fall in earnings. Regardless of which price deflator is used, the real earnings of low-wage workers fell sharply. Wage declines were largest for male high school dropouts, who suffered a 20 percent decline in their real earnings between 1979 and 1993. Falling wages are not confined to a small group of workers. Even experienced, college-educated men suffered a decline in earnings over this period.

Compensation in the form of benefits also has become more unequal. Whereas in 1979, 57 percent of high school graduates and 39 percent of high school dropouts received employer-provided pensions, in 1993 these figures had fallen to 45 and 21 percent, respectively. By contrast, there was little change in pension provision for college graduates. The distribution of medical benefits has followed a similar pattern, as Freeman points out in Chapter 2.

About half of the increase in inequality can be accounted for by differences in skills, as indicated by education, age, and work experience. Returns to schooling increased sharply after 1979 and have now reached a postwar high. As the study by Jensen and Troske in Chapter 5 reveals, inequality rises during recessionary periods, in which the ratio of skilled to unskilled workers in the labor force ratchets upward. This pattern mirrors that of European unemployment, which rises during recessions and diminishes only modestly during expansions.

Falling relative wages for less skilled workers has not led to higher participation rates for these Americans. On the contrary, the rise in the skill premium has been accompanied by a *declining* share of less skilled workers in the labor force—in all occupations. From the 1970s through the 1990s, annual hours worked for men in the bottom deciles of the pay distribution fell while those in the upper deciles rose or were steady. Thus, inequality in hours worked increased along with inequality in hourly pay, producing even greater income disparities.

More than half of the growth in inequality remains unexplained. Even among workers with observationally equivalent skills, wage disparities have risen. For example, among college graduates, the wage ratio between the 90th and 10th percentiles rose by 22 percent between 1979 and 1997.

The distribution of family income has followed that of wages. The top 20 percent of families obtained virtually all of the gain in income over the past 20 years, and within that group most of the gains went to the top 5 percent. As it turns out, the wives of high-income men tend to be high earners themselves.

There is no evidence that the growing disparity of wages has been offset by increased labor mobility or that mobility is much higher in the United States than in Europe. On the contrary, the wage gains that used to accrue from job experience have diminished over the past 15 years. Among recent immigrants, mobility is likely to be an even greater problem, as 40 percent are high school dropouts. (Twenty-nine percent of dropouts are immigrants.)

Moreover, poverty and poor educational training seem to be becoming more entrenched in urban areas. Research by Chris Mayer has documented that the share of the poor living in census tracts with a poverty rate of more than 40 percent increased from 16 to 28 percent, while the share living in tracts with poverty exceeding 20 percent rose from 55 to 69 percent.[2] This greater concentration of poverty is likely to hamper individuals' access to good primary and secondary schools and the financial support to pursue higher education.

Despite the general dynamism of the U.S. labor market, there are some signs that structural employment has increased. As Lynch indicates in Chapter 7, the duration of unemployment has increased, and the share of unemployed workers who are permanently displaced in recent years is high in comparison to similar points in earlier business cycles. Job losses due to the abolition of positions or shifts have increased in recent years, largely among older, white-collar, and more educated workers. The costs of job loss are large and enduring; recent studies suggest that, even six years after job displacement, earnings remain about 9 percent lower than before.

Slow aggregate wage growth and rising income disparities have been most pronounced in the United States.

Inequality rose to some degree in most of the advanced market economies in the 1980s and 1990s. However, the widening in the wage distribution has been most pronounced in the United States (which had the largest wage disparities to start with), began the earliest, and has continued into the 1990s, as Blanchflower and Slaughter demonstrate in Chapter 3.

Some European countries have experienced rising unemployment rather than higher wage inequality. However, this pattern is not uniform. The United Kingdom, Canada, and New Zealand faced both higher earnings inequality and rising unemployment. On the other hand, the Netherlands, Japan, Austria, and Sweden experienced low or declining unemployment and only a small rise in earnings inequality. France and Germany have seen substantially higher unemployment but little change in earnings inequality.

Overall wage growth in the United States has been slower than in other countries. In the 1980s average real hourly compensation of blue-collar manufacturing workers rose in the United Kingdom (by 2.6 percent), Japan (by 1.6 percent), France (by 0.9 percent), and Germany (by 1.3 percent). In contrast, pay for these workers fell by 12 percent in the United States. As a result, low-paid workers in America earn less than their counterparts abroad, even though average incomes in the United States are significantly higher. Low-paid German workers earn roughly twice as much as low-paid Americans. Even in the United Kingdom, whose GDP per capita is two-thirds that of the United States, low-income workers earned 32 percent more than their American counterparts in 1995. Overall, one-third of American workers earn less in purchasing-power-parity terms than comparable workers overseas. Adjusted for hours worked, the disparities are even greater.

On the other hand, the U.S. economy has created many more jobs than European countries. In 1974 the ratio of employed workers to the population aged 15 to 64 was the same in the United States and Europe (about 65 percent). By 1995 the ratio stood at 73.5 percent in the United States and 60 percent in Europe. However, U.S. job growth has been concentrated in high-wage and low-wage occupations, making it harder for American workers to move up the income scale.

This rise in U.S. wage disparities coincides with "globalization" of the American economy, which, most economists agree, has been beneficial for U.S. living standards.

The labor market trends just described have coincided with a rapid expansion in global trade, especially trade in manufactures between industrial and developing nations. As a share of industrial country output, imports of manufactured goods from developing countries rose fivefold in the two decades after 1970.

Labor and capital flow increasingly across national borders. U.S. foreign direct investment and portfolio capital flows have surged over the past two decades, with a growing share directed toward emerging markets. At the same time, immigrant inflows into the United States have reached record levels. An estimated 1.2 million immigrants (about 900,000 legal and 300,000 illegal) entered the United States in 1996. As a result, the foreign-born share of the American population roughly doubled between 1970 and 1997 to about 10 percent.

Not surprisingly, the global integration of goods, capital, and labor markets has been implicated in the slow wage gains and rising inequality of the past two decades. Some have called for renewed protection of American industry, sometimes in the guise of labor and environmental standards. However, most economists still emphasize the overall benefits of economic integration.

And, in fact, the benefits are many. U.S. consumers have enjoyed lower-cost imported goods. Television sets, microwaves, automobiles, and computers have become less expensive and more reliable. Were it not for job creation in the high-wage export and technology sectors, the slowdown in U.S. productivity and earnings would likely have been greater. The evidence suggests that foreign direct investment has contributed to the growth of U.S. exports, which are produced with more advanced technologies by higher-skill, better-paid workers. To the extent that trade augments competition and expands potential markets, productivity is enhanced, although economists debate the degree of change.

The availability of low-wage (and often skilled) immigrant labor has reduced the cost of doing business in the United States, while increased competition has contributed to the process of disinflation. It is no accident that the U.S. economy is enjoying an unprecedented combination of low inflation, low unemployment, and rapid productivity growth. Immigration has also lengthened the age profile of the American labor force and may ease the pressures on the Social Security system in future years. For these and other reasons, the U.S. performance is the envy of many industrial countries.

There is less consensus among economists about the distributional impact of globalization. However, few see a "smoking gun" in trade with developing countries.

Much of the research on the rise in wage inequality has focused on the "demand side" of the labor market. Since both employment and the relative wages of less skilled workers have fallen since 1980, economists have concluded that the demand for their services has declined. Among the demand-side explanations, attention has been focused on the effects of foreign trade, investment (including outsourcing of production), and technological progress.

According to classical trade models, expanded commerce with low-wage countries ought to augment wage disparities since trade rewards those factors of production that a country has in abundance. Generally speaking, the relative wages of less skilled workers in poorer countries are expected to rise, as are the wages of skilled workers in the more advanced countries. Conversely, the rate of return to capital in low-income countries should fall (relative to labor), whereas wealthier nations should experience a rise in capital income.

The debate over globalization and its impact on wage inequality has received considerable attention—despite the limited empirical evidence in support of a link—because theory suggests there should be a connection. However, if there is a link, it is considerably more complicated than conventional models would suggest.

One strand of research analyzes the impact of trade on the employment of less skilled workers by measuring the quantity of labor that is displaced. This research indicates that commerce with developing countries can account for no more than 10 to 20 percent of the rise in wage inequality in the United States during the 1980s. However, these models are poorly specified, in that the volume of trade is determined endogenously and depends on many factors. In early studies researchers identified the growing U.S. trade deficit as a key contributor to rising wage disparities, even though the deficit primarily reflected macroeconomic phenomena (the low U.S. saving rate and strong dollar) rather than microeconomic factors such as the distribution of skilled labor and/or changes in labor institutions. Wage inequality continued to rise in the late 1980s, even as the deficit narrowed. As economist Paul Krugman has asserted, the amount of imports from developing countries is simply too small to have induced the sizable wage disparities now evident in the United States.[3]

More recent research recognizes that it is the potential rather than the actual supply of foreign goods that influences prices of traded products and the wages earned by their producers. The threat of competition from abroad—either through imports or outsourcing of production—may exert a strong influence on prices and wages. To the extent that such pressures influence relative wages, a corresponding change in the relative prices of goods produced with more skilled labor vis-à-vis those produced with less skilled labor would be expected.

This body of research, which is surveyed in Chapter 3, finds trade to have little or no impact on relative wages—even controlling for the impact of technological improvements on the prices of some goods, such as computers.

In principle, price-based studies can account for the "threat effect" of foreign competition—even when no trade actually occurs—on wages in the industries exposed to it. However, their accuracy is dependent on the proper specification of the sectors exposed to import competition; the import penetration ratio may not be the best measure of such competition. These studies also suffer from compositional and quality biases in the relative price indices as well as nontrade influences on prices that may not be adequately controlled for. Both the price- and quantity-based studies have shortcomings, but they reach the same conclusion: Trade with developing countries has had only a limited impact on the relative wages of U.S. workers.

Closely related to foreign trade is foreign direct investment (FDI) abroad. There are two potential threats to low-skilled U.S. workers from such investment: the shifting of manufacturing jobs overseas via outsourcing and the "hoarding" of high-wage jobs in the home countries of offshore multinationals that invest in the United States. Research on these influences, which is thoughtfully summarized in Chapter 4, suggests that FDI abroad by U.S. multinationals actually *enhances* U.S. exports, thus contributing to the creation of higher-wage jobs in this country.

As Chapter 4 points out, jobs in export industries pay 13 to 15 percent more than those in nonexporting firms, provide 11 percent higher benefits, experience 20 percent faster job growth, and are 9 percent less likely to go out of business. Andrew Bernard and Brad Jensen have confirmed that when other plant characteristics that are correlated with wages (e.g., size, capital intensity, and productivity) are controlled for, exporting is associated with higher wages for both production and nonproduction workers.[4] Other research has shown that outsourcing leads to increased demand for skilled workers but *not* higher relative wages for them.

There is little evidence that FDI, by itself, triggers increased imports of goods from emerging markets that compete with those produced by less skilled U.S. workers. However, the threat to relocate production abroad, regardless of whether the firm faces competitive pressures to do so, can be used to negotiate smaller wage increases. As Dani Rodrik points out in his book, *Has Globalization Gone Too Far?*, the elasticity of demand for labor would tend to rise as a result of such threats as well as the volatility of earnings and the incidence of nonwage costs.[5] While such influences are difficult to measure, research by Slaughter and others suggests that the elasticity of labor demand is higher in industries where there is greater international competition.[6] Moreover, trade with other industrial countries can be just as potent in restraining wages as trade with emerging markets.

The principal alternative explanation for the rise in demand for skilled labor is skill-biased technology. However, the technology story, by itself, is not persuasive.

For many economists, the most plausible explanation for rising wage inequality is technological progress that demands more skilled workers. Typically, the impact of technology is measured as the residual—that which cannot be explained by other factors. Research by Alan Krueger and others has attempted to identify a direct link between technological progress and relative wages.[7] These studies have found that the demand for skilled workers has grown more rapidly in industries that make larger capital investments, undertake greater research and development expenditures, and use more business equipment, such as computers. However, the direction of causality is not clear: The presence of skilled labor may facilitate the adoption of more advanced technology.

Another strand of research attempts to differentiate the impact of technology-related changes in the labor market from those induced by shifts in product demand by decomposing changes in the ratio of production to nonproduction workers (and their relative earnings) into those that occur *between* and *within* industries. Technological change is thought to change the relative proportions of skilled and unskilled workers within a given industry or firm. On the other hand, if trade is the cause of increased wage dispersion, it is assumed that the reallocation of labor should occur mainly between industries (or firms); those industries that use relatively more unskilled labor would shrink in response to import competition. In an influential 1994 paper, Eli Berman, John Bound, and Zvi Griliches found that most of the increased demand for skilled workers occurred within industries, which they interpreted as evidence in favor of a technology-based explanation for rising skill premiums in the U.S. labor market.[8]

The pervasive shift toward more skilled labor across U.S. industries—and in many other industrial and developing countries—suggests to many economists that a broad process of technological innovation is under way.[9] If globalization were behind the decline in wages of less skilled workers, some sectors (or industries, or countries) might be expected to use their services more intensively. However, this appears not to be the case.

As Chapter 5 demonstrates, aggregate studies miss much of the story, since most of the increase in wage dispersion has occurred within industries. Even among plants in the same detailed industry classification, there is tremendous heterogeneity along a number of dimensions, such as the rate of technology adoption, foreign investment, export performance, productivity, and employment patterns. Research by John Haltiwanger has shown that industry attributes at the four-digit Standard Industrial Classification (SIC) level can account for less than 10 percent of the variation over time in the growth of employment, output, total factor productivity, and investment.[10]

Plant-level studies find that most of the increase in the demand for skilled labor has occurred within plants in the same industry. However, no single variable (technology-related or otherwise) can account for much of this trend, nor its cyclical component. Moreover, between-plant changes in the relative wages of skilled workers have been the primary cause of the workers' increased earnings. The reallocation of labor among plants with different characteristics is an important source of aggregate changes in relative wages. Most of the increase in wage inequality appears to be the result of growing disparities among firms.

Plants that hire more skilled workers are likely to see a rise in productivity and average wages, with little or no shift in relative earnings if differently skilled workers play complementary roles. On the other hand, the closure of less productive plants that employ more unskilled labor would result in a fall in their relative earnings. It is not clear whether these within- and between-plant changes in employment and wages should be attributed to trade, technology, or both.

In Chapter 5, Jensen and Troske note that, even controlling for other attributes, there is a positive correlation between export performance and the use of advanced technology.[11] However, the causal mechanism is not defined. It may be that the use of advanced technology or the decision to export leads firms to use more capital, employ more skilled workers, and pay higher wages. Alternatively, large capital-intensive firms may be more likely to adopt advanced technologies or to export as a result of economies of scale or other factors.

If technology is the main reason relative wages have risen so sharply in the United States, it is a puzzle why productivity has not grown more rapidly. Nor is it obvious that technology's impact should have been greater in the 1980s than in the 1970s, and in the United States rather than in other industrialized countries.

Labor institutions have also influenced the extent and pattern of inequality.

All major industrial countries have experienced large shifts in the industrial and occupational structure toward sectors and jobs that use a greater proportion of skilled workers. Moreover, the share of manufacturing in total employment has declined everywhere but in Japan. There is no evidence that the expansion of trade or technological progress occurred more slowly in other countries than in the United States.

Even so, the United States experienced a much sharper, and earlier, rise in inequality. America also has faced a larger increase in inequality among groups of workers with similar skills. These contrasting experiences reflect differences in the supply of labor across countries as well as changes in labor institutions.

As Chapter 3 points out, the distribution of wages in countries with strong labor institutions is almost always more compressed than elsewhere. Unions tend to reduce inequality by standardizing pay rates among workers within a given establishment or across establishments. The threat of unionization also forces nonunion employers to raise pay and/or benefits in order to keep unions out. The swift decline in union strength in the United States, along with the fall in the real minimum wage, is correlated with the early and sharp widening of the U.S. wage gap. Union density has declined dramatically in this country since 1970—from about 27 percent of the labor force to 15 percent at present. America's unionization rate is the lowest in the world. (The figure for France, although lower, is not comparable.)[12] After 1990 union density also fell markedly in the United Kingdom, a country that has seen a sharp increase in wage inequality as well.

Minimum wages also compress the pay structure, at least for those who are employed. The sharp fall in the real U.S. minimum wage over the past two decades and the weakening of wage councils in the United Kingdom fit the pattern of rising wage inequality in these two countries. In contrast, increases in France's minimum wage appear to have prevented an erosion in real wages at the low end of the pay scale.

There appears to be a trade-off between wage inequality and unemployment. However, the pattern is not clear-cut. Some countries (the Netherlands, Austria, Japan, and Sweden) enjoy both low unemployment and moderate wage dispersion, while others (Australia, Canada, the United Kingdom, and New Zealand) suffer from high unemployment and large earnings disparities. Most Europeans enjoy more generous social benefits than do Americans, mitigating the impact of unemployment on household income and the social stigma associated with joblessness. To discern the full impact of prolonged unemployment, all sources of income and the lifetime earnings profile should be examined.

Labor institutions clearly matter, but it is not obvious why the regulations protecting workers have declined in many countries. Weakening labor standards may be a result of increased global competition. However, if global trade and investment played a role in the demise of labor institutions, their impact should be evident from the price and wage studies just cited.

Trade, foreign investment, and technology have not, by themselves, caused the dramatic widening of the U.S. wage structure. However, these may be mutually reinforcing elements of a broader process of market integration that has increased the demand for skilled workers.

Limitations in data, interpretation, and testing have prevented the identification of individual causes of rising wage inequalities. Measuring skills, the impact of trade, and technological progress is quite difficult, as is devising price indices that are free of compositional and quality biases. The large increase in residual inequality should make people wary of skill-based explanations for growing wage disparities. Ultimately it may prove impossible to disentangle the various influences as they are closely related and, often, mutually reinforcing.

As Chapter 4 and 5 demonstrate, a firm's size, participation in export markets, foreign direct investment abroad, and technological progress go hand in hand. Those firms that pay the highest wages and hire relatively more white-collar workers are those that export, invest overseas, employ the latest technologies, and are large.

As Adrian Wood has suggested, "defensive innovation" may be a response to competition in export and import markets.[13] Global trade may facilitate the transfer of skill-biased technologies among industrial countries and toward emerging markets, which would account for the increased demand for skilled labor everywhere. The expansion of markets increases the incentives for innovation and rewards small (perhaps unmeasureable) differences in skill with large payoffs. The attributes of workers may matter less than the productivity of the industries or firms in which they work. Strategic decisions by firms are extremely important for worker outcomes, particularly when there is limited mobility of labor across industries.

Similarly, foreign investment may be "defensive" in character. If so, trade must be cited as a fundamental cause of wage disparity, insofar as it creates competitive pressures and facilitates the segmentation of the production process. Then, the activities of multinational corporations do no more than hasten the inevitable.

Changes in labor institutions may be a consequence of expanded trade and foreign investment rather than an independent cause of increased wage disparities. Indeed, labor institutions may change in response to wage inequality, insofar as the interests of workers would tend to diverge.

As these examples suggest, it is time for a broader conceptualization of the process of globalization and how it can affect the demand for labor. The conventional framework of analysis is too narrow, resting as it does on the restrictive assumptions of perfect competition, diversified product markets, and intersectoral factor mobility. Models that incorporate threat effects, strategic advantage, increasing returns to scale, and dynamic technological progress are better suited to explaining the phenomenon of rising wage inequality in the current global environment.

Even if these influences were conceptually separable, it would be a challenge to devise tests that could accurately distinguish between them, as the studies in this volume demonstrate.

Changes in the relative supply of less skilled workers as a result of immigration also may have played a contributing role in the rise in wage inequality.

The character of U.S. immigration has changed over the past two decades, as Chapter 6 points out. The educational attainment of newly arrived legal immigrants has diminished over time; among those who immigrated in the 1990s, 39 percent are high school dropouts. (Immigrants make up 11 percent of the workforce and 29 percent of those without a high school diploma.) In contrast, 34 percent of 1980s arrivals and 26 percent of those who arrived before 1980 were dropouts. The educational achievement of illegal immigrants may be even lower; among those who were granted amnesty under the 1986 Immigration Reform and Control Act, 74 percent lacked a high school diploma.

As a result of their more limited skills, recent immigrants' earnings have fallen farther behind those of their native counterparts. Whereas in 1970 the average annual earnings of recent male immigrants was 81 percent that of natives, by 1990 that figure had declined to 65 percent.

Lower earnings of less skilled immigrants have contributed to a widening of the wage distribution in some parts of the country. Immigration has not only skewed the distribution of income by increasing the number of workers in the lowest-paying jobs. It appears that immigrants also have depressed the earnings of low-skilled native workers. Chapter 6 estimates that the wages of less skilled workers were reduced by an estimated 0.7 percent for every 1 percent increase in the immigrant composition of a given occupation. Since low-skilled native workers are employed in occupations whose immigrant ratio averaged 15 percent, these workers suffered an estimated 10.5 percent drop in wages relative to others with the same individual and occupational attributes.[14]

George Borjas, Richard Freeman, and Lawrence Katz also have found that post-1979 immigration can explain between 27 and 55 percent of the decline in relative wages of high school dropouts.[16] However, no more than 10 percent of the fall in wages of high school graduates relative to college graduates could be attributed to immigration.

The American educational system, which has failed to meet the demand for skilled workers, also must bear some of the responsibility for the decline in relative wages.

Variations in skills are considerably less in other countries than in the United States, as noted in Chapter 7. Moreover, international variation in skills has tended to match changes in wage inequality from 1979 to 1990. In Germany and other countries, there are high minimum educational standards and clear incentives for students to do well in school—even for students who have no plans to attend college. Apprenticeship training is available for those who do not go on to university, leading to higher skill attainment among those in the bottom half of the ability distribution.

Most puzzling of all is why parents and students have not responded to the rise in skill premiums by attaining more education. As noted earlier, the wage gap between more and less skilled workers has nearly doubled over the past 15 years, while college enrollments have fallen. Part of the problem may be the rising cost of tuition; the General Accounting Office (GAO) estimates that tuition at four-year public colleges and universities has risen three times faster than median household income between 1980 and 1995. Student aid has not kept pace with tuition levels, so families are relying more on loans and personal finances to attend college. Access to educational financing may be limited for students from poor families, particularly in urban areas, making inequality ever more entrenched.

In the face of rising costs and limited financing, many students are forced to delay entry into college, temporarily suspend training, or drop out of school despite the high wage premium.

On-the-job training contributes to significantly higher business productivity, according to research surveyed in Chapter 7. Yet American businesses underinvest in training, due to high turnover rates and the large number of small firms in this country. (The cost of training, including downtime, is high.) Japan and Germany seem to have overcome these challenges through programs that facilitate joint investment in on-the-job training, certification of employer-provided skills acquisition, employment guarantees for workers, and extensive government financial support.

Funding for and the quality of education at the primary and secondary grades in the United States also have diminished. The portion of the federal budget allocated to education and training has fallen sharply over the past 20 years. Per capita spending on education and training (as a share of the population aged 5 to 24) has declined from over $4,700 in the 1970s to less than $3,500 at present, in inflation-adjusted terms. Of the more than $500 billion currently spent on education by federal, state, and local governments, some $211 billion is allocated to higher education (for which students can obtain their own funding), leaving relatively little money for publicly financed primary and secondary education.

The time to implement remedies is now.

Identifying precisely the causes of rising wage inequality is desirable but not essential to devising appropriate remedies. There are three possible approaches to the problem: (1) attempt to reverse the underlying causes of the wage gap; (2) boost workers' skills; and (3) implement ameliorative programs for those who cannot easily adjust. The ideal remedies are neutral with respect to productivity or are growth-enhancing (i.e., skills training that raises the productivity of less skilled labor).

Regardless of the evidence, in many people's minds globalization will remain inextricably linked to the problem of job insecurity and falling wages. Public concerns must be addressed somehow, or the benefits of freer international trade and financial flows will be lost as a consequence of poorly conceived remedies. There is clear evidence that trade, technology, and foreign direct investment raise overall wages, not just those of skilled workers. Rather than restrict incentives for productivity-enhancing external commerce, government policy should seek to preserve and expand access to overseas markets through reciprocal reductions in tariff and nontariff barriers. Labor standards can be incorporated into trade agreements, provided these do not merely serve as obstacles to further progress. Regional initiatives to liberalize trade may be an effective interim strategy toward a more liberal and equitable global trading system.

To ease the adjustment process, policymakers might consider taking steps to improve the skills profiles of new immigrants through skills-based admission criteria. Attention needs to be given to improving the quality of education in the United States, especially at the precollegiate level. The establishment of high minimum educational standards, augmented funding for primary and secondary education, increased opportunities for self-financing of higher education, and the creation of effective worker retraining and adjustment programs should be high on the agenda.

Some training programs have a proven track record. The Job Training Partnership Act (JTPA) programs for disadvantaged adults; residential programs for at-risk youths; the San Jose Center for Employment and Training; some welfare-to-work programs; and job search assistance all show returns of 40 percent or more for each dollar spent. Small and medium-size employers could be given tax credits for formal training programs and/or allowed to treat training expenditures as investments for tax and accounting purposes. Finally, it would be wise to improve the unemployment insurance system, which has been geared toward temporary job losses, not permanent job shifts and retraining needs.

For those who are too old or otherwise unable to adjust through retraining efforts, steps must be taken to ameliorate the burden of adjustment via transfer programs such as the earned-income tax credit, trade adjustment assistance, food stamps, and the like.

Can we afford it? Some estimates of the cost of ameliorating wage inequality range as high as $400 billion. However, not all of this money would need to be spent by the government, or in a single year. A well-targeted 10 percent annual increase in spending on education and training could go a long way toward raising the earnings of those with a high school education or less. These costs should be weighed against the risks to the economy and society of a break in the social compact that has yielded decades of unprecedented prosperity. If appropriate remedies to rising wage disparities are not identified and implemented, the backlash against globalization now spreading around the world will find willing supporters in the United States.

Notes

1. Jeffrey G. Williamson, *Industrialization, Inequality and Economic Growth* (Brookfield, Vt.: Edward Elgar, 1997).
2. Chris Mayer, "Does Location Matter?" *New England Economic Review*, Special issue (May/June 1996): 26–40.
3. Paul Krugman, "Growing World Trade: Causes and Consequences," *Brookings Papers on Economic Activity* no. 1 (1995).
4. Andrew B. Bernard and J. Bradford Jensen, "Exporters, Skill Upgrading, and the Wage Gap," *Journal of International Economics* 42 (February 1997): 3–31.
5. Dani Rodrik, ed., *Has Globalization Gone Too Far?* (Washington, D.C.: Institute for International Economics, 1997).

6. Matthew Slaughter, "International Trade and Labor-Demand Elasticities," *National Bureau of Economic Research Working Paper* no. 6262 (November 1997).

7. See for example, Alan A. Krueger, "How Computers Have Changed the Wage Structure: Evidence from Microdata, 1984–1989," *Quarterly Journal of Economics* 108, no. 1 (February 1993): 33–60.

8. Eli Berman, John Bound, and Zvi Griliches, "Changes in the Demand for Skilled Labor within U.S. Manufacturing: Evidence from the Annual Survey of Manufactures," *Quarterly Journal of Economics* 109, no. 2 (May 1994): 367–97.

9. For example, Robert Lawrence and Slaughter find that the ratio of (higher paid) non-production to production workers tended to increase both in the industrial country parent company and in its developing country affiliate. See "International Trade and American Wages in the 1980s: Giant Sucking Sound or Small Hiccup?" in Martin Neil Baily and Clifford Winston (eds.), *Brookings Papers on Economic Activity: Microeconomics* 2 (1993): 161–211.

10. John Haltiwanger, "Measuring and Analyzing Aggregate Fluctuations: The Importance of Building from Microeconomic Evidence," *Federal Reserve Bank of St. Louis Review* (May/June 1997): 57–78.

11. These controls are important, since large plants are more likely to use advanced technologies, to export, to be relatively capital intensive, to be more productive, and to pay higher wages.

12. *World Labor Report 1997–98* (Geneva: International Labour Organization, 1998), table 1.2.

13. Adrian Wood, "How Trade Hurt Unskilled Workers," *Journal of Economic Perspectives* 9, no. 3 (Summer 1995): 57–80.

14. The authors employed a number of tests to establish that immigrants are not simply concentrated in the lowest-paying jobs.

15. George Borjas, Richard Freeman, and Lawrence Katz, "Searching for the Effect of Immigration on the Labor Market," *National Bureau of Economic Research Working Paper* no. 5454 (February 1996).

2

The New Inequality in the United States

RICHARD B. FREEMAN

THE UNITED STATES currently is faced with a degree of economic inequality that exceeds anything we have seen since the Great Depression. From the 1980s, if not earlier, through the mid-1990s, inequality rose to levels that have made even conservative analysts, business gurus, and billionaires take notice.[1] Despite a period of substantial economic growth—between 1983 and 1995 gross domestic product (GDP) grew by 41 percent in real terms, or by some $1,100 per employee—and an employment record that was the envy of the world (24 million extra jobs were created over the same period), normal working Americans have not done well in the job market. On average, real earnings have stagnated for the bulk of the workforce. Among fully employed workers on the bottom rungs of the earnings distribution, real earnings fell while earnings rose for the most highly paid workers in the economy.

This chapter examines the facts behind the "new inequality," considers their consequences for the nation, and concludes with suggestions as to how the United States might reverse the new inequality if it so desires.

The chapter makes four basic points:

First, the distribution of earnings in the United States has widened greatly, dividing the society into an increasingly well-off group of high-wage, high-skilled workers and an increasingly impoverished group of low-paid, less skilled workers. Underlying the wider distribution have been deteriorating real earnings and benefits for lower-paid workers and stagnating earnings for average workers.

Second, inequality in the United States exceeds that in other advanced countries, with lower-paid Americans earning less (in purchasing power parity units) than lower-paid workers in those peer countries. In addition, Americans work more to maintain a good standard of living than workers in other advanced countries.

Third, while it is difficult to determine the relative contribution of various proposed causes for the new inequality, income differences are unlikely to diminish rapidly in the foreseeable future. Thus, the country must face the social consequences of labor market and family income inequality unprecedented since the Great Depression.

Finally, policies to ameliorate, if not reverse, the rise in inequality are likely to be expensive and possibly socially divisive. The new inequality requires hard choices about the benefits and costs of policies designed to raise the real earnings of those on the bottom rungs of our income distribution at the expense of those who are highly paid.

Documenting the New Inequality

For most of U.S. economic history, the "rising tide" of economic growth raised all boats. The real earnings of low-skill workers increased, in many periods more rapidly than those of skilled workers, reducing wage differentials and overall income inequality. Economic growth benefited all and reduced inequality, without any need for special redistributive policies. The new inequality, however, breaks sharply with this pattern. The rising tide did not raise the incomes of low-paid workers as well as those of high-paid ones. The job market for low- and medium-skill workers deteriorated while that for higher-skilled workers improved. No one expected these changes; nor is anyone certain for how long they will persist. But there is no debate over what happened.

THE DISTRIBUTION OF EARNINGS HAS WIDENED

The distribution of earnings measures the wages, salaries, and self-employment income of all workers in the economy, organized from the highest paid to the lowest paid. It is normally represented by a histogram that shows the proportion of workers paid different amounts. Since a distribution contains many numbers, analysts use various statistics to summarize it and to show how it changes over time.

One commonly used summary statistic is the ratio of the earnings of persons in the top percentiles of the distribution—for instance, the upper 10 percent or the upper 20 percent—to the earnings of persons in lower percentiles—for instance, the median (50th percentile) or the bottom 10th or 20th percentile. When earnings in the top percentiles rise more rapidly than earnings in the lower percentiles, the distribution of earnings widens. The first two lines in Table 2–1 record the change in the earnings of men and women workers in the upper and lower quintiles of the earnings distribution from 1979 to 1995. The upper quintile of men had roughly stable earnings over this period, while the lower quintile had a sizable drop in real earnings. The upper quintile of women had sizable gains in earnings while the lower quintile had an 8 percent loss in real earnings. The result of these changes is an increase in the pay differential between higher- and lower-earning workers in the distribution.

Any rise in inequality has two components: an increase in "skill premium," defined as pay differentials between workers with different levels of skill, usually measured by education, experience, or occupation; and an increase in earnings inequality among workers with the same measured skills. The remaining lines in Table 2–1 record percentage changes in the earnings of more and less skilled workers, defined by education, occupation, and experience. In each case, the more skilled groups obtained larger gains in earnings than the less skilled ones, most of whom suffered declines in their real earnings from 1979 to 1995.

The change in earnings by education group brought the premium to schooling to an all-time post–World War II high. The change in earnings by age occurred despite a drop in the relative number of young workers,

Table 2–1   Percentage Changes in Earnings, by Skill Group, 1979–1995

	Men (%)	Women (%)
Top quintile workers	1%	21%
Bottom quintile workers	–17	–8
College graduates	1	20
High school graduates	–17	–4
Less than high school graduates	–27	–11
Professionals	6	18
Administrative support (clericals)	–14	2
Machine operators	–16	–9
Laborers	–21	n.a.
Starting high school graduates	–27	–19
Experienced high school graduates	–21	–4
Starting college graduates	–11	3
Experienced college graduates	–3	21

Note: Starting workers have 1 to 5 years of experience; experienced workers have 16 to 22 years of experience.
Source: Calculated from Lawrence Mishel, Aaron Bernstein, and John Schmidt, *The State of Working America, 1996–1997* (Washington, D.C.: Economic Policy Institute, 1997), tables 3.5, 3.7, 3.8, 3.19, 3.20, and 3.22.

which should have improved the relative pay of the young but did not do so. Among occupations, the increased pay of chief executive officers and sports figures receives national attention, but the concentration of gains in high-paying occupations is more general: Wages increase more in professional, managerial, and other white-collar skilled occupations than in blue-collar and service sector occupations. As a result, accruing white-collar labor market skills pays more now than in the past.

The earnings distribution widened not only among skill groups but within skill groups as well. Among workers with the same years of schooling or in the same occupation, higher-paid workers had larger increases in earnings than lower-paid ones. For instance, in 1979 the ratio of the earnings of the top decile of college graduates to that of the lowest decile of college graduates was 3.46 whereas in 1995 the ratio was 4.22—a 22 percent increase.[2] I have examined the distribution of earnings in separate occupations and found that inequality rose in the vast majority.[3] Among carpenters, engineers, and clerks, for example, there is a greater gap in pay between the highly paid and the lower paid now than in the past. Since much of the difference in pay among employees occurs within measured groups, moreover, even if the differences between groups—such as the educational or age premium—fell to their 1979 level, overall pay inequality would still be much higher than in earlier years.

Another way to represent the changing distribution of earnings is in terms of the proportion of workers paid in specified earnings bands. We can, for instance, estimate the proportion of workers paid a given percent less or more than the average and the proportion between these two figures. When the earnings distribution widens, the proportion in the middle group necessarily falls. Whether this shows up largely as an increase in the proportion of people with high earnings or as an increase in the proportion of those with low earnings depends on the particular metric used. Among men, when proportions are computed around the *median*, the widening takes the form of an increase in the proportion of those with high earnings; if proportions of workers are computed around the *mean*, the widening takes more the form of an increase in the proportion of those with low earnings. (See Table 2–2.) The reason for this is that male wage gains are so concentrated among those with high pay that the mean increased sharply relative to the median. As a result, the proportion falling a certain percentage below the mean increased relative to the proportion falling a given percentage below the median. Among women, the proportions around both the median and mean show that much of the widening took the form of a shift of women into relatively lower-paying groups. Since female

Table 2–2 Changes in Proportions of Workers in Different Parts of the Earnings Distribution, 1979–1993

	1979 (%)	1993 (%)	Change (%)
Men			
Low earnings (63% or less of the median)	20%	23%	3%
Middle earnings (from 63% to 153% of the median)	60	51	–9
High earnings (153% or above of the median)	20	26	6
Low earnings (56% or less of the mean)	20	26	6
Middle earnings (58% to 136% of mean)	60	53	–7
High earnings (136% or above of the mean)	20	21	1
Women			
Low earnings (75% or less of the median)	20%	30%	10%
Middle earnings (from 75% to 155% of the median)	60	37	–3
High earnings (155% or above of the median)	20	23	3
Low earnings (68% or less of the mean)	20	41	21
Middle earnings (from 68% to 130% of the mean)	60	33	–27
High earnings (130% or above of the mean)	20	26	6

Source: Tabulated from outgoing rotation group files of CPS. I selected the percentages above and below the medians and means so that the initial proportions in the high-, middle-, and low-income groups were 20 percent, 60 percent, and 20 percent, respectively.

pay increased on average, however, this does not mean that the real earnings of these women fell, although for the lowest deciles, female earnings did fall in real terms. Rather, the shape of the distribution changed to the detriment of lower-paid workers. Finally, since the earnings of men fell in the 1980s and 1990s, measures of the shares of men earning below or above given constant dollar earnings, such as multiples of poverty wages, show that the entire widening consisted of rising proportions of low earners.[4]

Issues of measures aside, all of these summaries of the data tell the same story: In the 1980s and 1990s earnings became more unequal in the United States.

RISING INEQUALITY IN BENEFITS

During the 1950s and 1960s companies offered to lower-paid blue-collar workers many privately provided benefits, such as pensions and health insurance, that formerly had gone largely to higher-paid white-collar workers. Unions negotiated pensions and other fringe benefits for their members; many unionized firms extended those benefits to nonunion workers inside the company; and many nonunion firms did likewise. Increases in fringe benefits add to the cost of labor and to employee compensation. Had companies extended benefits to low-paid workers or increased expenditures on fringes rapidly for low-paid workers in the 1980s and 1990s, say, because of the rising cost of health insurance, hourly pay figures might overstate the rise of inequality. Total compensation might have risen for the lower-paid workers more than for the higher-paid ones, even though hourly wages rose less.

Table 2–3 documents that there was no such expansion of fringe benefits to low-skilled workers. Among men, less skilled workers were *less* likely to receive fringe benefits in the 1990s than in the past. In 1979, 57 percent of high school graduates and 39 percent of high school dropouts had employer-provided pensions; in 1993 these figures had dropped to 45 percent and 21 percent respectively. By contrast, there was little change in pension provision for college graduates. As for employer-provided health insurance, in 1979, 78 percent of male high school graduates and 58 percent of men with less than a high school education were covered by employer-provided health insurance; in 1993, the proportions had fallen to 62 percent and 35 percent. The proportion of workers whose employers paid all of the premiums also dropped sharply, although here the decline extends to college graduates as well. Among women, the situation is similar but less pronounced. The probability that a less educated woman had an employer-funded pension or health insurance plan was lower in 1993 than in 1979 while the probability that a college graduate woman had these benefits barely changed.

The U.S. Department of Labor has calculated the rate of health insurance coverage among workers by hourly pay and reports huge inequalities in employer coverage by hourly earnings in 1993. At the bottom of the earnings distribution, 36 percent of workers earning less than $5.00 per hour worked for an employer who offered a health insurance plan and only 14 percent were covered; 62 percent of workers earning $5.00 to $7.49 per hour worked for an employer who offered a plan and 35 percent were covered. At the high end of the earnings distribution, 92 percent of employers of the workers earning $15.00 or more per hour offered an employer health care plan, and 83 percent were covered.

In short, accounting for fringe benefits raises inequality in the earnings distribution.

Table 2–3 Trends in Employer-Provided Benefits, by Education and Gender, 1979–1993

	Men			Women		
	1979/80 (%)	1993 (%)	Change (%)	1979/80 (%)	1993 (%)	Change (%)
Pensions						
Less than high school graduates	39	21	–18	23	16	–7
High school graduates	57	45	–12	40	38	–2
College graduates	68	65	–3	57	60	3
Health Insurance						
Less than high school graduates	58	35	–23	36	26	–10
High school graduates	78	62	–16	56	49	–7
College graduates	85	79	–6	67	68	1
Employer All						
Less than high school graduates	24	10	–14	15	5	–10
High school graduates	35	19	–16	25	14	–11
College graduates	36	24	–12	31	22	–9

Source: Susan Houseman, "Job Growth and the Quality of Jobs in the U.S. Economy," *Upjohn Working Papers* 95-39, August 1995, tables 9 and 10, based on March CPS files.

INEQUALITY AND FALLING REAL EARNINGS

Should we worry about rising inequality? Consider the following situation. A's income rises by 100 percent, from $1,000 per week to $2,000 per week; and B's income rises by 20 percent, from $500 per week to $600 per week. Because A's gain is much larger than B's gain, inequality has risen, but both workers are better off. In countries where people are deeply committed to egalitarianism, a rise in inequality of this form would upset many persons. But Americans generally do not get worked up over invidious comparisons of income. As long as real earnings and living standards are rising for us all, why begrudge the highfliers their exceptional gains? Why not put aside envy or jealousy and let everyone enjoy the fruits of economic progress?

If the new inequality of the 1980s and 1990s was accompanied by economic gains for all, with high-paid workers obtaining exceptional increases in pay while low-paid workers had smaller gains, no one would be ringing alarm bells about the distribution of earnings. But the widening of the American earnings distribution is not a matter of very large gains for the rich and moderate gains for the low paid. On the contrary, it is a story of stagnant real wages for the average worker, falling real wages for low-paid ones, and large gains for the highest-paid ones.

Until the early 1970s the history of the American job market was one of rising average real wages. From 1900 to 1973 the real hourly pay of American workers rose by about 2 percent per year. Compounded, 2 percent doubles every 35 years, guaranteeing increases in living standards from one generation to the next. Until the 1980s, moreover, every American worker could expect increases in pay with additional years of work experience. For workers who remained with an employer and did their jobs, wages invariably grew more than inflation. As for new entrants into the job market, sons and daughters could expect higher starting pay than their parents had received when they entered the market.

The trend rate of growth of average real wages from 1973 or thereabouts to the mid-1990s breaks with the historical pattern. The most widely used statistical measures of wages—hourly earnings reported by workers on the U.S. Current Population Survey (CPS) of households or hourly earnings reported by employers on the national employer survey—divided by the consumer price index (CPI) have trended downward since 1973. (See Table 2–4.) The big losers in the earnings distribution are males. The real median earnings of full-time wage and salaried men fell by 13 percent while those of women rose by 7 percent. Over the shorter period, 1987 to 1996, the Bureau of Labor Statistics' employment cost index, which includes the cost of fringe benefits, shows a drop for all workers of 7.8 percent. Other earnings series recorded in the table, however, show modest gains in real earnings. Hourly compensation for the business sector reported by the Council of Economic Advisers rose by 10 percent from 1973 to 1996 while total compensation from the national income and product accounts increased by 16 percent. Even these gains, however, are a marked slowdown from the historical trend. The National Income and Product Accounts (NIPA) increase of 0.7 percent per year, for instance, is just one-quarter the 2.8 percent per year trend increase in earlier decades.[5]

However, measures of nominal wages deflated by consumer prices arguably understate the growth of real earnings in the United States. The principal problem is that the CPI and other price deflators do not fully measure improvements in the quality of goods. If these indices overstate inflation, dividing them into nominal earnings understates the growth of real earnings. The magnitude of the CPI bias is a matter of debate. The index is one of the most carefully developed statistical series in the United States, and the Bureau of Labor Statistics (BLS) improves it nearly every year. Still, many experts believe that the CPI

Table 2–4 Changes in Real Earnings in the United States, 1973–1995

Mean, average hourly earnings for production workers, in all private industry	–12%
Median weekly earnings of full-time workers	
Male	–13%
Female	7%
Mean compensation per hour, business sector	10%
Mean compensation per hour, all economy (through 1994)	16%

Note: All series deflated by CPI, except for line 4.
Source: Line 1: U.S. Council of Economic Advisers, *Economic Report of the President, 1996,* table B-43.
Line 2: *Employment and Earnings Bulletin 2307.* Monthly January issues and unpublished data, Washington, D.C.: U.S. Dept. of Labor, Bureau of Labor Statistics. U.S. Bureau of Labor Statistics, *International Comparisons of Manufacturing and Unit Labor Cost Trends,* July 17, 1996, Washington, D.C.: U.S. Dept. of Labor, Bureau of Labor Statistics.
Line 3: U.S. Council of Economic Advisers, *Economic Report of the President, 1996,* table B-45.
Line 4: Lawrence Mishel, Aaron Bernstein, and John Schmidt, *The State of Working America, 1996–1997* (Washington, D.C.: Economic Policy Institute, 1997), table 3.2. Based on national income and products accounts data, deflated by personal consumption deflator.

overstates inflation by as much as 1.0 percent per year.[6] If this were true, average real wages would have risen in the past two decades rather than fallen. The Federal Reserve Bank would be controlling inflation better than it recognizes, which would raise questions about whether monetary policy is overly restrictive. If, on the other hand, the CPI overstates inflation by, say, 0.3 percent to 0.5 percent per year (as some BLS analysts believe), real wages still would have fallen for the average male worker.

Regardless of where one comes out in this debate, the fact remains that compared to the past, the trend growth rate in real earnings has taken a dive.[7] There is nothing "magical" about a 0 percent growth of real wages that makes workers who earn 0.1 percent or –0.1 percent particularly different. Whatever the "true" rate of growth of real wages in the United States is, moreover, there is no denying that real wage growth has fallen relative to the past and also has fallen relative to real wage growth in other advanced countries (all of whom use CPI-style price deflators). In every country that is a member of the Organization for Economic Cooperation and Development (OECD), except for the United States, wages deflated by national price indices rose in the past two decades. For instance, OECD data show that in the 1980s, real hourly compensation for production workers in manufacturing increased by 2.6 percent per year in the United Kingdom, by 1.6 percent in Japan, by 0.9 percent in France, and by 1.3 percent in

Germany while they fell in the United States.[8] BLS estimates of average annual compensation for *all* workers in manufacturing show an increase in real earnings from 1973 to 1995 in the United States of 0.5 percent per year compared to 1.8 percent in Japan, 0.9 percent in France, 2.2 percent in Germany, and 2.4 percent in the United Kingdom. There is nothing intrinsic in CPI deflators to produce declining or stagnating measures of real wages. Until the past 20 or so years they never did, and they have done so in the 1980s and 1990s only in the United States.

LOW-PAID WORKERS

There is no debate over what happened to the real earnings of workers near the bottom of the U.S. earnings distribution in the 1980 and 1990s. As indicated in Table 2–1, they fell by sufficiently large amounts to be negative even with an alternative price deflator. The real earnings of high school dropout men age 25 to 34 fell by about one-fifth; those of high school graduate men in the same age bracket fell by only slightly less; the real hourly earnings of men throughout the lower rungs of the earnings distribution dropped sharply; and the real earnings of women in the lower rungs, who are the lowest-paid workers in the society, also fell sharply.

EMPLOYMENT OF LESS SKILLED WORKERS

If falling wages for less skilled workers created a job boom for them, it might be argued that increased inequality was positive even for them. Better to work at low wages in the United States than to be on the dole in Europe.

But with rising inequality, the employment of low-skill workers did not increase absolutely or relative to that of high-skill workers. Rather, the trend has been toward *reduced work* from the lower-skilled groups whose earnings fell. The most striking evidence that the American jobs miracle bypassed low-paid workers is found in statistics on the annual hours worked by adult men according to their position in the wage distribution.[9] From the 1970s through the 1990s, annual hours worked for men in the bottom deciles of the distribution fell while hours worked for those in the upper deciles were stable or rising. (See Table 2–5.) Inequality in hours worked increased along with inequality in hourly pay, producing an even greater increase in annual earnings inequality.

The decline in hours worked by low-skilled workers whose wages also fell arguably represents a rational supply response to reduced

Table 2–5 Mean Annual Hours Worked, by Wage Decile, Male Workers, 1970–1990

Wage Decile	1970	1990	Change, 1970–1990 (%)
0–10	2,133	1,693	−21%
10–20	2,268	1,940	−14
20–30	2,293	2,026	−12
30–40	2,192	2,076	−5
40–50	2,204	2,096	−5
50–60	2,170	2,132	−2
60–70	2,146	2,100	−4
70–80	2,085	2,085	0
80–90	2,011	2,066	3
90–100	1,742	1,776	2

Source: Tabulated from U.S. Census of Population public use data files, 1970 and 1990. The number of observations for the 1970 sample is 121,078; for the 1990 sample, 135, 434.

wages. Why work if work offers less economic reward than, say, crime? An alternative interpretation is that even huge real wage cuts were insufficient to create adequate demand for less skilled young labor. Regardless of which interpretation is preferred, falling wages clearly did not resolve the employment problem of less skilled men.

ADVANCEMENT AND MOBILITY

Inequality is intrinsically related to mobility. If everyone were paid the same, inequality would be zero. In such a world no one could improve his or her earnings through hard work, good ideas, or luck. No one would have a financial incentive to invest in skills or take risks. If someone found an opportunity to produce and earn more, inequality would increase. At least one person would be better and no one worse off; surely a better situation than if there was no inequality. More likely, the new opportunity would raise everyone's well-being.

Is the increased inequality evident in the United States of the 1980s and 1990s due largely to greater mobility in the economy?

No. A natural way to explore mobility is to estimate the probability that workers move between positions in earnings distributions over some specified time period. In any given period, after all, some workers will rise in the pay distribution while others will fall. If many workers change places, there is considerable mobility. This mobility can make standard measures of inequality based on the distribution at one point in time misleading. By contrast, if the "transition probabilities" of moving from one part in the earnings distribution to another are small, mobility will be slight and measures of inequality at a moment in time would capture the full reality of the distribution of earnings. At this writing, three studies have looked at changes in U.S. earnings mobility over time with sufficient scientific care to yield valid results.[10] Each uses a different data set. Two of the studies find that mobility decreased.[11] One finds that it has been unchanged.[12] There is *no* evidence that the rise in inequality was due to a rising mobility.

Another way to look at mobility is to examine changes in earnings as workers age and the economy progresses. Historically, American workers earned higher earnings with increased seniority and work experience. A person at 45 could expect to earn more than he or she did at 35, which is more than he or she made at 25. Table 2-6 shows that this pattern of advancement was broken in the 1980s and 1990s for American men with less than a college degree. Over the fourteen-year period from 1979 to 1993, male high school graduates who were 25-29 in 1979 suffered a loss of real earnings as they aged to 39-43 in 1993. Male high school graduates aged 30-34 in 1979 suffered an even larger loss in real earnings as they aged. By contrast, college graduates continued to earn sizable increases in pay as they aged over this period. In the decade of rising inequality, the earnings of less educated workers failed to improve as they aged, implying that chances to advance had decreased rather than increased over time.[13]

When there is considerable transitory churning or fluidity in the job market, measures of the distribution of earnings at a point in time misrepresent the permanent level of inequality of interest. Over their lifetime, A and B might have the same earnings, but A does well in one year and B does well in another. Individuals will be more insecure in a world with more churning than in one with less churning, but inequality will be less than standard measures indicate.

Table 2-6 Percentage Increases in Median Hourly Earnings for Male Workers as They Age, 1979-1993

Age	High School Graduates (%)	College Graduates (%)
25-29 in 1979; 39-43 in 1993	-6%	32%
30-34 in 1979; 44-47 in 1993	-12	13

Source: Calculated from NBER files of Current Population Survey, *CPS Outgoing Rotation Group Files.*

Is the new inequality the result of more churning in the job market?

No. One way to see if inequality increased largely because of more transitory churning is to follow the earnings of individuals for several years. Studies that do this find that a considerable proportion of inequality, possibly one-third, is variation in earnings over the life cycle.[14] But this proportion has not changed over time, so the rise in inequality cannot be ascribed to it. And no one claims that increased pay differences by broad skill classes—between college graduates and high school graduates; between lawyers vs. laborers—are due to churning in which the college/high school graduate or lawyer/laborer switch jobs every few years.

Random variations in earnings aside, if there is considerable permanent earnings mobility over the life cycle, measures of inequality that treat all age groups together will overstate the degree of inequality. Over their lifetimes, C and D may have the same present value of earnings, but at age 25 C earns little as a medical student while D earns a healthy paycheck as a salesman. At age 45 the situation is reversed: C earns more than D—the return on her investment in education. What looks like inequality is, in fact, opportunity and equality. C and D had the same options but made different choices that show up in a different pattern of earnings.

Is the new inequality due to changes in earnings by age among workers with unchanged differences in lifetime earnings?

No. Economists agree that the present value of lifetime income is the best measure of income for analyses of distributions. Lifetime incomes do not confuse the low earnings of the medical student with the low earnings of unskilled workers. To calculate lifetime incomes, earnings at different ages are examined. Data on earnings by age show that differences between education groups and between occupations have increased at all age levels, implying increased lifetime differences between those groups. For reasons having to do with the timing of investments and returns to on-the-job training, earnings 7 to 12 or so years after someone graduates from school offer a good proxy for lifetime earnings. If increased inequality among workers with the same schooling reflects increased inequality in lifetime incomes, it should show up in greater inequality among those with 7 to 12 years of experience. In fact, inequality has risen substantially among high school and college graduates 7 to 12 years after graduation.

The bottom line is that the new inequality is simply that: greater inequality, not greater mobility or greater churning or greater variation in the shape of income streams among those with the same lifetime earnings.

REDUCED EMPLOYMENT STABILITY?

Job security is important to most workers. The notion that if a person puts in a day's work, an employer will keep the person employed, unless the firm suffers losses of profits that require shutdown or restructuring, is part of the "social contract" in most advanced countries. Indeed, in most jobs, workers accrue additional skills that make them more valuable to employers so that both employer and employee seek a stable employment relationship. While U.S. firms have never been as committed to "lifetime employment" as Japanese firms, and U.S. workers have always been more mobile than Japanese or German workers, many employees have historically had secure jobs and spent many years with the same employer.

In the period of the new inequality, this pattern began to erode among male workers, with the greatest erosion occurring among those who were less skilled. Rates of job separation seemed to trend upward, particularly for less skilled men but even for the more educated.[15] The proportion of male workers reporting that they had been with the same firm for 10 years or 26 years fell.[16] Among women, by contrast, years with an employer rose slightly as women increased their commitment to careers, withdrawing from work to raise children less frequently than in the past.

INCOME PER CAPITA AND FAMILY INCOMES

Despite increased inequality and stagnation in real earnings, the living standards of most Americans could have improved substantially in the period of the new inequality. In fact, measured by the mean income, the well-being of American families increased from 1979 through the 1990s. That average or mean income per family increased does not, however, gainsay the significance of the widening of the earnings distribution for our country. Rather, it emphasizes the fact that it is the distribution of incomes, not the rate of growth of the economy, that makes this period so different from previous American experience.

To estimate average income for a group, the incomes of all members are summed; and that figure is divided by the number of people in the group. If the incomes of a few rise a lot, per capita income can grow even when the incomes of most people fall. Consider an economy with five people in which income falls by $500 for A, B, C, and D but increases by $3,000 for E. Per capita income rises by $200 (($3,000 - $500 \times 4) / 5 = 200$), but everyone except E is worse off. The distribution has changed so that 80 percent of the population has lower living standards while one person has improved his or her position. Since per capita calculations divide incomes by population rather than by numbers of workers, moreover, per capita incomes can even rise when the incomes of all workers fall. This occurs because more people work or work more hours. Family income goes up when a man's pay falls by 20 percent if his spouse enters the workforce and earns more than 20 percent of his initial earnings or if he takes a second job and earns 20 percent or more of his initial earnings.

In fact, this is basically what happened in the United States in the 1980s and 1990s. Between 1979 to 1994 (years in which unemployment was about the same rate), gross domestic product (GDP) per family rose by nearly one-quarter and mean family incomes rose by 10 percent.[17] But most of the gain went to those with high incomes, particularly to families with two well-educated earners. Median family income was roughly constant. The incomes of persons in the lower two quintiles of the distribution fell, and the incomes in the middle quintile rose slightly. The top 20 percent of families obtained essentially all of the gain in income, and within that group the vast bulk of the gain went to the upper 5 percent. Table 2–7 shows that the gain in mean family income from 1979 to 1994 was $4,419, but that most of this gain went to families in the upper 5 percent of the family income distribution.[18] Looking over a longer period, in 1993 median household income in the United States was roughly the same as in 1974, but the percent of persons living in poor families rose from 11.2 percent in 1974 to 15.1 percent in 1993—because the distribution had widened.[19]

One reason why gains of family incomes were so concentrated was that the increased employment, hours worked, and earnings of women were concentrated among high-income families. The spouse or partner of a professional man or woman probably works at a high-wage job. The spouse or partner of a less educated man or woman may not work or is likely to have a low-paying job. A less educated woman may be a single head of household or have a low-wage or unemployed spouse. In years past, women from low-income families tended to work more and contribute more to family income than women from high-income families, reducing inequality in family incomes. But in the 1970s and 1980s the employment rate and earnings of women with husbands in the upper percentiles of the wage distribution rose relative to that of women with husbands in the lower percentiles of the wage distribution.[20] Today two-earner families are at the top of the income distribution, while single-earner families, particularly those headed by female single parents, are near the bottom of the distribution.

In sum, the change in family incomes mirrors the change in individual earnings.

Table 2-7 Changes in the Mean Level of GDP Family and Per Capita Income and the Distribution of Changes, 1979–1994

GDP/Family	23%
Disposable personal income per capita	23
Average family income	10
Median money income of families	−1
Average family income for quintiles	
Lowest quintile	−11
Second quintile	−5
Third quintile	−1
Fourth quintile	7
Top quintile	24

Note: Family income figures are not adjusted for the size of the family. Adjustments using the family's poverty line by Lynn Karoly show that for the years 1973 to 1993, the change for the lowest group is negligible but the income of the median and higher groups increased more rapidly than in the unadjusted figures. The trend in inequality is bigger in the adjusted data. Karoly, "Anatomy of the U.S. Income Distribution: Two Decades of Change," *Oxford Review of Economic Policy* 12, no. 1 (Spring 1996), table 1.
Sources: Line 1: Calculated from data in U.S. Council of Economic Advisers, *Economic Report of the President* (Washington, D.C.: U.S. Government Printing Office, 1996).
Line 2: Reported in ibid.
Line 3: Lawrence Mishel, Aaron Bernstein, and John Schmidt, *The State of Working America, 1996–1997* (Washington, D.C.: Economic Policy Institute, 1997), table 1.9.
Line 4: U.S. Council of Economic Advisers, *Economic Report of the President.*
Line 5: AFL-CIO Department of Research, *America Needs a Raise* (February 1996), chart 2-4. These figures differ somewhat from this in Mishel, Bernstein, and Schmidt, *The State of Working America,* which shows a smaller increase for the fourth quintile and an even greater concentration of gains for the top quintile.

World Leader in Rising Inequality

Is the tide of inequality largely a U.S. phenomenon, or is it something affecting all advanced countries?

The United States has historically had a high level of inequality. The main reason for that is not the nation's heterogenous population. The United States has a diverse ethnic population, and the rising number of immigrants from less developed countries in recent years has added workers at the bottom of the earnings distribution. But the distribution of earnings is exceptionally wide among all ethnic groups. Blacks, whites, and Hispanics all have a highly unequal distribution of earnings, as do Americans with two parents of Swedish heritage.[21]

A major reason for the high inequality in earnings in the United States is that the nation relies extensively on market forces to determine pay; most other countries also rely on collective bargaining, minimum wage regulations, and other institutions to set pay. Distributions of wages set by institutions are invariably more compressed than distributions of wages set by markets.[22] Institutions reduce the leeway that firms have to pay rates that differ from the national average and reduce the leeway that supervisors have to vary pay among workers in a given job. In some countries, such as Norway or Sweden or Italy, national wage-setting has consciously sought to reduce wage differentials, with some success.

Still, given the more unequal distribution of earnings in the United States than in other advanced countries, a smaller rise in inequality in the 1980s and 1990s might have been expected in the United States than elsewhere. If a modern information-based economy demands higher wage differences among workers than the industrial economy of the past, the United States was arguably ahead of the game. Other countries would have to increase inequality to catch up. But this is not what happened, with us.

INEQUALITY GREW MORE IN THE UNITED STATES

Table 2–8 shows that inequality, as measured by the ratio of the earnings of men in the 90th decile to earnings of those in the 10th decile, rose in the majority of advanced market economies in the 1980s and 1990s. English-speaking countries had the most pronounced increase in inequality. Excluding tiny New Zealand, the United States led the pack in increased inequality. In most countries the rise of inequality was modest. In three countries inequality fell, substantially in Germany. By the mid-1990s the United States was an even more extreme outlier in inequality among advanced western countries than in the past.

Declining real earnings for low-paid Americans and rising real earnings for low-paid workers in other advanced countries has produced the anomalous situation that low-paid workers in the United States—still the most successful economy in the world—have lower living standards than low-paid workers in other advanced economies. (See Figure 2–1.) According to OECD estimates of hourly U.S. pay, a male worker in the bottom decile of the U.S. earnings distribution earns 38 percent of the U.S. median whereas a bottom-decile worker in Europe earns 68 percent of the European median and a bottom-decile worker in Japan earns 63 percent of the Japanese median. Using purchasing-power-parity prices that measure the cost of the same consumption bundle across countries to transform foreign earnings into U.S. dollars, the greater inequality in the United States translates into lower pay for 10th-decile Americans than for 10th-decile workers elsewhere. German low-paid workers earn roughly twice as much per hour as low-paid Americans.

Table 2-8 Levels and Changes in Earnings Inequality Among Advanced OECD Countries, Measured by 90th to 10th Decile Male Earnings, 1979–1995

	1979 or Other Early Year	1995 or Other End Year	Annual Change
Huge Rises in Inequality			
New Zealand	2.72 ('84)	3.16 ('94)	0.044
United States	3.18	4.35	0.027
Italy	2.29	2.64 ('93)	0.025
Canada	3.46 ('81)	3.74 ('94)	0.021
United Kingdom	2.45	3.31	0.020
Some Rise in Inequality			
Australia	2.74	2.94	0.013
Japan	2.59	2.77 ('94)	0.012
Austria	2.61 ('80)	2.77 ('94)	0.009
Netherlands	2.51 ('85)	2.59 ('94)	0.009
Sweden	2.11	2.20 ('93)	0.008
Finland	2.44 ('80)	2.53 ('94)	0.006
Denmark	2.14 ('80)	2.17 ('90)	0.003
France	3.39	3.43 ('94)	0.002
Declines in Inequality			
Belgium	2.29 ('85)	2.25 ('94)	−.004
Norway	2.05 ('80)	1.98 ('91)	−.006
Germany	2.38 ('83)	2.25 ('93)	−.013

Source: Calculated from OECD, *Employment Outlook, July 1996* (Paris: OECD, 1996), table 3.1. The 1994 Austrian figure is calculated from changes in the 80/50 decile statistic reported in the table, assuming the 90/80 decile earnings ratio is the same in 1994 as in 1989. The Belgium figures are adjusted for a change in reporting between 1988 and 1989.

Even in the United Kingdom, which has just two-thirds U.S. GDP per head, low-paid workers earn more than Americans. OECD *Employment Outlook 1996* statistics on the lowest decile of *weekly* earnings show low-paid Americans closer to the median (48 percent) than do the OECD statistics on hourly earnings. But these data still show that the United States is far out of line with other countries, with low-paid Americans having lower earnings than low-paid workers in advanced European countries and Japan.[23]

It is not just the bottom decile of American workers that trails workers in other advanced countries, however. Approximately one-third of American workers are paid less in purchasing power units than comparable workers overseas. Not until the 30th to 40th decile of earnings do Americans do better than Europeans. That so many American work-

Figure 2–1 Real Hourly Earning of Low–Decile Men

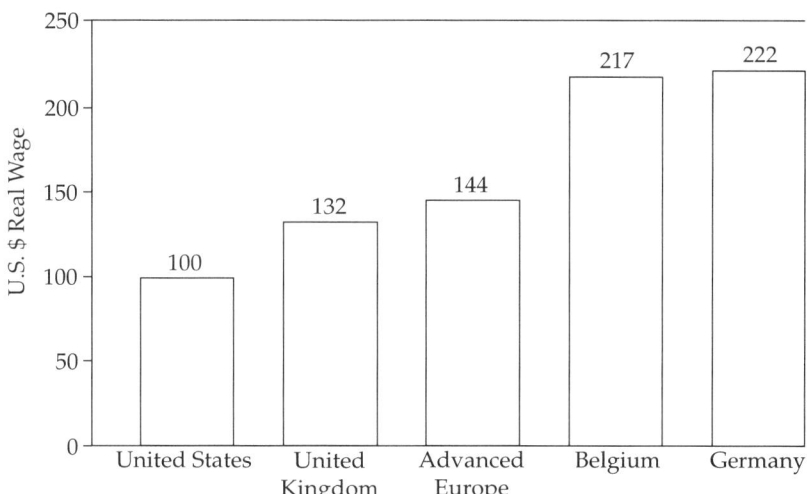

Note: The ratio of the 10th decile to the mean for the United States is 38; United Kingdom, 59; Advanced Europe, 68; Belgium, 73; Germany, 71.
Source: Author's calculations based on hourly earnings figures in OECD, *Employment Outlook* (Paris: OECD, 1993).

ers fare poorly compared to their peers in other countries shows that the problem of low pay is not "simply" a matter of low-skill immigrants or poorly educated inner-city minority youths.[24] It is a problem of the entire distribution of income.

Because taxes are higher in many countries than in the United States, comparisons of pay before taxes may exaggerate the disadvantage of low-paid Americans. This would be the case if taxes gave nothing back in value to employees. But in most countries taxes provide national health insurance, pensions, housing subsidies, and other social benefits, the bulk of which Americans purchase from their earnings. Comparisons of wages before taxes are thus likely to understate the U.S. disadvantage in pay among low-paid workers.

Finally, comparisons of wages based on market exchange rates, which are appropriate for calculating business costs, show even greater differences between low-paid Americans and low-paid workers in other countries. Among advanced countries, differences in labor costs are such that production workers are a bargain for business in the United States. For example, using exchange rates, in 1995 U.S. production workers in manufacturing were paid roughly half as much as German production workers. Given the difference in the distribution of earnings between the two countries, this implies that in exchange rate terms, U.S. low-decile workers cost employers roughly one-quarter what German low-decile workers cost employers. Despite these costs of labor, the United States runs huge trade deficits while the European Union runs rough trade balances.

BUT THE UNITED STATES DOES BETTER IN EMPLOYMENT

Measured by employment-population rates or unemployment rates, the U.S. labor market has far outperformed European labor markets. In 1974 the ratio of employment to population aged 15 to 64 was the same in the United States and in OECD Europe: 64.8 percent. In 1995 the employment-to-population rate was 73.5 percent in the United States and 60.1 percent in OECD Europe. For over a decade the unemployment rate was roughly 3 percentage points lower in the United States than in Europe.

Some analysts stress that much of U.S. job growth consists of low-paid, unskilled, fast-food-type jobs. The implication is that there is something wrong about hamburger flipping, bagging at a checkout counter, and related work. Other analysts stress that U.S. job growth consists largely of high-paying jobs.[25] The implication is that employing more lawyers or engineers resolves the problem of a widening earnings distribution.

There is truth in both assertions. Among industries, most American job creation has been in the service sector, particularly retail trade, which pays less than, say, manufacturing. Among occupations, the greatest increase in jobs has been in professional and managerial work, which pays more than the average occupation. If we divide industries into quintiles on the basis of average earnings, we find that nearly two-thirds of growth of private nonfarm employment has occurred in industries with wages in the lowest two-fifths of the earnings distribution whereas virtually no growth occurred in industries in the upper fifth. If we divide occupations by earnings, we find that rapid growth in high-paying as well as in low-paying occupations.[26]

But there is also disingenuity in both assertions. There is nothing wrong with working for McDonald's or the local supermarket. Low-paid, unskilled, fast-food (or other) jobs are a fine way for teenagers or others entering the job market to gain work experience and earn pocket cash. If employers created more such jobs, demand for low-skill work would increase and the wages of those workers would rise. More "bad jobs" are good, not bad, for low-paid workers. Moreover, when unions organize low-paid workers in the service sector, as they have done among supermarket workers in many cities, they can raise pay in even "bad" jobs without risking loss of employment to overseas competition. The problem in the United States is not too many low-skill entry jobs but too few opportunities for workers in those jobs to move to more skilled work as they age or for them to raise their pay over time. On the other side, there is no news in the fact that the U.S. occupational structure shifted toward higher-level jobs in the 1980s and 1990s. The job structure has been upgraded for the entire twentieth century, as the workforce has become more educated and skilled. Continuance of this trend does not gainsay the widening of the earnings distribution.

Economists at the U.S. Bureau of Labor Statistics have examined what has happened to the occupational and industrial dimensions of jobs taken together. This is the natural way to amalgamate divergent trends by occupation and industry, both of which affect the economic status of workers. One study divided employment into 90 industry-occupation groups and categorized these groups into high-, medium-, and low-paying on the basis of their pay.[27] The growth of employment from 1983 to 1995 and from 1989 to 1995 was concentrated in high-paying and low-paying jobs. Indeed, the number of jobs paying in the middle of the distribution actually fell in the 1990s. Even if the BLS had found no change in the industry-occupation mix of jobs by level of pay, however, there still would have been divergence in earnings due to the rising pay gap between industry-occupation groups and the rising dispersion of pay within the groups.

THE JOBS MIRACLE: EMPLOYMENT OF WOMEN, NOT OF LESS SKILLED MEN

If the main reason for the jobs boom in the United States was falling real wages, then employment should look much better for the groups that suffered the biggest wage drops compared to their peers in Europe—namely less skilled and younger men—relative to groups whose real wages rose or fell less—namely, women.

Comparing employment rates for less skilled workers in the United States and Europe shows that, for the most part, the U.S. jobs miracle bypassed less educated men. In the early 1990s, employment-population rates for out-of-school 20- to 24-year-olds were lower in the United States than in most advanced OECD European countries despite much lower relative pay in the United States.[28] In the late 1980s American men with less than four years of high school were less likely to be employed than

European men with comparable low levels of schooling.[29] Taking all out-of-school men as a group, Table 2–9 records employment-population rates for young men not attending school in the United States and the four major European economies, Germany, France, the United Kingdom, and Italy, in 1989 and 1994. The employment rates vary with the business cycle, rising more sharply in Europe than in the United States from 1989 to 1994. Still, in 1994 the United States had higher youth employment than France, Italy, and the United Kingdom but a lower rate than Germany. In 1989 the U.S. rate of employment was lower even than in France for 22- and 26-year-olds and was second lowest to the United Kingdom among 26-year-olds. The higher rate of employment for German than for American young men presumably reflects the success of the German apprenticeship system in giving even less skilled young persons workable skills. All of these figures, moreover, understate the problem faced by less educated young American men, many of whom are incarcerated for committing crimes and thus are not counted in the employment statistics.

If the great American jobs miracle did not benefit low-skilled men, who were the main beneficiaries?

The group whose employment increased most in the United States is women, whose employment-to-population rate rose from 54.5 percent in 1985 to 58.9 percent in 1995. By contrast, the employment-to-population rate for men was 70.9 percent in 1985 and 70.8 percent in 1995. The jobs miracle of 1985 to 1995 in the United States was largely a *female* jobs miracle. In 1970 the employment-to-population rate for men was higher than it was in 1995, so that absent an increase in population, male employment would have fallen for those years. That the gain in female employment was accompanied by an increase in the pay of

Table 2–9 Percentage Employed of Age Group Not Attending School, Men Age 18, 22, and 26, U.S. and Major European Economies, 1989 and 1994

Country	Age 18		Age 22		Age 26	
	1989	1994	1989	1994	1989	1994
United States	68.5	66.6	78.8	77.5	85.6	86.5
Germany	90.9	85.8	86.9	84.5	90.7	88.5
France	50.8	46.9	79.2	66.4	89.4	84.8
Italy	67.2	54.5	74.6	60.3	88.0	78.7
United Kingdom	68.7	65.6	80.1	69.2	82.0	84.3

Source: OECD, *Employment Outlook, July 1996* (Paris: OECD, 1996), table 4.9.

women relative to men—the only case in which a lower-paid group rose in the earnings distribution—argues against any simple "cut pay, create jobs" interpretation of the U.S. jobs boom. The real wages of low-skilled women certainly fell, but they fell much less than the real wages of low-skilled men did.

In short, the United States created many jobs when most other advanced countries did not. But even with falling pay for less skilled workers, particularly young men, the United States did no better than European countries in finding work for these workers. One interpretation of this fact is that the huge fall in pay was not necessary for employing low-paid workers. But there is a more negative reading: an even greater fall in pay was required to employ these workers in the face of declining labor demand.

HOURS OF WORK

Americans work considerably more hours than Europeans, and, given declines in hours worked in Japan, are now working roughly as many hours over the year as the Japanese. In the mid-1990s employees in the United States worked 200 to 400 more hours during a year than employees in Europe—five to ten full weeks. In 1995, for example, the OECD reports that Americans put in 1,743 hours compared to 1,534 hours for Germans, 1,542 hours for the French (1992), and 1,409 hours by the Dutch. In 1996 the OECD upped its estimates of U.S. hours worked to 1,945, producing an even larger U.S.-Europe gap in hours and higher reported hours for Americans than for the Japanese.[30] The major reason why Americans work so much is that we take just two or so weeks a year in vacation compared to the four to five weeks common in Europe. In addition, 6 percent of Americans hold a second job; 18 percent of workers do job-related work at home; overtime hours have risen substantially; and fewer Americans work part time than Europeans.

With a higher fraction of the workforce employed and putting in more hours in the United States than in Europe, it might be expected that Americans would be eager for time off. Most surveys of preferences for work show the opposite: Americans want to work more than Europeans and report themselves working harder and more willing to sacrifice family activities for work than Europeans.[31]

Why are Americans so devoted to long hours? One possible explanation is that this is a response to the economic incentives of stagnating real earnings, high inequality in earnings, and job insecurity. Families now need two full-time earners, working long hours, to maintain rising living standards. Individuals risk failing in the workplace if they do not put in as many hours as their peers and may win the promotion if they outdo their peers. Some would call this a rat-race equilibrium.

Whatever its cause, excessive hours of work detract from well-being—or at least that is what standard economic analysis of behavior suggests. Money aside, most people would rather spend time on hobbies, going to concerts or ball games, relaxing with families, and so on than putting in that extra hour of work. In years past the United States led the world in reductions of working time. The United States was among the first countries to establish the 40-hour week and to give paid vacations to ordinary workers. As recently as 1970, Americans worked fewer hours than, say, Germans. It is only in the past 20 years, as inequality has risen, that Americans have chosen work over leisure. That working Americans have short vacations and work so many hours implies that comparisons of GDP per capita overstate the American edge in living standards compared to those in Europe.[32] Americans have more material possessions than Europeans but less free time in which to enjoy them.

U.S. VS. EUROPEAN MOBILITY

Many Americans view mobility as being massively greater in the United States than in Europe. The U.S. society is more open than European ones are. The only "counts" and "dukes" in the United States are Basies and Ellingtons, who advanced through ability. Comparisons of mobility between the United States and western Europe show, however, only modest country differences in the proportion of workers changing positions in the earnings distribution.[33] For example, between 1986 and 1991, 51 percent of American full-time wage and salary workers moved from one quintile (fifth) in the U.S. distribution to another quintile. This exceeded mobility in Germany, Sweden (where 47 percent moved quintile position), Italy (where 49 percent moved), and France (where just 43 percent moved), but not in Denmark and the United Kingdom (where 52 percent moved) or Finland (where 56 percent moved).[34] What distinguishes the United States is not so much mobility from one percentile of the distribution to another as it is the extent to which mobility affects earnings. Since the American earnings distribution is exceptionally wide, any given movement has a greater effect on earnings in the United States than elsewhere. For instance, if an American moves from the 10th decile to the median, he or she will more than double earnings whereas a Swede moving from the 10th decile to the median obtains less than a one-third increase in earnings. Measured in this manner, the United States has greater upward and downward returns to mobility than other advanced countries.

In sum, it is the high level of inequality, not the dynamics of mobility, that differentiates income distribution in the United States from that of other advanced countries.

Whodunit?

It would make a good story if the new inequality could be attributed to a single cause: Trade, or technology, or changes in the minimum wage, or the influx of women into the job market . . . or greedy corporate executives, or (name your favorite villain). The evidence rejects any monocausal explanation. It seems that several factors have been at work, and analysts weigh their importance differently.

Trade has contributed to the problems of low-wage workers. Losses in pay or employment for those competing with foreign imports, particularly from less developed countries (LDCs), are the flip side of the benefits that trade brings the nation. Ross Perot in the United States and Sir James Goldsmith in Europe claim that trade is the big enchilada, but most studies reject this explanation of rising inequality in the United States or of unemployment in Europe.[35] The estimated effects of trade in shifting the demand for labor toward less skilled workers are not big enough to dominate wage determination in a large modern economy. And the pattern of changes in wages between men and women makes a trade-is-the-villain story difficult to sustain. Less skilled women are highly concentrated in apparel, textiles, shoes, and other sectors that compete most intensely with LDC imports. If the traded goods sector determined wages in the entire economy (as in simple trade models), these workers would have suffered the greatest loss of wages. But while less skilled women have had cuts in real pay, the group with the biggest drop in earnings is less skilled men, who do not compete as much with LDC workers. Trade surely affects the structure of wages, but it does not seem to be the dominant factor, as posited in the simplest trade model. It is not dominant because most Americans, particularly women, work in service sector jobs not directly affected by trade. Women displaced from import-competing activities have found employment in retail trade and other service sectors, where demand for labor is growing.

Immigration also has contributed to the problems of low-wage native-born Americans. Fully one-third of the high school dropout workforce in the United States is foreign born. If they were not here, surely the wages and employment of their native-born counterparts would be higher. But our best estimates suggest that the increased flow of low-skill immigrants is not "the" cause of falling earnings for less skilled

Americans. A significant proportion of less educated immigrants have less than a grade school education and are more likely to complement the work of the vast bulk of Americans than to compete with Americans in the job market. If immigration were the sole factor at work, the earnings distribution would be changing modestly. Much of the rise in inequality in the United States has occurred among workers with similar skills, including those unaffected by immigration—for instance, mechanics or lawyers.

The *decline of trade unions* has contributed to inequality. Unions reduce inequality in pay among their members by standardizing pay among workers within establishments and by equalizing pay across establishments. They reduce inequality of pay between high- and low-paid workers by raising the pay and benefits of their largely blue-collar private sector members closer to that of higher-paid executives and professionals. They reduce the inequality of pay in nonunion firms by inducing those firms to raise pay or benefits to avoid unionization. Imagine that unionism was 30 percent of the private sector, as it was in the 1960s, instead of 10 percent as in 1996. Would earnings inequality be less? Yes. Studies suggest that about one-fifth of the rise in inequality is due to the decline of unions.[36] When the U.S. earnings distribution was most compressed (although still more unequal than in Europe), unions were a far stronger social force than today. Many factors have undoubtedly contributed to the decline in unionization, including sluggish union response to the changing economic world and a change in employer attitudes toward unions, motivated in part by competitive pressures. Employers are generally more averse to unionism now than they were in the 1950s and 1960s, when most firms accepted unions as a fundamental part of the American labor system.

The reduced real value of the *minimum wage* in the 1980s also has contributed to rising inequality. The Reagan administration kept the minimum wage from rising with inflation in the hope that a reduced real minimum wage would create a jobs bonanza for low-skilled workers. Instead, the falling real minimum wage contributed to the drop in wages in the lower rungs of the income distribution without noticeably raising employment of less skilled workers. Even with ensuing increases in the minimum wage, its ratio to average hourly earnings is remarkably low by historical standards.

The *influx of women* into the job market also may have contributed to the problems of low-wage workers. An increase in the supply of labor drives wages down, and more and more women have supplied labor to the workforce. Since women earn 70 percent to 80 percent of what men earn, many of them fall in the lower rungs of the male earnings distribution, potentially adding to the labor supply of workers in those pay brackets. But women's pay has risen relative to that of men, and women and men with even the same pay/skills are employed in very different industries and occupations. It is difficult to see why more women workers adversely affected men's wages but not their own. Assume, for the sake of argument, that all of the increase in female labor supply was due to a shift in the supply curve. Then women's wages should have fallen relative to male wages and pay ought to have been driven down in those parts of the economy where women predominate. The wages of low-skill women did fall, but wages fell more for low-skill men and in the manual jobs held by such men. By itself an exogenous increase in female labor supply cannot generate the observed pattern of change in wages.

The Clinton administration has favored *technology* as the culprit, and many economists concur. There is evidence that the technological change involved with computerization has adversely affected low-skill workers, but as analysts have looked more closely at the evidence, the case that the technology is the big enchilada is underwhelming.[37] Why hasn't the same technology not produced massive inequality in other advanced countries? Why have productivity increases been moderate if we have entered a brave new world of accelerating technology? Why do industries that use new technologies most extensively fail to displace less skilled workers more rapidly than others? Every generation deals with new technology and often blames it for whatever ills occur: In the 1960s there was the great automation scare. No one denies the potential importance of technological change, but its effects may be overstated.

Another factor has been a *slowdown in the growth of the supply of college graduates* relative to less educated workers. In the 1970s Jan Tinbergen, a Nobel Prize–winning Dutch economist, wrote that inequality was a race between the increasing demand for highly educated workers due to technology and the increasing supply of these workers due to education.[38] For most of western economic history, the increase in the supply of skills offset the increase in the demand for skills, maintaining or reducing pay differentials. In the 1970s in the United States and other advanced countries, the increased supply dwarfed the increase in demand, reducing educational premiums. The returns to higher education fell in the 1970s (the result of a huge influx of new college graduates), and the rate of growth of the college workforce decelerated in the 1980s, contributing to the rise in the earnings advantage of more educated workers. In countries where the educated workforce grew rapidly in the 1980s, pay differentials between more and less educated workers did not widen much, if at all, and even fell in some cases. The

1970s slowdown in the flow of young persons into college, which reduced the rate of increase in the number of graduates in the 1980s, is not sufficient to explain the massive rise of inequality, but it is a significant factor. My best estimate is that it accounts for perhaps 20 to 30 percent of the rise in educational differentials, but it cannot account for the huge rise in the dispersion of pay within education groups.

The debate over how much weight to give the "suspects" has enlivened economic conferences and journals. The debate is important in one respect. If we knew for certain the causes of the rise in inequality, we might have a better notion of how the distribution will change in the future—whether earnings will continue to diverge, or whether the new inequality will stabilize or decline. But for the purpose of deciding how, if at all, the nation should respond to the new inequality, the issue of causality is largely irrelevant, because there is no necessary link between the causes of a problem such as inequality and its consequences or potential cures. Someone impoverished by economic change is impoverished regardless of whether the cause is trade, immigration, technology, or declining unionization. And, whatever the cause of a problem, something quite different may cure it. The biggest single factor behind the new inequality may be technology, as many analysts believe, but surely the cure is not destroying our computers and marching on the Massachusetts Institute of Technology or CalTech with Pat Buchanan's pitchforks. The cure could be a more progressive tax system, with tax cuts targeted at the poor, or better education or training for low-paid workers, or unionization of low-wage workers—changes that have no connection at all with technological change.

What Will the New Inequality Do to Us?

The new inequality will almost certainly affect the United States in significant ways. An economy in which workers are sharply divided by income must operate differently from one dominated by a large, confident middle class. Since the huge widening of the earnings distribution is a recent phenomenon, however, no one can say with any surety what changes it will bring to our economy and society. Still, logic and the evidence available indicate that the new inequality is likely to exacerbate economic and social problems and possibly alter the very nature of American society.

The clearest consequence is that persons in the lower parts of the income distribution are poorer than they otherwise would have been. Being poor in the United States is not the same as being poor in a less developed country, but it is a meager and deprived economic existence.[39] Poor persons spend 30 percent of their income on food, 36 percent on shelter and utilities, and much of the rest on other necessities such as clothing or transportation. One-fourth fail to meet rent or mortgage payments at least once during a year; one-third fail to pay utility bills during a year; one in 11 has services cut off by the gas, electric, or oil company; and one in 6 suffers a disconnected telephone. While most poor people have color televisions and other consumer appliances, many do not have telephones. Poor people are more likely to live in a crime-prone neighborhood and to be the victim of crime than other Americans; they are less healthy and have shorter lifetimes than the wealthy; their children are more likely to have health problems and troubles in school. Very poor people risk homelessness. When people are on a financial edge, changes in earnings that may seem modest to higher-income Americans can be critical.

The widening of the income distribution already has had adverse effects on the economic well-being of a substantial number of American children. Historically, poverty was concentrated among elderly people and children, particularly those living in single-parent families, largely because neither group worked. In 1970 the rate of poverty for elderly persons was 25 percent; for children, it was 15 percent. For both groups the rate of poverty was trending downward. By 1993, Social Security and private pensions had reduced the rate of poverty among the elderly population to 12 percent. By contrast, the rate of poverty among children rose to 22 percent in 1993—a figure that exceeds child poverty rates in most advanced countries. In the 1990s American children in the lowest quintile of the income distribution were absolutely poorer (using purchasing-power-parity currency adjustments to convert foreign currencies into dollars) than low-income children in 15 other advanced countries. At the other end of the distribution, U.S. children in the top-quintile families had markedly higher real incomes than top-quintile children in other countries.[40]

The widening of the earnings distribution contributes directly to child poverty because the sharpest loss in real incomes has been to young persons just beginning their working life. Persons in families headed by someone under age 25, for example, had incomes in 1993 roughly one-third less than that of similarly aged persons in 1973. To the extent that the widened distribution helped fuel the rise of the single-parent home by making it harder for low-skilled men to maintain a family, moreover, it has added to child poverty indirectly as well.

For persons with high incomes and their family and friends, by contrast, additional inequality has some benefits. A rich person can hire a poor person as gardener, maid, nanny, or whatever. Not surprisingly, the personal services sector of the U.S. economy has grown with the rise of inequality. If the middle class shrinks and buys fewer tickets to basketball games or concerts, moreover, there will also be more places for the rich at those events.

Many higher-income persons are, however, troubled when fellow Americans and their families struggle in a land of plenty. Those distressed by the poverty of others range across the political spectrum, from liberals to conservatives; from members of chambers of commerce to members of community groups to union members; from religious fundamentalists to nonbelievers. Indicative of our attitudes toward those in trouble, Americans volunteer more time and donate larger shares of their income to nonprofit charitable activities than the citizens of any other country (most of whom rely on a large welfare state to take care of those in trouble).

But the primary effect of the new inequality on the well-to-do will not be increased charitable feelings or altruism, although it is hoped that there will be increased private charitable activities. The primary effect will be a worsening of social problems that affect all citizens, including the rich who do not care about how their poorer neighbors fare.

One potential cost of inequality is a continued growing prison and jail population and costly criminal justice system. The number of American men involved in crime is staggering. In 1995, 1.5 million American men were incarcerated, or one man for every employed man. By 2000, nearly 3 percent of the American male workforce will be incarcerated, and about 10 percent will be incarcerated, paroled, or on probation. These numbers are a decimal point away from comparable statistics in other countries. Mass incarceration may explain why the rate of crime stabilized in the 1980s and began to fall in the 1990s. But incarceration is an incredibly expensive way to control crime. Incarcerating a criminal for a year costs about as much as sending a person to Harvard. In 1995 the state of California budgeted more for prisons than for higher education. A society that spends more on prisons than on universities is a society in trouble.

There is no smoking gun linking crime to falling real wages or employment opportunities for the less skilled, but the economic logic is clear: Whatever makes legitimate work less attractive to young men makes crime more attractive. With so many criminals incarcerated, the crime rate should have plummeted. The crime rate has fallen but has not plummeted because many nonincarcerated young men find crime a preferable alternative to legitimate work, even though they face severe penalties when they are caught. We are not sure how earnings from crime changed (possibly they rose because of demand for drugs), but we do know that the real earnings of low-skill young men fell in the 1980s and 1990s and that most of these men recognize that they can do better "on the street" than in legitimate work.[41]

Further support for the economic story of crime is found in the demographics of the criminal population. Roughly three-quarters of prison inmates are high school dropouts—the group whose earnings have deteriorated so sharply in the past 20 years. While high school dropouts are a decreasing proportion of the workforce, they continue to make up the bulk of the incarcerated population. A disproportionate number are young blacks, whose employment opportunities are especially poor. Would some of these young men forgo crime if the economy offered them jobs with living wages and opportunity for advancement? Of course. How many would do so, and the savings in the costs of prisons, police, and courts, and in the social losses due to crime are, however, not well determined. Which, if any, government training program could get these young men into the normal economy is also problematic: Job and Training Partnership Act (JTPA) programs have not succeeded with this group, although benefit-cost evaluations suggest that the Jobs Corps has been a worthwhile social investment.

Continued homelessness is another likely consequence of high inequality. When the homeless burst on the scene in 1981–1982, the Reagan administration saw them as a temporary problem that would disappear with economic recovery—a reasonable but erroneous expectation. When the economy recovered, homelessness remained. The bulk of homeless people are from the low-skilled, low-wage groups whose employment/earnings prospects have deteriorated. Many cannot earn enough to rent even the lowest-quality housing. As the income distribution has widened, moreover, fewer middle-class families move to better housing and free older dwellings for poor families. This means fewer spaces for those at the tail end of the earnings distribution.[42]

Inequality is likely to adversely affect the family structure as well. Falling earnings/job prospects for young men are as antifamily a "policy" as can be imagined. If a young man cannot earn enough to support a family, he will not do so, although he may still father a child. He may become involved in crime. Hundreds of thousands of children in single-parent homes in the United States have fathers in jail or prison. Millions of children receive no child support or little support from fathers whose real earnings have trended downward. If low-skilled young men had better earnings prospects, would they be more responsible participants in a family? Of course—although again, how many would change their behavior we cannot readily say.

Some medical experts suggest that inequality has harmful health consequences. Mortality is inversely related to income and/or education and the relation has grown pronounced in the United States since 1960 or so.[43] States with more unequal distributions of income by some metrics have higher mortality rates.[44] Blacks, moreover, have shorter life expectancies than whites. Poor families are less likely to inoculate children against diseases than other families.[45] Teenagers from poor communities are more likely to be homicide victims. But cross-section relations cannot be generalized to changes over time. Until *changes* in inequality or *changes* in the real incomes of low-paid Americans are linked to *changes* in health status, the claim that the divergence of earnings has adversely affected the nation's health is problematic. The increased disparity in death rates by economic status may be due to the widening disparity in incomes, but perhaps other factors are at work.

What are the consequences of inequality for business and the economy more broadly?

Economists have studied the effects of inequality on the growth of GDP per capita—the single best indicator of economic performance and the development of markets—and have found that growth across countries is inversely related to inequality.[46] East Asian countries, such as South Korea or Taiwan, with low inequality have grown more than countries with highly unequal distributions, such as many in Latin America. Why? Some speculate that in societies with high levels of inequality, people fight over the distribution of the national output rather than work to increase national output. As the divide between bosses and employees grows, many employees come to view business unfavorably and may be attracted to policy interventions harmful to the national product. Absent a perfect capital market where individuals can borrow on their future earnings, moreover, inequality reduces the chances for poor people to invest in education and skills. When a large segment of the workforce lacks skills, moreover, their inefficiency may adversely affect the performance of skilled persons who rely on them for some tasks. The engineer or scientist who works with highly competent technicians or crafts workers will have higher productivity than the one working with poorly trained or illiterate workers.

A more unequal earnings distribution will benefit some businesses at the expense of others. Businesses that provide goods and services to the super-rich and those that cater to the new poor will prosper. The businesses that produce for the middle class will, by contrast, face smaller markets. Consumer credit defaults may rise, as many individuals find themselves unexpectedly sliding down the earnings distribution. Savings by normal citizens, already low, may fall or fail to rise to provide the funds needed for investment. Since businesses adjust to market opportunities, one potential outcome is more Neiman Marcuses and more WalMarts—a division in retailing that mirrors the division in the distribution of earnings. Similarly in terms of the use of labor, the division between "good employers" and "bad employers" could very well grow. An increasing gap in the pay between more and less skilled workers offers profitable opportunities for some employers to hire cheap, low-skill labor and to treat them poorly. High-paying firms may contract out low-skill services, removing those workers from their wage and benefit packages. Already sweatshops have returned to the United States, and most major firms contract cleaning services to small enterprises that pay low wages and offer few benefits.

More speculatively, a widening income distribution may increase social tensions, reduce stability, and create opportunities for demagogues of diverse bents. Animus against chief executive officers, Wall Street, free trade, and the like is one logical consequence of rising inequality. Animus against immigrants or ethnic groups other than one's own may grow. Policies to aid disadvantaged groups lose appeal.[47] If Pat Buchanan's "peasants with pitchforks" (the phrase used to describe his low-income populist supporters) take to the streets, who knows in which direction they will turn? When one man's earnings are falling despite his efforts, whom shall he blame? Perhaps it's the next person's fault. If year after year that person is getting wealthier and that man is getting poorer, who knows what demagoguery might appeal to him?

Looking at the problem from an even wider perspective, American democracy has been premised on a reasonable degree of equality among citizens. Whether that democracy can function as well when incomes are highly unequal as when they are more equally distributed is an open question. If a person believes that the well-to-do or special monied interests control politics, why bother to vote or to commit to the democratic process? Where is that person's pitchfork, anyhow?

This list of costs—crime, insecurity, family, business decisions, political attitudes—is neither exhaustive nor definitive. Some costs may be larger than would be expected. Others may be smaller. Riots and urban disorder have occurred spasmodically in U.S. history, usually when the expectations of impoverished or discriminated persons exceed their rate of progress in the society, and usually to the surprise of most observers. Racial tensions often are fueled by economic insecurity and feelings of being left out or left behind.

What most worries me about the new inequality, however, is not disorders by persons in the lower rungs of the income distribution but something very different. It is acceptance of the new inequality by the better-off parts of society. I worry that the United States may be on the road to a stable divided economy in which we accept the division of society into the well off and the poor as the way things are and proceed normally. I have used the phrase "apartheid economy" to describe this possible scenario—an economy in which the rich live aloof in their suburbs and expensive apartments with little link to the poor in their slums or to the declining middle class struggling to keep its head above water.[48] People have a remarkable capacity to adjust to social/economic situations that they once viewed as intolerable. Compare the nation's initial response to homelessness to its current acceptance of homelessness as part of the American scene. When was the last time you saw a homeless man on the street and thought "this is not America—we must do something"? Or walked four or five blocks from the White House and thought "this is not America—we must do something"?

What Might We Do?

Determining the best strategy for ameliorating the new inequality would require a major national study of the pros and cons of diverse policies to improve the fortunes of low-paid Americans, assessing both the effects and costs of various initiatives. I have not done such a study and neither has anyone else. Thus I limit this section to a brief menu of responses that seem worth study. For heuristic purposes, I have organized the policies into seven thematic packages.

STRATEGY 1: LET THE LABOR MARKET WORK

The first option is to do nothing special in the hope that the competitive market will itself remedy the inequality problem. It might do this by encouraging enough persons to invest in skills to flood the market with educated workers and drive down the high returns to skill. On the supply side, we already see increased enrollments in institutions of higher education in response to the high premium for education. Between 1980 and 1993 the proportion of 18- to 19-year-olds enrolled in school rose from 46 percent to 62 percent while the proportion of 20- to 21-year-olds enrolled in school rose from 32 percent to 43 percent.[49] Blacks, who had especially high dropout rates from high school and low academic achievement scores, have improved in both areas, despite the problems of the inner cities where many live. Increases in the supply of educated workers alleviate the rise of inequality by providing upward mobility to some, reducing the number of less educated people seeking work, and increasing the demand for less skilled workers whose jobs complement those of the more skilled. The question is not whether the labor market will reduce inequality but whether it will do so sufficiently, quickly, and powerfully. My suspicion is that the market correction will reverse only part of the increase in inequality in the next decade; the requisite flood of college graduates seems too large.[50] But if, for reasons I fail to foresee, the demand for labor suddenly shifts in favor of less skilled workers, we could have a repeat of the 1970s, when wage differentials fell noticeably. The market would then cure much of the inequality problem by itself, and the best policy might be "do not interfere."

STRATEGY 2: MACROECONOMIC EXPANSION

There is another way in which the market may potentially reduce the new inequality: through economic growth that produces low unemployment. Supply-siders and traditional Keynesians believe that faster economic growth cures most economic woes. While the expansion of the 1980s and 1990s did not improve earnings in the lower parts of the income distribution, perhaps the mid-1990s expansion will do so, as the 1960s expansion did. The drop in unemployment rates in 1995 to 1997, to 6 percent, then 5 percent, and then below 5 percent, did increase the real pay for low-skill and low-paid workers. Historically, tight labor markets reduce skill differentials, as employers find "shortages" of even less skilled workers. Areas in the United States that have enjoyed low unemployment rates at various times have seen the wages of even less skilled young blacks rise substantially.[51] If the United States can maintain a low rate of joblessness for an extended period of time and avoid a major recession, perhaps the market will restore the real earnings of low-paid people, with no additional policy intervention. More aggressively, it might be asked which, if any, policies could be tailored so that economic expansion benefits low-paid workers. Perhaps we might lower the taxes on low-income families as the economy grows, much as we automatically raise Social Security payments for elderly persons with rises in the consumer price index.[52] Some radical supply-side thinking on how to assure that low-paid workers gain in the next growth spurt is sorely needed.

STRATEGY 3: ENCOURAGE PRIVATE COLLECTIVE RESPONSES

One natural response of workers facing economic troubles is to organize trade unions to bargain collectively with employers. Forming a union in the United States is, however, contentious and difficult. The percentage of workers unionized in the private sector continues to fall, despite substantial interest by workers in unionization, particularly among those with low pay and limited skills.[53] Even modest policy reforms to reduce the costs of organizing to workers are highly divisive, as many in the business community view unions as an adverse economic force. But irrespective of people's views about unions, policies to ease the formation of unions by workers who want them merit consideration as a way to raise the pay of low-paid workers. The "new" AFL-CIO has begun to put significant resources into organizing. Increased unionization may turn out to be both a natural collective market response to the new inequality and impoverishment of low-paid workers and a partial cure for the problem.

The effort of many firms, nonunion as well as union, to forge new and more positive relationships with employees, to use profit-sharing more widely, and to involve employees in decision making to a greater extent than in the past offers other ways for institutional changes in workplaces to ameliorate the rise of inequality.[54] These innovations are, however, concentrated in firms that already pay high wages and have progressive human resource policies, so they are unlikely to improve the economic well-being of low-paid workers.

Outside the labor market, the most significant institutions for collective problem-solving are private charities and nonprofit "independent-sector" organizations. The Reagan and Bush administrations encouraged the private sector, including major corporations, to undertake more welfare state–type activities, with moderate success. But a strategy to help low-paid workers through independent-sector activity will need considerably more private charitable contributions by individuals and firms than have been available even in peak giving and volunteering years. Perhaps the tax code could be changed to spark greater independent-sector activity. Perhaps more government funds should flow through that sector. Finding the most effective way to use private charities to alleviate the problems of impoverished Americans should be part of any serious assessment of responses to the new inequality.

STRATEGY 4: MITIGATE THE HARDSHIP

When people work hard but do not make enough to rise above poverty, it is natural to look at taxes and benefits to increase their economic well-being. Such redistributions put cash into the pockets of those needing it, although they do not change labor market fundamentals.

On the tax side, there are diverse ways to reduce taxes on low-income families. The Earned Income Tax Credit (EITC), which gives tax rebates to those with very low incomes, is a negative income tax for working families. At one time both conservatives and liberals favored the EITC, and the Clinton administration increased the EITC in its first year in office. Most tax reform packages, including consumption or value-added taxes or various flat taxes with single rates, can be tilted progressively, so that the gains in economic efficiency they might bring would not come at the expense of lower-paid workers.[55] Packaged with other programs, moreover, the progressive nature of the federal budget might be able to be maintained or increased.

An alternative way to mitigate hardship is to provide more benefits to poor people. Criminals prey on the poor, so that increased police protection in poverty neighborhoods has some appeal. People's income may be low, their housing poor, but please let them and their children be safe. Greater support for child care, more comprehensive medical coverage for low-wage workers, increased food stamps, and other alternatives—vouchers for schooling or housing—could also mitigate poverty by augmenting the living standards of those with low incomes.

Mitigation programs are costly. Someone pays, directly through taxes or indirectly through an expanded government deficit, and Americans have become highly suspicious of taxes that benefit others, with the exception of Social Security. But perhaps there are creative ways around this problem: If privatization of Social Security will benefit many high-income workers, perhaps some of those benefits can be taxed to redistribute to lower-paid workers. Mitigation programs also have unintended adverse effects on economic incentives and behavior. If people are given money or benefits when they have low income, they may not try as hard to better themselves. Employers may give workers a smaller wage increase if the government is subsidizing living standards. These are serious problems in western Europe, where countries have large welfare state benefits, but are largely irrelevant in the United States, given our low safety net. The disincentives of mitigation policies can be reduced but not eliminated through artful program design.

STRATEGY 5: INVEST IN SKILLS

A very different set of policies seeks to increase the skills and productivity of the workforce so that individuals can earn more in the labor market. Higher education subsidies can make college-going easier, particularly for those from poverty backgrounds. The United States has a host of such policies—Pell grants, guaranteed student loans, state funding of community colleges—which could be expanded, and the Council of Economic Advisers has suggested that the nation consider income-contingent student loans as well.[56] Supporting higher education when the educational premium is huge might seem to be an odd way to help low-skill workers since higher education subsidies benefit those who will have sizable earnings later, but it has virtue by potentially speeding the long-term upgrading of the workforce.

A different set of invest-in-skill policies involves education and job training programs for less skilled workers. These also can take various forms, from government training programs to GI bill–type awards for any training a young person deems valuable. Some government-sponsored training programs have been relatively successful, but even the most successful are likely to have only modest effects on the earnings of less skilled workers.[57] A three- to six-month government training program is not going to restore a greater than 20-year fall in the real earnings of less skilled workers.[58] Most distressing, no one has managed to find the right programs for high school dropouts, who constitute such a large share of the bottom deciles of the income distribution and who are disproportionately involved in crime and on welfare.

Perhaps the right places for additional investment in skills are elementary and high schools. Perhaps it is even earlier—at the preschool level. Perhaps the issue is less one of money than of the organization of the school system. Milton Friedman, the Nobel laureate champion of the market economy, believes that vouchers for education will in the long run improve educational quality and the skills and pay of persons in the bottom parts of the U.S. wage distribution. The German educational system brings low scorers on academic achievement tests closer to the median than the U.S. system.[59] Perhaps there is something to be learned from the German experience.

Skill strategies are appealing because they address the fundamental problem of raising the productivity of low-skilled workers. But they do little for current employees and risk burdening an educational/training system with more than it can manage.

STRATEGY 6: STRUCTURAL WAGE
AND EMPLOYMENT PROGRAMS

Structural wage and employment programs seek to raise the pay or benefits of specified groups of workers or to increase their employment relative to that of others.

The most direct way to raise the earnings of low-paid workers is through legally mandated increases in pay or benefits. A person's pay is exceptionally low. Get Congress to increase it with a higher minimum wage. An employer does not offer health insurance. Get Congress to mandate that all employers provide it under some guise. Research on the minimum wage suggests that modest increases buttress the bottom of the earnings distribution with little loss of employment.[60] But even advocates of the minimum wage recognize its limitations. Some benefits go to secondary earners from high- or middle-income homes. Some of the burden of paying for the minimum wage falls on low-income families through higher prices for the goods and services produced by minimum-wage workers. And while a modest minimum wage may not cost jobs, a "high" minimum would surely run into serious employment problems, though one person's definition of "high" may differ from another's.

Mandated health insurance or other legally required expenditures may have a smaller effect on labor costs than minimum wages, because some firms will redistribute labor compensation from direct pay to the mandated cost. The incidence of such a "tax" is likely to fall mostly if not entirely on workers, substantially reducing any redistribution toward covered groups. The Clinton administration's failed health care plan shows the extreme care with which such schemes must be developed; what sounds good in principle may prove disastrous in the details.

An alternative way to improve the job market for less skilled workers is with programs that subsidize their employment. Tax credits or subsidies to private employers to hire less skilled workers have in the past had some modest positive employment effects, although they risk stigmatizing the workers they are designed to help.[61] Public sector job creation also has proven modestly successful, although workers do not seem to benefit over the long run and there are problems of substitution between workers in a program and other workers.[62] While employment schemes do not directly affect the pay of low-skill workers, they increase the demand for such workers and thus place upward pressure on wages.

STRATEGY 7: CIRCLE THE WAGONS

Circling-the-wagon policies call for the United States to restrict trade and immigration in the hope that this will benefit lower-paid Americans.

There is an economic logic to autarkic policies. Compared to the bulk of the world, the United States has a highly skilled workforce. We export goods that use skills and import goods that are produced by less skilled workers. If we reduced our trade, particularly with less developed countries, we would create jobs for low-skilled Americans and raise their wages. This is the protectionist solution to our inequality problem, and is a singularly expensive one. The costs of creating jobs by protectionism are so high (even without foreign retaliatory tariffs) as to be nearly impossible to justify. For example, Hufbauer and Elliot estimate the average consumer cost for a job saved by tariffs to be around $170,000.[63] It is hard to imagine circumstances under which the benefits of "saved jobs" would be worth these costs. Better to increase taxes a bit and write checks to those workers through, say, the EITC, or to subsidize employers to hire them.

What about policies to reduce immigration of less skilled workers? Estimates by Borjas, Freeman, and Katz suggest that reductions in the number of less skilled immigrants could raise the wages of low-skilled Americans modestly.[64] But the failure of the huge drop in the number of young Americans entering the job market after the baby boom to improve the economic position of young workers suggests that any such "restrict supply policy" will not resolve the entire inequality problem.[65] It is even possible that if fewer less skilled workers immigrate to the United States, the nation simply will import more goods made by low-skilled labor overseas. Reducing immigration by itself may not be that effective in a global economy where trade and capital flows can substitute for immigrants.

Circling-the-wagon strategies are anathema to most economists, but I put them on the list because they have a logic and are supported by enough people to be treated as a serious option.

Finding a Solution

In this chapter I have summarized the evidence on the increase in inequality in earnings and incomes in the United States in the 1980s and 1990s and have documented that the new inequality is due largely to the falling real earnings of lower-paid workers. The statistics show that the widening of our earnings and income distributions and impoverishment of low-paid Americans is not the artifact of some political debate but a real development in the U.S. economy. Both logic and evidence suggest that the new inequality will have deleterious effects not only on Americans in the lower rungs of the income distribution but on the rest of society as well. I have sketched out some possible private and public sector policy responses to raise the economic well-being of the low-paid, while recognizing the range of uncertainty about the effectiveness of policies, particularly in the absence of a major national study that brings our collective knowledge and wisdom to bear on the problem.

The next step in addressing the new inequality is, I believe, obvious: to examine in depth the pros and cons of the policies that might resolve it. As my list of strategies indicates, by policies I do not necessarily mean governmental actions. I use the term broadly to include the strategies of letting the labor market work and relying on growth and full employment. Our goal must be to find what will work to improve the real earnings of those on the bottom rungs of our income distribution, regardless of its political or philosophical pedigree. Moreover, we must search for the right mix of policies that will help low-paid workers without endangering the great success of the U.S. economy in job creation. The widening distribution of earnings and impoverishment of low-paid Americans should rank high in our national agenda of problems to solve. At the risk of sounding like some hot-air politician on the hustings, I believe that by reasoning and working together, we can solve this problem as we have solved so many others and can restore the "American dream" of a rising living standard to our less skilled and low-paid fellow citizens as well as to highly skilled and high-paid workers. Such at least is the motivation for this chapter.

Notes

1. I refer to Kevin Phillips, Peter Drucker, and George Soros.
2. Calculated from Lawrence Mishel, Aaron Bernstein, and John Schmidt, *The State of Working America, 1996–1997* (Washington, D.C.: Economic Policy Institute, 1997), table 3.23.
3. Because the census changes definitions of occupations, there are problems with classifications, but whether one uses one-digit or two-digit or three-digit occupations, or whether one excludes occupations for which definitions change markedly or uses computer programs to bridge them, the pattern is clear: inequality rose within occupations.
4. Mishel, Bernstein, and Schmidt, *The State of Working America,* table 3.10.
5. There are various reasons for the differences among series. The surveys cover different groups of workers, and utilize different measures of earnings, ranging from annual earnings to usual weekly earnings. Some series include fringe benefits, while others do not. The series may miss a sizable number of low-wage young men in inner cities and/or the earnings of workers in the "underground" economy. These problems do not mean that any particular survey gets the facts wrong but that one should examine all of them to obtain a balanced picture. See Katherine Abraham, James Spletzer, and Jay Stewart, "Divergent Trends in Alternative Real Wage Series" (Bureau of Labour Statistics, October 19, 1995).
6. Michael J. Boskin, Ellen R. Dulberger, Robert J. Gordon, Zvi Griliches, and Dale Jorgensen, "Toward a More Accurate Measure of the Cost of Living," *Advisory Commission to Study the Consumer Price Index (CPI) Final Report to Senate Finance Committee* (1996).

62   Richard B. Freeman

7. Robert Gordon reports that the rate of growth of the real consumption wage was just one-fifth as great from 1987 to 1995 as it was from 1963 to 1972, and was one-half as great from 1987 to 1995, even after he makes a huge correction for the possible bias in the CPI. Gordon, "The American Real Wage since 1963: Is It Unchanged or Has It More than Doubled?" Northwestern University, December 1995.

8. *Historical Statistics* (Paris: OECD, 1995).

9. This limits the sample to persons who work at least one week in the year. Richard B. Freeman, "The Limits of Wage Flexibility to Curing Unemployment," *Oxford Review of Economic Policy* 11, no. 1 (Spring 1995): 63–72; Chinhui Juhn, Kevin M. Murphy, and Robert H. Topel, "Why Has the Natural Rate of Unemployment Increased over Time?" *Brookings Papers on Economic Activity* 2 (1991): 75–126.

10. A fourth study, by Michael Cox and Richard Alm, is unfortunately based on largely erroneous analysis. See their "By Our Own Bootstraps: Economic Opportunity and the Dynamics of Income Distribution," *Federal Reserve Bank of Dallas Annual Report* (1995): 4. This study shows huge movements of Americans from the bottom parts of the earnings distribution to the top parts of the distribution. The degree of mobility they find is massive, far beyond what any other study has ever turned up. For instance, they claim that only 5.1 percent of persons in the lowest 20 percent of the earnings distribution remain there 16 years later while 29 percent rise to the top decile. The main reason for this is that they include teenagers and students, who have low earnings at the outset of their career but high earnings later on. The average income in the lowest 20 percent in 1975 is a bare $1,153, which could not conceivably hold for adult workers. See Peter Gottschalk, Notes on "By Their Own Bootstraps," mimeo., Boston College, April 22, 1996.

11. Moshe Buchinsky and Jennifer Hunt, "Wage Mobility in the United States," *National Bureau of Economic Research (NBER) Working Paper* no. 5455 (February 1996); and Maury Gittleman and Mary Joyce, "Earnings Mobility and Long-Run Inequality: An Analysis Using Matched CPS Data," *Industrial Relations* 35, no. 2 (April 1996): 180–196.

12. Peter Gottschalk and Robert Moffit, "The Growth of Earnings Instability in the U.S. Labor Market," *Brookings Papers on Economic Activity* 2 (1994): 216–254. Richard Burkhauser also reports little change in U.S. mobility between the 1970s and 1980s. See "Income Mobility and the Middle Class," *Seminar on Understanding Economic Inequality* (American Enterprise Institute, April 15, 1996) exhibits F, G, using the Panel Survey of Income Dynamics.

13. Stephen Rose reports a slowdown in the lifetime income growth of low-skill individuals on the Michigan Panel Survey of Income Dynamics from the 1970s to the 1980s. Rose, *On Shaky Ground: Rising Fears about Incomes and Earnings* (Washington, D.C.: National Commission on Employment Policy, October 1994). The Department of Labor shows a similar pattern in

the *National Longitudinal Survey of Youth* (Washington, D.C.: U.S. Government Printing Office [USGPO], 1994). That the rate of growth of earnings over the lifetime has fallen is thus verified in various data sets.

14. Gottschalk and Moffit, "The Growth of Earnings Instability in the U.S. Labor Market."

15. Henry S. Farber, "Trends in Long Term Employment in the United States, 1979–1996," *Princeton University Working Paper* no. 384 (June 1997).

16. Ibid.

17. Why the 13 percentage point difference? The major reason is that GDP is measured in real terms by dividing nominal GDP by the GDP deflator whereas mean family income is measured in real terms by dividing nominal family income by the CPI. From 1979 to 1994, the GDP deflator increased by 90 percent while the CPI increased by 104 percent.

18. These are my calculations based on table 1.9 in Mishel, Bernstein, and Schmidt, *The State of Working America*. The table shows that the average family income of the top 5 percent increased by $87,295. This is equivalent to $4,365 per family. Other tabulations may yield somewhat different fractions of gain accruing to the top, but they will still show the same pattern of concentration.

19. In 1974 median household income was $31,175 in 1993 dollars; it was $31,241 in 1993, using the CPI-U-X1 deflator.

20. Chinhui Juhn and Kevin Murphy, "Wage Inequality and Family Labor Supply," *NBER Working Paper* no. 5459 (February 1996), table 3.

21. Anders Bjorklund and Freeman, "Generating Equality and Eliminating Poverty: The Swedish Way," in Freeman, Swedenborg, and R. Topel (eds.), *The Welfare State in Transition: Reforming the Swedish Model* (Chicago: University of Chicago Press, 1997).

22. Why? One important reason is that institutions depend on voters, and usually more than 50 percent of the voting group (it could be union members) will have earnings below the mean and thus benefit from some compression of market-determined distributions.

23. *Employment Outlook, July 1996* (Paris: OECD, 1996), table 3.1.

24. In fact, immigration has been significant to other countries, as well as to the United States. Australia, Canada, Sweden, Austria, and France have also been major recipients of immigration in the 1970s–90s.

25. *Economic Report of the President* (Council of Economic Advisers, U.S. Department of Labor, April 23, 1996).

26. *American Workers and Economic Change* (New York: Committee for Economic Development, 1996), figs. 9 and 10.

27. Randy Ilg, "The Nature of Employment Growth," *Monthly Labor Review* 119, no. 6 (June 1996): 29–36.

28. *Employment Outlook, July 1994* (Paris: OECD, 1994), table 1.20.
29. *Employment Outlook, July 1989* (Paris: OECD, 1989), chap. 2, annexes 2A, 2B.
30. My tabulations of the Current Population Survey suggest that the OECD 1996 estimates exceed U.S. hours worked while the OECD 1995 estimates understate U.S. hours worked. To err on the side of caution, I give the more conservative OECD numbers in the text. The Japanese hours reported by the OECD do not include employees at small Japanese firms, and thus may understate Japanese hours worked. See *Employment Outlook, July 1996* (Paris: OECD, 1996) and *Employment Outlook, July 1995* (Paris: OECD, 1995).
31. Linda Bell and Richard B. Freeman, "Why Do Americans and Germans Work Different Hours?" in Friedrich Butler, Wolfgang Franz, Ronald Schettkat, and David Soskice (eds.), *Institutional Frameworks and Labor Market Performance: Comparative Views on the U.S. and German Economies* (New York: Routledge, 1995), pp. 101–131.
32. Linda Bell and Richard B. Freeman, *Working Hard,* Paper presented at the *SERF*/Upjohn Institute Conference on Working Hours (Ottawa, Canada, June 13–16, 1996).
33. *Employment Outlook, July 1996* (Paris: OECD, 1996).
34. Ibid.
35. See Richard B. Freeman, "Are Your Wages Set in Beijing?" *Journal of Economic Perspectives* 9, no. 3 (Summer 1995): 15–32; and "The Limits of Wage Flexibility to Curing Unemployment," *Oxford Review of Economic Policy* 11, no. 1 (Spring 1995): 63–72.
36. David Card, "The Effect of Unions on the Distribution of Wages: Redistribution or Relabelling?" *NBER Working Paper* no. 4195 (October 1992); John DiNardo, N. Fortin, and T. Lemiuex, "Labor Market Institutions and the Distribution of Wages, 1973–92," ms, University of Montreal (1994); and Freeman, "How Much Has De-Unionisation Contributed to the Rise in Male Earnings Inequality?" in Sheldon Danziger and Gottschalk (eds.), *Uneven Tides* (New York: Russell Sage Press, 1992), pp. 133–163.
37. Alan B. Krueger, "How Computers Have Changed the Wage Structure: Evidence from Micro Data," *Quarterly Journal of Economics* 108, no. 1 (February 1993): 33–60; Mishel, Lawrence, and Bernstein, *The State of Working America, 1994–95* (Washington, D.C.: Economic Policy Institute, 1995).
38. Jan Tinbergen, "Substitution of Graduates by Other Labour," *Kyklos* 27, no. 2 (1974): 217–26.
39. Maya Federman et al., "What Does It Mean to Be Poor in America?" *Monthly Labor Review* 199, no. 5 (May 1996): 3–17.
40. Lee Rainwater and Timothy Smeeding, "Doing Poorly: The Real Income of American Children in a Comparative Perspective," *Working Paper* 127, Syracuse University, April 1995.

41. Freeman, "Why Do So Many Young American Men Commit Crime and What Can We Do About It?" *Journal of Economic Perspectives* 10, no. 1 (Winter 1996): 25–27.

42. Brendan O'Flaherty, *Making Room: The Economics of Homelessness* (Cambridge, Mass.: Harvard University Press, 1996).

43. Gregory Pappas, Susan Queen, Wilbur Hadden, and Gail Fisher, "The Increasing Disparity in Mortality between Socioeconomic Groups in the U.S., 1960 and 1986," *The New England Journal of Medicine* 329, no. 2 (July 8, 1993): 103–9.

44. Bruce Kennedy, Ichiro Kawachi, and Deborah Prothrow-Stith, "Income Distribution and Mortality: Cross-sectional Ecological Study of the Robin Hood Index in the United States," *British Medical Journal* 312, no. 20 (April 1996): 1004–7.

45. U.S. Department of Health and Human Services, "Trends in the Well-Being of America's Children and Youth: 1996" (Washington, D.C.: USGPO, April 1996).

46. Roland Benabou, "Inequity and Growth," in Ben S. Bernanke and Julio Rotemberg (eds.), *NBER Macroeconomics Annual, 1996,* vol. 12 (Cambridge, Mass.: MIT Press, 1997).

47. Manning Marable, "Full Employment and Affirmative Action," *Uncommon Sense Series Paper* no. 7 (National Jobs for All Coalition, 1996).

48. Richard B. Freeman, "Toward an Apartheid Economy?" *Harvard Business Review* 74, no. 5 (September–October 1996): 114–126.

49. U.S. Bureau of the Census, *Statistical Abstract* (Washington, D.C.: USGPO, 1996), table 234.

50. John Bishop, "Is the Market for College Graduates Headed for a Bust? Demand and Supply Responses to Rising College Wage Premiums," *New England Economic Review,* Special Issue (May/June 1996): 115–136.

51. Richard B. Freeman, "Labor Market Tightness and the Declining Economic Position of Young Less Educated Male Workers in the United States," in Fiorella Padoa-Schioppa (ed.), *Mismatch and Labour Mobility* (New York: Cambridge University Press, 1990).

52. What I have in mind is a scheme like this: if GDP per hour worked increased by 2 percent, workers paid below $10.00 who do not receive a 2 percent pay increase might get a reduction in taxes proportionate to the difference between 2 percent and their pay increase.

53. Freeman and Joel Rogers, "Findings from the Workplace Representation and Participation Survey," mimeo., National Bureau of Economic Research (1995).

54. Jerry Jasinowski, "Improving the Economic Condition of the American Worker" (Manufacturing Institute, April 1996).

55. Frank Sammartino, "The Impact of Tax Reform on Income Distribution," (Washington, D.C.: NPA, 1996).

56. Council of Economic Advisers, *Economic Report of the President* (Washington, D.C.: USGPO, 1996).

57. U.S. Department of Labor, *Report on the American Workforce* (Washington, D.C.: USGPO, 1995).

58. James Heckman, "Assessing Clinton's Program on Job Training, Workfare, and Education in the Workplace," *NBER Working Paper Series* no. 4428 (August 1993).

59. Stephen Nickell, "The Collapse in Demand for the Unskilled: What Can Be Done?" in Freeman and Gottschalk (eds.), *Generating Jobs: How to Increase Demand for Less-Skilled Workers* (New York: Russell Sage Foundation Press, 1998), pp. 297–319.

60. Card and Krueger, *Myth and Measurement* (Princeton, N.J.: Princeton University Press, 1995).

61. Katz, "Wage Subsidies for the Disadvantaged," in Freeman and Gottschalk (eds.), *Generating Jobs: How to Increase Demand for Less-Skilled Workers,* pp. 21–52.

62. Gottschalk, "The Impact of Changes in Public Employment on Low-Wage Labor Markets," in Freeman and Gottschalk (eds.), *Generating Jobs: How to Increase Demand for Less-Skilled Workers,* pp. 72–101.

63. Gary Clyde Hufbauer and Kimberly Ann Elliot, "Measuring the Costs of Protection in the United States," (Washington, D.C.: Institute for International Economics, 1994).

64. George Borjas, Freeman, and Katz, "Searching for the Effect of Immigration on the Labor Market," *AEA Papers and Proceedings,* Session: Globalization and the U.S. Labor Market, vol. 86, no. 2 (May 1996).

65. *Employment Outlook, July 1996.*

3

The Causes and Consequences of Changing Income Inequality

David G. Blanchflower and Matthew J. Slaughter

THIS CHAPTER attempts to reconcile the views of labor economists and trade economists. Labor economists and trade economists tend to operate differently, and it is a hard task to move people out of the paradigm they know.

The chapter has three goals. First, it attempts to synthesize the research to date on the contribution of international trade to rising income inequality in the United States and to labor market developments in other countries. The basic conclusion is that despite using very different methodologies, to date, on balance, most labor and trade economists agree that trade has accounted for a relatively small share of rising U.S. income inequality across skill groups. Other factors that play an important role seem to be demand shifts from skill-biased technological change, a deceleration in the growth of skilled-labor supply, and institutional factors such as declining unionization and falling real minimum wages.

Second, the chapter attempts to sketch out where research on trade and labor markets might go from here. In particular, we emphasize that research into how globalization has affected labor markets is far from complete. Trade economists in particular have tended to work from one perspective: the standard Heckscher-Ohlin trade model. This model has proven very useful, but it is not the only way of conceptualizing how global integration might affect labor markets. Given this, the literature's current consensus that trade has played a smaller role than factors such as skill-biased technological change could be revised in the future. Additional research on globalization's role should try to balance sound theory with careful empirical work. Moreover, future research also should try to explain better the sharp rise in within-group (or "residual") wage inequality. Most of the research to date has focused on wage inequality across groups, but within-group inequality has been a major part of the overall inequality picture. To the extent that trade, technology, or other hypotheses cannot address this issue, our overall understanding of the causes of rising inequality will be limited.

Finally, the chapter discusses whether public policy solutions to rising inequality depend on understanding the exact causes. While the ongoing academic debate about the causes of rising inequality might help policy, an accurate understanding of these causes is not necessarily a precondition for most well-targeted policies. If policymakers want to help those whose relative (and, in many cases, real) incomes have fallen, sensible policies can be formulated without knowing these causes. The ongoing disagreement about causes does not imply there is disagreement about possible solutions.

The remaining sections summarize the basic facts about changing income distributions and the research to date about the causes, suggest directions for future research, and conclude by discussing the relevance (or lack thereof) of all this research to public policy.

The Research to Date

THE BASIC FACTS

The Current Population Surveys and other similar works have provided the main information about earnings inequality. Economists, primarily labor economists, have analyzed these data, which report on the earnings levels of millions of individuals, to determine the basic facts. Similar data files are available in many other advanced countries, and there has been a growing effort to compare and contrast the evidence for those countries with those for the United States.[1]

Since the early 1970s the U.S. labor market has changed in three distinct ways. First, earnings have become much more unequal between more skilled and less skilled workers. For example, in 1979 male college-educated workers earned on average 30 percent more than male high school–educated workers. By 1995 this premium for college-educated workers had risen to about 70 percent. Within the class of male high school–educated workers, workers at the 90th percentile of the wage distribution earned 60 percent more than workers at the 50th percentile in 1979. By 1995 this "90/50" gap had reached 83 percent. The overall wage distribution reveals a similar picture of rising inequality. Between 1979 and 1994 the ratio of the earnings of a male worker at the ninth decile compared with one at the median rose from 1.73 to 2.04. At the same time the earnings of that median male worker rose from 1.84 to 2.13 times the earnings of a worker at the first decile.[2]

The rise in U.S. earnings inequality observed is far from a global phenomenon. While many member countries of the Organization for Economic Cooperation and Development (OECD) experienced increases in earnings inequality during the 1980s, with the exception of the United Kingdom, the orders of magnitude were well below those experienced in the United States. Table 3–1 reports average five-year changes in the ratios of the ninth decile to the median and the median to the first decile. Only the United Kingdom and the United States have continued to experience a rapid rise in inequality into the 1990s, albeit it at a slower rate than occurred in the 1980s. While the tendency toward increased inequality appears to have slackened somewhat, only a few countries, notably Canada, Finland, and Germany, have actually experienced a decline in earnings dispersion over the last five or ten years.

Table 3–1 Average Five-Year Changes in Inequality since 1979

	1979–1989		1989–1994/95	
	D9/D5	D5/D1	D9/D5	D5/D1
Australia	.02	.02	.06	−.04
Austria	.02	.00	.00	.07
Belgium	−.01	−.02	−.02	−.02
Canada	.03	.08	−.01	−.13
Finland	.03	.00	−.02	−.10
France	.02	−.01	.01	.00
Germany	.01	−.12	−.03	−.08
Italy	−.03	−.23	.19	.32
Japan	.05	.00	−.02	−.07
Netherlands	.03	.00	.02	.01
New Zealand	.04	.05	.02	−.03
Sweden	.02	.01	.03	.00
United Kingdom	.09	.05	.03	.02
United States	.12	.11	.06	.07

Note: D9/D5 is the value of the ninth decile over the first decile. D5/D1 is the value of the fifth decile over the first decile.
Source: OECD, *Employment Outlook, July 1996* (Paris: OECD, 1996), table 3.1.

It should also be noted that the rise in U.S. inequality appears to predate increases occurring elsewhere.

While most OECD countries did not experience a sharp rise in inequality, many confronted increased unemployment. Table 3–2 presents the range of unemployment outcomes from 1973 through 1993 for a number of OECD countries. It is certainly true that, on average, earnings inequality did increase less, while unemployment increased more in Europe than it did in North America from 1979 to 1994. However, a number of countries are important exceptions. Of particular interest is the United Kingdom, which experienced *both* a rise in earnings inequality *and* a rise in unemployment.[3] Countries with a similar mix (albeit with less inequality) are Australia, New Zealand, and Canada. The unemployment experience of Belgium looks much like that in the United Kingdom despite the fact that it experienced a decline in inequality over the period. Unemployment in the Netherlands has been low and declining in the 1990s, alongside only a small rise in earnings inequality. Similar to the Netherlands are Austria, Japan, and Sweden. The experience of other OECD countries has been more mixed.

The second important change in the U.S. labor market has been that average real earnings have been growing much more slowly. In the 100 years to 1973, real average hourly earnings rose by 1.9 percent per year.

Table 3–2 Percentage Unemployment Rates, 1973–1993

	1973	1979	1985	1989	1993
OECD	3.3%	5.1%	7.8%	6.4%	8.0%
OECD Europe	3.0	5.6	9.9	8.5	10.4
of which EU	2.7	5.4	10.5	8.7	11.0
Australia	2.3	6.1	8.1	6.1	10.8
Austria	1.0	2.1	3.6	3.1	4.2
Belgium	2.4	7.5	12.3	9.3	10.3
Canada	5.5	7.4	10.4	7.5	11.2
Finland	2.3	5.9	5.0	3.4	17.7
France	2.7	5.9	10.2	9.4	11.5
Germany	1.0	3.2	8.0	6.8	8.8
Italy	6.2	7.6	10.1	11.8	10.8
Japan	1.3	2.1	2.6	2.3	2.5
Netherlands	2.2	5.4	10.9	8.3	6.2
New Zealand	0.2	1.9	4.1	7.1	9.4
Sweden	2.5	2.1	2.8	1.3	8.2
United Kingdom	2.2	4.6	11.5	6.1	10.2
United States	4.8	5.8	7.1	5.2	6.7

Source: OECD, *Labour Force Statistics, 1973–1993* (Paris: OECD, 1995).

Since 1973 Consumer Price Index (CPI)–deflated real wages have *fallen* by about 0.4 percent per year. The combination of flat average wages and rising inequality means that tens of millions of American workers have experienced stagnation or even absolute declines in their real earnings in recent decades. U.S. workers at the low end of the earnings distribution have suffered the most, particularly those in the lowest decile. For example, the real hourly earnings of high school–educated males fell by 20 percent from 1979 to 1993.[4] In contrast, there has been considerable growth in real earnings at the top of the earnings distribution. Senior managers and executives have experienced large increases in real earnings over the last couple of decades, especially when total compensation, including stock options, is included.

In contrast to the United States, in most OECD countries, including the United Kingdom, there has been strong real earnings growth across the wage distribution. For only two countries (New Zealand and Australia) has a rise in earnings inequality implied weak growth or even declining real wages for workers at the bottom half of the earnings distribution.[5] In most industrial countries, low-paid workers have experienced real earnings growth over the last two decades.[6]

There is mixed evidence whether families are able to mitigate the impact of increased earnings variability. Susan Dynarski and Jonathan Gruber report that households have responded to earnings variation by smoothing their consumption.[7] They find that roughly half of this consumption smoothing occurs through offsetting income flows, in particular through the tax and transfer system, with the other half coming through savings and dissaving. This consumption smoothing is fairly complete: Dynarski and Gruber report that only about 10 percent of the variation in a household head's earnings is translated into variation in nondurables consumption and 17 percent in durables. Consumption expenditures, particularly on durable goods, do appear to be much more responsive to unemployment-induced earnings reductions for low-education or low-wealth groups than for high-education or high-wealth groups. In contrast, however, Orazion Attanasio and Steven J. Davis report for the United States that, among the less educated, real household consumption fell sharply during the early 1980s in parallel with sharp declines in real wages for those groups.[8] Among the college educated, both real consumption and real earnings rose throughout the 1980s. Attanasio and Davis conclude that this strong correlation across groups between real consumption and real earnings represents a failure of the hypothesis of between-group consumption insurance.

The third important fact is that in most countries, the rise in inequality has occurred not only between workers of different skill levels but also among workers *within* a given skill level. Among workers in the same occupation or with the same years of schooling and age, the higher-paid ones had larger increases in earnings than the lower-paid ones. Moreover, it appears that earnings inequality has risen within virtually all occupations. Panels A through C of Figure 3–1 illustrate the changes in inequality within groups for the United States, Great Britain, and France, respectively. Movements in inequality within groups, sometimes called "residual inequality," tracks closely overall change.[9] It rose steadily in the United States from the 1970s, while it declined in Great Britain in the 1970s but rose in the 1980s. In contrast, residual inequality was generally flat throughout the 1970s and 1980s in France. In the United States rising residual inequality accounts for approximately half

Figure 3–1 Within-Group Wage Inequality

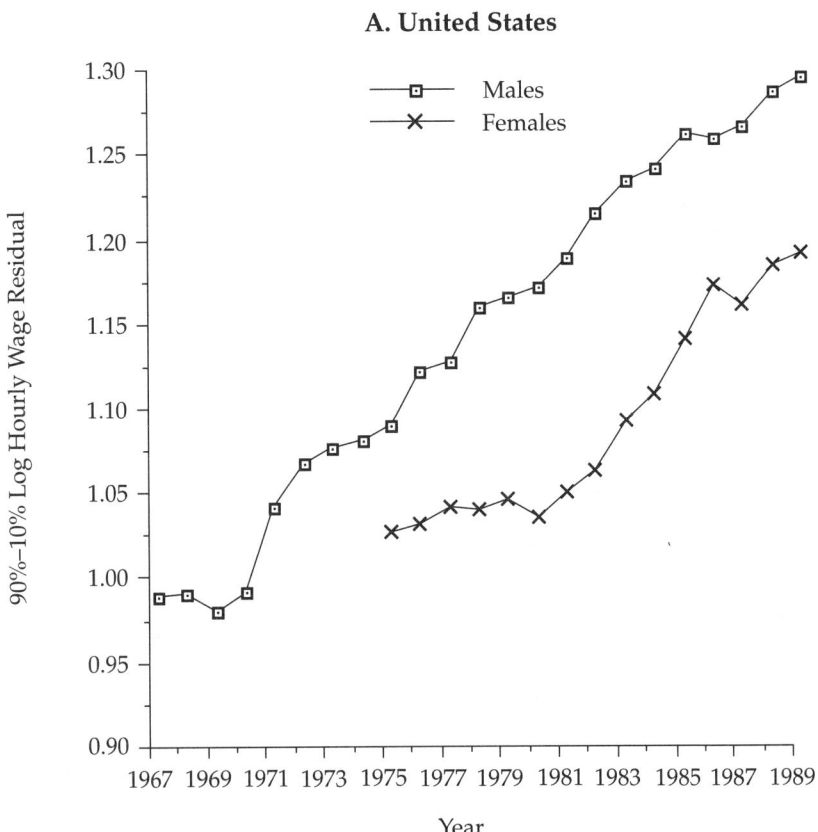

Figure 3–1 Within-Group Wage Inequality (*Continued*)

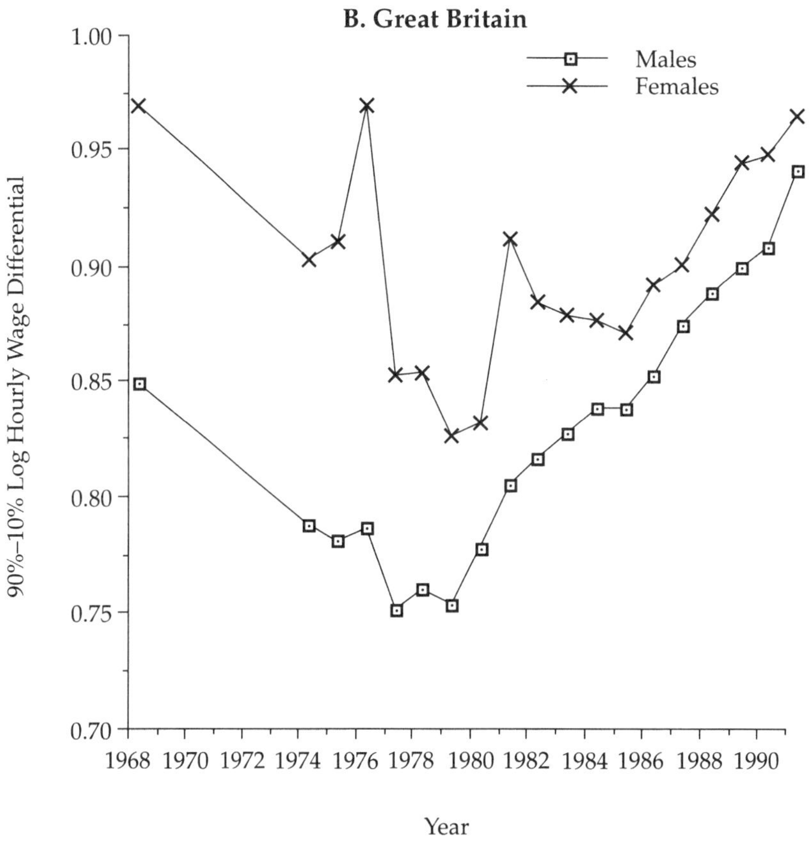

of the overall rise in wage inequality. Even if the differences between groups, such as the educational or wage premium, were to return to their 1979 levels (perhaps through an increase in the supply of skilled workers), overall inequality in the United States would still be higher than in earlier years.

In our view, any comprehensive explanation for the changes in wage inequality that have occurred over the past two decades has to be consistent with the rather different experiences that have occurred across countries. Moreover, it also must address rising inequality within skill groups as well as across groups. In what follows we examine possible explanations.

Figure 3–1 Within-Group Wage Inequality (*Continued*)

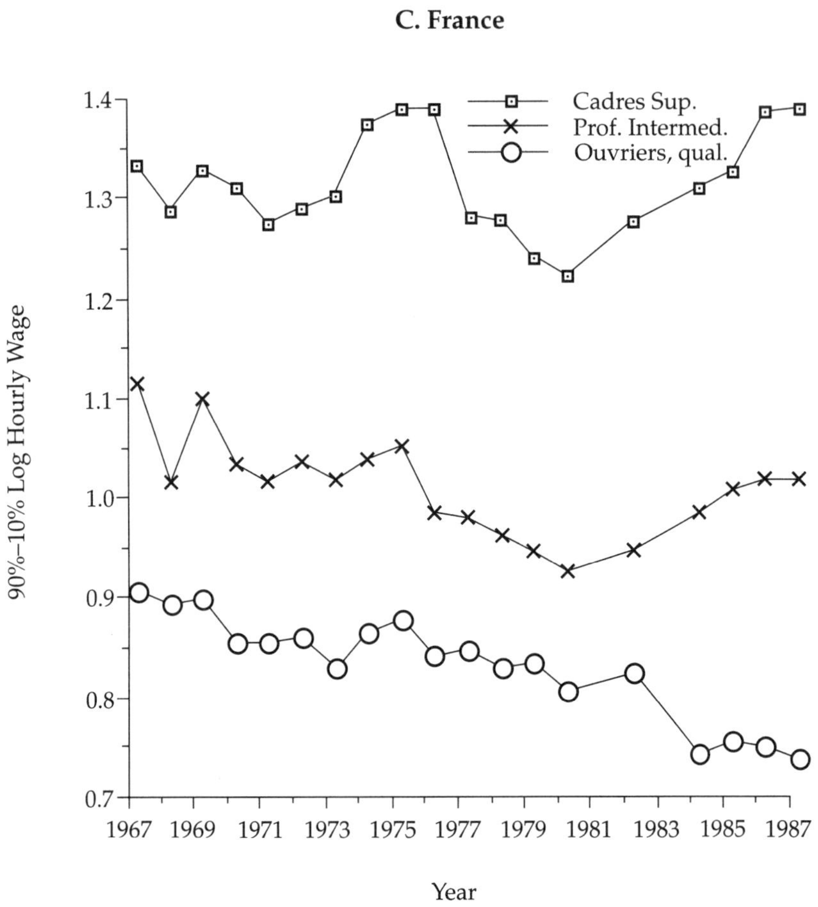

C. France

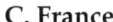

Source: Lawrence F. Katz, Gary W. Loveman, and David G. Blanchflower, "A Comparison of Changes in the Structure of Wages in Four OECD Countries," in Lawrence F. Katz and Richard B. Freeman (eds.), *Differences and Changes in Wage Structures* (Chicago: University of Chicago Press and National Bureau of Economic Research, 1995).

THE FRAMEWORK OF CAUSES: DEMAND, SUPPLY, AND INSTITUTIONS

There are three main candidates to explain rising inequality: shifts in relative labor demand, shifts in relative labor supply, and changes in labor market institutions. Within the set of demand-side and institutional explanations, those that have received the most attention are international trade, technological change, the composition of aggregate demand, the decline in the real minimum wage, and deunionization. On the supply side, changes in the supply of educated workers have been emphasized as an importance influence. Presumably some combination of all of these has contributed to increased wage dispersion.

One broad point of consensus is that a primary cause of rising inequality has been a shift in relative labor demand toward more skilled workers. Lawrence F. Katz and Kevin M. Murphy document that for the U.S. economy overall, supply changes alone cannot explain rising income inequality.[10] The main reason is that for most time periods and skill groups, both the relative earnings and relative supply of more skilled workers have been rising. Relative earnings can increase along with relative supply only if relative demand is increasing as well. Katz and Murphy conclude that demand growth has been an important component of the change in factor prices since 1963 and particularly during the 1980s. David H. Autor, Katz, and Alan B. Krueger also report an acceleration of the demand shift between the 1970s and 1980s relative to earlier decades.[11] Looking at just the manufacturing sector, Eli Berman, John Bound, and Zvi Griliches and Robert Z. Lawrence and Matthew J. Slaughter find the same trend: that even though the relative wage of more skilled workers has been rising, within most industries firms have been employing relatively more of these workers.[12] These facts point strongly toward a shift in labor demand.

THE INFLUENCE OF INTERNATIONAL TRADE ON LABOR DEMAND

Both trade and labor economists have studied whether international trade has contributed to the demand shift away from less skilled workers. To date, the majority of trade economists working in this area have tested trade's role in a Heckscher-Ohlin framework. The standard assumptions are that all countries make the same sufficiently diversified mix of products under perfect competition and with all factors (in particular, skilled and unskilled labor) perfectly mobile across industries. In this context the Stolper-Samuelson theorem predicts that international trade influences relative factor demands and thus factor prices.

The basic idea underlying all versions of the Stolper-Samuelson theorem is straightforward. International trade affects the prices of products, which, in turn, affect factor prices by changing relative factor demands.

Any trade-induced change in a country's product prices alters the relative profit opportunities facing its price-taking firms, which respond by shifting their resources toward (away from) those industries in which relative profitability has risen (fallen). This entails a shift in country-wide demand for factors of production: Demand rises (falls) for the factors used relatively intensively in the now relatively profitable (unprofitable) sectors. Given fixed factor supplies, changed factor demands mean changed factor prices. Thus trade influences relative factor prices via changes in the terms of trade—which may result from trade liberalization and other causes.

A number of papers have tested whether the Stolper-Samuelson process has contributed to rising income inequality. Several have examined changes in U.S. product prices to see whether the prices of unskilled-labor–intensive products have fallen relative to the prices of skilled-labor–intensive products. Jagdish Bhagwati analyzes the aggregate U.S. terms of trade (i.e., the price of U.S. exports relative to the price of U.S. imports) and finds they fell during the 1980s.[13] This is evidence that skilled-labor–intensive products did not have relatively higher price increases (assuming exports employ skilled labor intensively relative to imports). Lawrence and Slaughter analyze various samples of industry-level U.S. manufacturing prices over the 1980s.[14] They find no clear evidence that skilled-labor–intensive products had relatively larger price increases. Jeffrey D. Sachs and Howard Shatz argue that computer prices should be excluded from any analysis because these prices are measured poorly.[15] For their restricted sample, Sachs and Shatz find that skilled-labor–intensive products had slightly higher relative price increases in the 1980s. Edward E. Leamer allows for various degrees of pass-through from technology changes (as measured by total-factor productivity growth) to product prices; he also analyzes the 1960s and 1970s as well as the 1980s.[16] For all pass-through specifications for the 1980s and the 1960s, he finds no concentration of price increases in skilled-labor–intensive industries. However, he consistently finds relative price increases for the skilled-labor–intensive products for the 1970s. Like Leamer, Robert E. Baldwin and Glen C. Cain control for the effect of technology on product prices, and they also conclude that trade seems not to have contributed to widening income inequality during the 1980s.[17] Finally, Krueger finds that for a sample of 150 of the 450 four-digit Standard Industrial Classification (SIC) industries, from 1989 to 1995 skilled-labor–intensive industries did experience slightly higher product-price increases.[18]

On balance, then, these product-price studies generally find little evidence that trade contributed much at all to increased income inequality during the 1980s. Some studies do find evidence of relative price declines for unskilled-labor–intensive products during the 1970s and the 1990s. However, on many measures these were not periods of rapidly rising earnings inequality.

In contrast to these product-price studies, many labor economists and some trade economists have analyzed the effect of trade flows—exports and imports. The difference in focus can be attributed in part to the fact that many labor economists have expressed concern about the quality of aggregate price data. For example, Freeman worries that "price data is subject to serious measurement problems. Import prices exist for relatively few industries and cover only some goods in those industries. Output prices suffer from an aggregation problem, since the sectors with imports presumably include domestic goods that differ in important dimensions from the imports. Changes in the quality of products not captured in the indices create measurement error, which may be correlated with the skill intensity of production."[19] In addition to concerns about data quality, many economists also worry that product-price studies do not control adequately for nontrade influences on these prices.

Given these concerns, various authors have searched for effects of trade in output or employment quantities. Bound and Johnson treat trade as a product-demand shock and find that it explains very little of the rise in inequality.[20] Berman, Bound, and Griliches assume that trade operates by shifting demand *across* industries only (which could be true, for example, with fixed-input production technologies and an unchanging set of industries produced).[21] Yet they calculate that the large majority of the manufacturing-wide demand shift occurred *within* industries. From this they conclude that trade played no important role. L. G. Kletzer uses industry-level data on the United States drawn from the March Annual Demographic Files of the Current Population Survey and finds that foreign competition accounts for a relatively small share of employment and wage changes.[22] Furthermore, Davis, J. Haltiwanger, and S. Schuh examine firm- and plant-level data from the Census of Manufactures over many years and find no evidence that either job creation or job destruction varies across industries according to the trade flows in those industries.[23]

Other studies have focused on trade volumes. Paul R. Krugman calibrates a simple general-equilibrium model of the U.S. economy to consider what changes in relative product prices and wages would be consistent with the observed increase in imports from less developed countries (LDCs).[24] In his model, the small amount of imports that enter the United States from LDCs (1.6 percent of total OECD output in 1990) corresponds to very small changes in relative product prices and relative wages—magnitudes he terms well within measurement error. George J. Borjas, Freeman, and Katz argue that the effect of trade on labor markets can be thought of as working through factor supplies, not factor demands: Imports from developing countries are treated as an increase in the U.S. relative endowment of less skilled labor while exports reduce it.[25] Using input-output tables to infer from observed U.S. trade flows the implicit quantities of factor services embodied in these flows, they calculate that the large U.S. trade deficits from 1980 to 1985 can account for approximately 15 percent to 20 percent of the total rise in income inequality. But they also conclude that this effect dissipated in later years as the trade deficit shrank relative to total output. Using a similar methodology, in a later paper they conclude that U.S. trade—particularly trade with less developed countries—accounts for less than 10 percent of either the rise in the college/high school wage differential or the drop in relative wages of high school dropouts.[26]

Many trade economists believe that these quantity studies—particularly the trade volume studies—have serious problems. A major issue has been the conditions under which trade volumes correctly identify the effect of trade on relative factor prices.[27] One serious problem with relying on trade volumes is they are endogenous outcomes: that is, trade flows are the outcome of decisions of producers and consumers worldwide. Trade volumes are not exogenous causes, and they can change for nontrade reasons, such as a rise in aggregate demand triggered by higher government spending.

The methodological issues surrounding the proper way to gauge trade's role have not been resolved. Nevertheless, what is important to emphasize is that the large majority of studies to date—*regardless of their methodology*—find only a small role for international trade in rising U.S. income inequality. Product prices, labor shifts, trade flows: All these data have been analyzed in different ways, and the recurring conclusion is that trade has not mattered much.

OTHER INFLUENCES ON LABOR DEMAND:
SKILL-BIASED TECHNOLOGICAL CHANGE

It is fair to say that, at present, many economists think that the biggest single cause of changes in the U.S. income distribution is technological change. In most studies, the conclusion that technology is the main culprit has not been drawn from direct observation or measurement.

Rather, it is the residual explanation—it is largely a name for our ignorance. The often-made argument is "it isn't X, Y, or Z so it must be skill-biased technical change."

A few recent papers provide direct evidence of this technological shift and link it to wage outcomes. Berman, Bound, and Griliches present several case studies that document the technological changes that have occurred in industries experiencing large shifts toward more skilled workers.[28] Following this work, Berman, Bound, and Steve Machin present evidence that many OECD countries have experienced rising relative employment of more skilled workers within the same industries.[29] This, they argue, is evidence that the skill-biased technological change is a global phenomenon. Krueger demonstrates evidence that people who use computers on the job tend to earn more than similar workers who do not use computers on the job.[30] And Autor, Katz, and Krueger analyze several plausibly direct measures of technological change (e.g., rising investment in office equipment) and find a high correlation across industries between these direct measures and indirect measures such as rising skilled labor shares of the total wage bill.[31]

But the evidence in favor of the skill-biased technological change hypothesis is not without its own set of problems. John E. DiNardo and Jorn-Steffen Pischke emphasize the difficulty in inferring causation between income inequality and measures of computer usage.[32] Rather than the computers causing higher wages for the users, it might be that the more skilled, higher-paid workers tend to choose jobs using computers. Also, the technology story is not easily reconciled with sluggish growth in average U.S. real wages. Real wages approximately equal labor productivity: if massive investments in new computer technologies have been made, why have these investments not lifted average labor productivity and, thus, wages? Finally, it might be wondered why, if technological changes have been similar across countries (as Berman, Bound, and Machin suggest), they have not produced similar inequality outcomes.

More generally, we would argue that research to date has not demonstrated that labor demand factors explain much of the *differential* growth of wage inequality among countries. In fact, all advanced countries have experienced large, steady shifts in the industrial and occupational structure of employment toward sectors and job categories that use a greater proportion of more educated workers.[33] Also, the share of employment in manufacturing declined everywhere except in Japan. Perhaps differential labor demand shifts help explain the experiences of different countries. But if this is the case, it will need to be demonstrated that different countries have experienced different combinations of trade policy changes as well as differences in the rate of new-technology adoptions, fiscal policies, and other factors affecting the demand for products and factors.

THE ROLE OF SUPPLY CHANGES

Current research does indicate that differences among countries in growth in the supply of workers has contributed to the greater rise in skill premiums in the United States than in other countries. In the United States in the 1970s, the baby-boom cohort moved from college to the labor market, increasing the relative supply of more skilled workers. But in the 1980s the baby boom busted and growth in the relative supply of more skilled workers slowed considerably. These changes help explain why the U.S. college–high school wage differential fell during the 1970s and then reversed around 1979. Table 3–3 illustrates the differential growth rates of college-educated workers in the United States, Britain, France, and Japan. Katz, G. Loveman, and David G. Blanchflower found that, under a set of plausible assumptions, such differences can account for a large portion of the declining U.S. skill premium in the 1970s and its rise in the 1980s.[34]

Some of the supply changes might reflect a nontrade aspect of globalization: immigration. There are two key facts here. First, immigration rates have risen sharply since around 1970. Second, since about that time U.S. immigrants' average skill levels have been declining. Today one-third of U.S. high school dropouts are foreign-born.[35] Recent immigrants might have helped expand the relative supply of less skilled workers during the 1980s and thus put downward pressure on the wages of less skilled U.S. natives who compete with these immigrants for jobs.

The evidence on immigration's contribution to rising income inequality is mixed. Some studies find that immigration-driven supply shifts have *not* contributed very much to wage dispersion. David Card cites many papers that report very small effects of immigrants on native wages: The ballpark figure is that a 10 percent increase in the fraction of immigrants in an area reduces native wages by less than 1 percent.[36]

But there is a methodological debate among labor economists on this point. Most of these studies have used cities (or metropolitan statistical areas) as the unit of observation. Borjas argues that this approach ignores the possibility that workers move across cities and

Table 3-3 Growth Rates of Male and Female College-Educated Workers in Four Countries

	Annual Log Growth Rates	
United States	1969–1979	1979–1989
Employees age 18–64	.043	.023
Population age 18–64	.043	.026
Britain	1973–1979	1979–1989
Employees age 16–60	.068	.037
Population age 16–60	.068	.037
France	1970–1980	1980–1989
Labor force age 15+	.039	.050
Population age 15+ (males)	.045	.039
Population age 15+ (females)	.026	.046
Japan	1971–1979	1979–1987
All employees age 15+	.050	.029

Source: Reprinted, with permission of the publisher, from L. Katz, G. Loveman, and D. Blanchflower, "A Comparison of Changes in the Structure of Wages in Four OECD Countries," in L. Katz and D. Freeman (eds.), *Differences and Changes in Wage Structure*, (Chicago: University of Chicago Press and NBER, 1995), p. 48.

regions.[37] This mobility can diffuse the impact of immigrants from their destination city throughout the national labor market. If native workers can leave a city when immigrants arrive or if outside native workers can choose not to relocate to that city, then the labor supply change in the destination city can be much smaller than the total immigrant inflow. Thus, wages decline everywhere, not just in the destination city (although presumably the nationwide decline is much smaller than the destination-city decline would be if native workers were immobile). To measure accurately the impact of immigrants on wages, the entire United States must be studied. With this national perspective, Borjas, Freeman, and Katz find that immigration has sharply pressured the earnings of the least skilled Americans.[38] Specifically, post-1979 immigration can account for between 27 and 55 percent of the decline in the relative wages of high school dropouts. However, immigrants can explain no more than 10 percent of the decline in the wages of high school graduates relative to college graduates.

Immigration seems to have mattered less in the rest of the OECD. Immigration flows have been small in the United Kingdom since 1980, yet they were substantial in the period of declining wage inequality before 1970. Similarly, immigrant flows into France and Germany appear to have coincided with a narrowing, not a widening, of the earnings distribution.

THE ROLE OF LABOR MARKET INSTITUTIONS

In addition to supply and demand, a third possible influence on relative wages is labor market institutions interacting with supply and demand. The two most important ones are unions and minimum wages. And the broad evidence here is that both have mattered: In the two OECD countries with the strongest rise in inequality during the 1980s (the United States and the United Kingdom), both of these institutions weakened in ways that tended to exacerbate inequality.

The decline in trade unions might be an important explanation of rising inequality. Unions reduce inequality by standardizing pay rates among workers within an establishment and across establishments. The threat of unionization also forces nonunion employers to raise pay or benefits to keep unions out. Thus, strong unions generally mean less inequality.

Table 3-4 reports union density rates across countries. In the United States, union density has declined dramatically since 1970.[39] The U.S. decline is greater than in other countries and predates declines elsewhere—as does the nation's rise in inequality. In the United Kingdom, unionization rose strongly in the 1970s and then declined subsequently. Again, this trend closely tracks the inequality changes over the period. In the rest of the OECD the evidence is more mixed. Some countries (e.g., Denmark and Sweden) saw increased union density over the period. Others experienced declines in union density in the 1980s, with some experiencing recovery or no further declines in the 1990s. Moreover, the decline in earnings inequality in the 1990s that occurred in a number of countries (Belgium, Canada, and Germany) is associated with stabilizing or even slight increases in density in a number of countries (Japan, Netherlands, Norway, Canada, and Germany).

Minimum wages obviously tend to reduce inequality, at least among the employed. The fall in the real minimum wage also seems to have contributed to rising inequality in the United States and United Kingdom. The real value of the minimum wage in the United States declined substantially over the period 1970 to 1990, and even with recent

Table 3-4 Union Density Across OECD Countries, 1970–1994

	1970	1980	1990	1993
Declining Density				
Austria	61.3	56.2	45.9	43.2
France	22.0	17.5	9.5	8.8 (1992)
Greece	–	47.7 (1977)	34.1	31.8
Japan	34.7	30.8	25.2	24.2
Portugal	–	60.7 (1984)	31.8	–
Turkey	–	29.2	21.5 (1989)	–
United States	27.3	22.3	15.9	15.3
Sharp Rises in Density				
Denmark	60.0	76.0	73.0	76.3
Finland	51.4	69.8	72.0	80.1 (1994)
Iceland	–	68.1 (1979)	96.4	–
Spain	–	12.5	16.1	22.0
Sweden	67.7	80.0	84.0	90.5 (1994)
1970s rises; Declines in 1980s and 1990s				
Australia	44.2	49.9	40.8	35.0 (1994)
Ireland	53.1	57.1	51.7	49.2 (1992)
Luxembourg	46.8	52.2 (1981)	49.7 (1987)	–
New Zealand	40.8 (1972)	47.7 (1981)	45.5	30.1
Switzerland	28.3	30.7	26.6	25.7 (1992)
United Kingdom	44.8	50.7	39.1	36.3
Declining density in 1980s; Stabilizing in 1990s				
Belgium	47.1	55.9	51.2	52.9 (1992)
Canada	31.0	36.1	35.8	37.4
Germany	33.0	35.6	32.9	33.2 (1994)
Italy	36.3	49.3	38.8	38.8 (1992)
Netherlands	38.0	35.3	25.5	25.5 (1994)
Norway	54.9	56.9	56.0	58.1 (1994)

Notes: Data for Canada, Greece, Iceland, Luxembourg, New Zealand (1970–1986), Portugal, and Turkey is membership including retired and unemployed members as a percent of wage and salary earners in employment. For the remaining countries it excludes from the numerator union members who were retired or unemployed.

Administrative data based on union files used with the following exceptions. Survey data used in the United States, 1980–; Australia, 1990–; New Zealand, 1989–. Confederation data used in France, Greece, Iceland, Luxembourg, Portugal (1990), Spain (1977–1979), and Turkey.

Source: Katz, Loveman, and Blanchflower, "A Comparison of Changes in the Structure of Wages in Four OECD Countries," pp. 54–55.

increases it remains very low by historical standards. In the United Kingdom, wages councils, which set sectoral pay rates for the young and the unskilled, were gradually abolished during the 1980s. Even though the abolition appears to have had little impact on employment, it appears to have reduced wages at the low end. Here again the United States and the United Kingdom look different from other OECD countries. For example, strong rises in France's minimum wage appear to have prevented a sharp erosion in real wages at the low end of the French wage distribution.[40]

Overall, then, the timing of changes in these institutions and wage inequality suggests a link between them. More systematic research has supported this view. Freeman argues that one-fifth of the total rise in inequality can be attributed to declining union power.[41] Blau and Kahn argue that more decentralized wage-setting mechanisms in the United States account for the greater rise in male wage inequality in the United States than in other countries.[42] And Nicole Fortin and Thomas Lemieux (and, relatedly, John E. DiNardo, Fortin, and Lemieux) argue that one-third of the total rise in U.S. wage inequality in the 1980s can be attributed to declines in unionization and the real minimum wage along with economic deregulation.[43]

Conclusion About the Current Evidence on Inequality Causes

Research to date does not allow the precise allocation of the relative contribution of demand, supply, and institutional forces to rising U.S. wage inequality. However, at this time most economists agree that trade has not been a major factor in the shift in labor demand away from less skilled and toward more skilled workers. Other factors playing an important role seem to be demand shifts from skill-biased technological change, a deceleration in the growth of the skilled-labor supply, and institutional factors such as declining unionization and falling real minimum wages.

Future Research: The Need to Test Other Aspects of Globalization

Where might research go from here? To answer this question, first we highlight some of the important differences in thinking among labor and trade economists. We will then discuss how bridging these differences might help direct future work.

THE DIFFERENCES BETWEEN LABOR ECONOMISTS AND TRADE ECONOMISTS

As the research has progressed, methodological debates have emerged—at times quite spirited. There have been disagreements between trade economists, between labor economists, and between trade economists and labor economists. At the risk of overgeneralizing, it is probably fair to say that many of the "trade vs. labor" debates reveal fundamental methodological differences between the two fields. Trade economists tend to value clear general-equilibrium thinking, whereas labor economists tend to value careful empirical work. The reasons for this difference in relative values is not entirely clear. History might explain part of it. For a long time labor economists have had more and higher-quality data sets available than trade economists. Perhaps over time those lacking data concentrated on theoretical issues while those with data focused on empirical issues. Whatever the reasons for these taste differences, they clearly have driven many of the methodological debates. Some trade economists fault labor economists for being atheoretical while some labor economists fault trade economists for sloppy empirical work and untestable theories.

In particular, some trade economists argue that labor economists miss many of the important general-equilibrium insights of trade theory. Trade economists tend to prefer to think about—and to analyze empirically—many markets simultaneously. This is crucial, because many of trade theory's key insights, such as the Stolper-Samuelson theorem, rely on interactions among product and factor markets. Labor economists who focus on an individual labor market or markets will necessarily miss these general-equilibrium issues.

Some labor economists respond that because there are few appropriate instruments in the labor market to solve endogeneity problems, identification is difficult to achieve. When set alongside the serious aggregation and omitted variable biases associated with estimating general equilibrium models, there is a widely held view that such models are unlikely to produce useful insights. More generally, labor economists also seem skeptical about the validity of some of the basic assumptions of most trade theories.

For example, standard trade theory assumes that factor markets are perfectly competitive—that every factor earns its marginal revenue product. There is a good deal of evidence, however, that rent-sharing is prevalent and hence that labor markets should be characterized as noncompetitive.[44] This is especially true in Europe, and a growing body of evidence finds this even in the United States and Canada.[45] Similarly, standard trade theory assumes perfect interindustry factor mobility within countries. This implies, among other things, that the same factor should earn the same wage in all industries. Yet labor economists have assembled a large body of evidence that interindustry wage differentials are sizable, persistent over time, and stable across countries.[46]

RECONCILING METHODOLOGIES: WHAT CAN BE DONE?

It is probably true that most labor and trade economists could learn something from the other group. Labor economists probably should think harder about the theory underlying their data analysis, while trade economists should worry more about data quality and about how their theories accord with basic facts.

This learning could help push the research on trade and labor markets in a much-needed direction. The literature's current best guess that trade has played a smaller role than other factors, such as skill-biased technological change, should be prudently regarded as tentative, because this conclusion depends so strongly on research from one perspective: the Heckscher-Ohlin model. The model's detailed analysis of multiple factor and product markets makes it a natural tool to study a general-equilibrium problem such as trade and wages. However, many issues regarding how trade—and globalization more generally—affects labor markets remain understudied.

What has not been looked at? First, many nontrade aspects of globalization. We still know very little about how the U.S. labor market may have been affected by exchange-rate volatility or increased international capital mobility. Second, it may be that "nontrade" influences on labor demand are themselves driven by international trade. Might not the pace of technological change depend on (among other things) the competitive pressures generated by international trade? Adrian Wood calls this type of technological change "defensive innovation": Firms innovate only when forced to defend existing market positions against international competitors.[47] Another idea that warrants further exploration is that deunionization reflects (again, among other things) the competitive pressures generated by international trade.

These aspects of globalization seem plausible. There are anecdotes of firms adopting information technology in order to remain internationally competitive. Similarly, there are anecdotes of firms gaining bargaining strength against unions by threatening to hire foreign factors of production (via foreign direct investment or outsourcing to foreign suppliers).

The difficulty is to find appropriate empirical tests to distinguish between these competing explanations. Anecdotes help direct research, but as trade theory rightly emphasizes, they must hold up in general equilibrium. To the extent that the data permit, these issues, like the product price studies, are best addressed with broad data sets. On the other hand, these are subtle questions that may be better analyzed with industry- or firm-level data. Careful consideration should be given to balancing a general-equilibrium focus against industry-level and firm-level case studies for which better-quality data can be obtained.

Some researchers have moved beyond Heckscher-Ohlin models and factor-content studies to analyze the effects of globalization. For example, Robert C. Feenstra and Gordon Hanson consider the factor price implications of Ricardian trade among countries making different sets of products (distinct from the standard Heckscher-Ohlin assumption that all countries make the same set of products).[48] Slaughter considers whether foreign direct investment by multinational corporations has contributed to U.S. income inequality.[49] Borjas and Valerie A. Ramey analyze whether international trade has pressured imperfectly competitive industries to squeeze the rents earned by less skilled workers in those industries.[50] And Slaughter considers whether international trade has pressured U.S. labor markets not by changing the prices of factors but by changing the elasticities of demand for factors.[51] It is worth noting that in some cases, the results suggest an important role for trade in explaining rising inequality. More research along these lines will expand our understanding of trade and labor markets.

In proposing future research directions, more attention should be paid to explaining residual (within-group) inequality. This inequality likely will be difficult to reconcile with models that group factors of production based on observable characteristics. The problem affects not only standard trade models but many labor models as well. A comprehensive trade-based explanation of residual inequality will have to expand standard trade models to incorporate some explanation of this dimension of inequality.

Overall, research into how trade and other aspects of globalization have affected labor markets is far from complete. Therefore, economists' current best guess that trade and other globalization considerations have played only a small role may be subject to revision. If progress is to be made, research will need to develop theories with clear empirical predictions that can be tested against the available data.

Public Policy Responses to Rising Inequality: Do the Causes Matter?

Many sensible public policy responses to rising inequality can be undertaken without knowing the exact combination of the causes, primarily because the policy principle of targeting should be followed. That is, any policy undertaken to reduce wage inequality should attempt to create as few distortions—and thus generate as little economy-wide deadweight losses—as possible.

The appropriateness of the targeting principle can be debated. There are many philosophical and political arguments why aggregate efficiency gains may be weighted less relative to equality goals such as reducing inequality. Nevertheless, this principle seems to be the most appropriate one because in reality, it seems to have guided many recent U.S. economic policies. A good example of this has been the country's overall support of freer trade since 1945 through ongoing rounds of negotiations through the General Agreement on Tariffs and Trade (GATT).

The targeting principle suggests that many of the major research questions regarding rising inequality are largely irrelevant for formulating sound redistributive policies. For example, consider the major issue of whether the demand shift away from less skilled workers has been caused by international trade and/or skill-biased technological change. Both international trade and technological innovation generate aggregate gains for society, even in cases where they hurt particular groups within society. In light of these aggregate gains, redistributive policies should not attempt to restrict international trade or technological innovation. Doing so would incur unacceptably high costs for society overall.

On the supply side, however, knowing whether immigration is contributing to rising inequality might help inform policy debates. In particular, if the balance of evidence indicates that immigrants are putting downward pressure on less skilled wages, then policies such as tightening the skill criteria for immigrants might make sense. Even if this were the case, targeting suggests that if immigration generates aggregate gains for society, policies should not attempt to restrict immigration more than current policies already do.[52] Conceptually, one difficult issue here is how to define society: including or excluding the new immigrants?

As for labor market institutions, even if their decreased role has contributed to rising inequality, it is not clear that policies to reassert their role would be well targeted. Minimum wages, for example, are usually regarded as inefficient because of the costs they impose on firms and on displaced workers. The trade-off between the efficiency and equity of labor market institutions like the minimum wage is not entirely clear. Recent research suggests that the efficiency costs of minimum wages, when the level of the minimum is low, may be smaller than commonly supposed. However, there is still widespread belief that the trade-off is large enough that policies that target institutions are not the best ones.

All this suggests that the best solution is to target the problem—low incomes for less skilled workers—as directly as possible. This means short-term solutions such as earned income tax credits and (perhaps) long-term solutions aimed at facilitating the acquisition of skills through education and retraining.

Obviously, it is far from obvious how public policies can facilitate the acquisition of skills. For example, the broad goal of "better education" might be proposed. One issue this immediately raises is its long-term nature. Increasing the supply of more skilled workers through education takes decades; does this really help the less skilled workers already in the labor force and unlikely to return to school? "More retraining for current workers" might be the broad response to this issue. But for whom, and financed by whom?

More generally, the role public policy can and should play in education and training is an extremely complicated problem involving a large set of issues related to access, financing, methods, and standards. Existing research by economists and others demonstrates this quite clearly. Even the modest goal of limiting policy to just helping solve market failures is difficult, at least partly because the identity of these failures is not entirely agreed upon. But it is important to stress that these issues exist regardless of the causes of rising inequality—and solving these issues almost certainly does not require an exact understanding of the causes of rising inequality. How best to educate children, for example, is a policy problem independent of relative wages and issues such as how open a country is to international trade.

Unfortunately, there is no political consensus in the United States (or elsewhere) that action should be taken to counteract rising inequality. In the current U.S. political discussions, the problems of the less skilled is not a major issue. One argument against any policy response is that rising income inequality is a temporary development to which market forces will respond appropriately. In particular, on the supply side, people respond to higher returns to skill by acquiring more skills through education and retraining. Again, this argument returns to the issue of what role public policy should play in the process of skills acquisition.

However, it also returns to the point that these policy discussions largely do not depend on knowing the exact causes of rising inequality.

It is on this point that the two coauthors agree most strongly. While we still have very different opinions about how good research relates theory, testable hypotheses, and data, we agree quite strongly that the economics of proper policy interventions is relatively clear—and we conjecture that a large majority of economists agree on this point. There is still much to be learned about the causes and consequences of changing wage inequality, but these causes are largely irrelevant for designing appropriate policy responses.

Notes

The authors would like to thank Karen Parker, Dani Rodrick, and participants at the Council of Foreign Relations Study Group for their helpful comments.

1. For some of these papers, see Richard B. Freeman and Lawrence F. Katz (eds.), *Differences and Changes in Wage Structures* (Chicago: University of Chicago Press and National Bureau of Economic Research [NBER], 1995).

2. Statistics are from Organization for Economic Cooperation and Development (OECD), *Employment Outlook, July 1996* (Paris: OECD, 1996), table 3.1. These basic facts on relative earnings come from the *Economic Report of the President* (Washington, D.C.: U.S. Government Printing Office, 1997), which devotes two chapters to labor markets and inequality. Inequality has risen across education, experience, and occupational groups as well as within these groups. The exact timing and magnitude of the changes vary somewhat with the measures used, but all standard measures show dramatic changes. For various cuts on the data, see John Bound and George Johnson, "Changes in the Structure of Wages in the 1980s: An Evaluation of Alternative Explanations," *American Economic Review* 82, no. 3 (June 1992), pp. 371–92; Steven J. Davis, "Cross-Country Patterns of Change in Relative Wages," in Olivier J. Blanchard and Stanley Fischer (eds.), *1992 Macroeconomics Annual* (New York: National Bureau of Economic Research [NBER], 1992); Lawrence F. Katz and Kevin M. Murphy, "Changes in Relative Wages, 1963–1987: Supply and Demand Factors," *Quarterly Journal of Economics* 107, no. 1 (February 1992), pp. 35–78; or Robert Z. Lawrence and Matthew J. Slaughter, "International Trade and American Wages in the 1980s: Giant Sucking Sound or Small Hiccup?" in Martin Neil Baily and Clifford Winston (eds.), *Brookings Papers on Economic Activity: Microeconomics* 2 (1993), pp. 161–211.

3. For a discussion of the lack of success of the Thatcher reforms of the United Kingdom labor market, see David G. Blanchflower and Richard B. Freeman, "Did the Thatcher Reforms Change British Labour Market Performance?" in

R. Barrell (ed.), *The UK Labour Market: Comparative Aspects and Institutional Developments* (Cambridge: Cambridge University Press, 1994).

4. Declines of this magnitude are reported by Richard B. Freeman, "Are Your Wages Set in Beijing?" *Journal of Economic Perspectives* 9, no. 3 (Summer 1995), pp. 15–32, and by Lawrence Mishel and Aaron Bernstein, *The State of Working America, 1994–95* (Armonk: M. E. Sharpe, 1994).

5. For more information on changes in real wages, see OECD, *Economic Outlook 1996* (Paris: OECD, 1996); and for the United States, United Kingdom, France, and Japan, see Lawrence F. Katz, Gary W. Loveman, and David G. Blanchflower, "A Comparison of Changes in the Structure of Wages in Four OECD Countries," in Richard B. Freeman and Lawrence F. Katz (eds.), *Differences and Changes in Wage Structures* (Chicago: University of Chicago Press and NBER, 1995), pp. 25–65.

6. OECD, *Economic Outlook 1996*.

7. Susan Dynarski and Jonathan Gruber, "Can Families Smooth Variable Earnings?" mimeo., MIT, July 1997.

8. Orazio Attanasio and Steven J. Davis, "Relative Wage Movements and the Distribution of Consumption," *Journal of Political Economy* 104, no. 6 (December 1996), pp. 1227–62.

9. It is called "residual inequality" as it arises, as it is usually estimated as a residual from a regression of log hourly wages on a set of education, experience, and race dummies with interactions, separately by year and gender. See Katz, Loveman, and Blanchflower, "A Comparison of Changes in the Structure of Wages in Four OECD Countries."

10. Katz and Murphy, "Changes in Relative Wages."

11. David H. Autor, Lawrence F. Katz, and Alan B. Krueger, "Computing Inequality: Have Computers Changed the Labor Market?" *Princeton University Industrial Relations Section Working Paper* no. 377 (March 1997).

12. Eli Berman, John Bound, and Zvi Griliches, "Changes in the Demand for Skilled Labor Within U.S. Manufacturing: Evidence from the Annual Survey of Manufactures," *Quarterly Journal of Economics* 109, no. 2 (May 1994), pp. 367–97; Lawrence and Slaughter, "International Trade and American Wages."

13. Jagdish Bhagwati, "Free Traders and Free Immigrationists: Strangers or Friends?" *Russell Sage Foundation Working Paper* (1991).

14. Lawrence and Slaughter, "International Trade and American Wages."

15. Jeffrey D. Sachs and Howard Shatz, "Trade and Jobs in U.S. Manufacturing," *Brookings Papers on Economic Activity* (1994), pp. 1–84.

16. Edward E. Leamer, "In Search of Stolper-Samuelson Effects on U.S. Wages," *NBER Working Paper* no. 5427 (January 1996).

17. Robert E. Baldwin and Glen C. Cain, "Shifts in U.S. Relative Wages: The Role of Trade, Technology, and Factor Endowments," *NBER Working Paper* no. 5934 (February 1997).

18. Alan B. Krueger, "Labor Market Shifts and the Price Puzzle Revisited," *NBER Working Paper* no. 5924 (January 1997).
19. Freeman, "Are Your Wages Set in Beijing?" pp. 28–29.
20. Bound and Johnson, "Changes in the Structure of Wages."
21. Berman, Bound, and Griliches, "Changes in the Demand for Skilled Labor."
22. L. G. Kletzer, "The Impact of Foreign Competition on Occupational Employment and Wages in U.S. Manufacturing, 1971–1992," mimeo., University of California, Santa Cruz, August 1996.
23. Stephen J. Davis, John C. Haltiwanger, and Scott Schuh, *Job Creation and Destruction* (Cambridge, Mass.: MIT Press, 1996).
24. Paul R. Krugman, "Growing World Trade: Causes and Consequences," *Brookings Papers on Economic Activity* (1995), pp. 327–77.
25. George J. Borjas, Richard B. Freeman, and Lawrence F. Katz, "On the Labor-Market Effects of Immigration and Trade," in George Borjas and Richard Freeman (eds.), *Immigration and the Work Force* (Chicago: University of Chicago Press, 1992), pp. 213–244.
26. George J. Borjas, Richard B. Freeman, and Lawrence F. Katz, "How Much Do Immigration and Trade Affect Labor-Market Outcomes?" *Brookings Papers on Economic Activity* 1 (1997), pp. 4–90.
27. Comprehensive surveys of many of the issues include: Jagdish Bhagwati and Vivek Dehejia, "Free Trade and Wages of the Unskilled: Is Marx Striking Again?" pp. 36–75; and Alan Deardorff and Dalia Haikura, "Trade and Wages: What Are the Questions?" pp. 76–107, both in Jagdish Bhagwati and Marvin Kosters (eds.), *Trade and Wages* (Washington, D.C.: American Enterprise Institute, 1994); see also J. David Richardson, "Income Inequality and Trade: How to Think, What to Conclude," pp. 33–55; and Adrian Wood, "How Trade Hurt Unskilled Workers," pp. 57–80, both in *Journal of Economic Perspectives* 9, no. 3 (Summer 1995).
28. Berman, Bound, and Griliches, "Changes in the Demand for Skilled Labor."
29. Eli Berman, John Bound, and Steve Machin, "Implications of Skill-Biased Technological Change, International Evidence," *NBER Working Paper* no. 6166 (October 1997).
30. Alan B. Krueger, "How Computers Have Changed the Wage Structure: Evidence from Microdata, 1984–1989," *Quarterly Journal of Economics* 108, no. 1 (February 1993), pp. 33–60.
31. Autor, Katz, and Krueger, "Computing Inequality."
32. John E. DiNardo and Jorn-Steffen Pischke, "The Returns to Computer Use Revisited: Have Pencils Changed the Wage Structure Too?" *Quarterly Journal of Economics* 112, no. 1 (February 1997), pp. 291–304.

33. Freeman and Katz (eds.), *Differences and Changes in Wage Structures*.
34. Katz, Loveman, and Blanchflower, "Comparison of Changes in the Structure of Wages."
35. Richard B. Freeman, paper prepared for the Council on Foreign Relations, 1996.
36. David Card, in "Immigrant Inflows, Native Outflows, and the Local Labor Market Impacts of Higher Immigration," *NBER Working Paper* no. 5927 (February 1997), cites Robert J. LaLonde and Robert H. Topel, "Labor Market Adjustment to Increased Immigration," in John M. Abowd and Richard B. Freeman (eds.), *Immigration, Trade, and the Labor Market* (Chicago: University of Chicago Press, 1991), pp. 167–200.
37. George J. Borjas, "The Economic Benefits from Immigration," *Journal of Economic Perspectives* 9, no. 2 (Spring 1995), pp. 3–22.
38. Borjas, Freeman, and Katz, "How Much Do Immigration and Trade Affect Labor Market Outcomes?"
39. David G. Blanchflower, *The Role and Influence of Trade Unions in the OECD*, Report to the Bureau of International Labor Affairs, September 1996; David G. Blanchflower and Richard B. Freeman, "Going Different Ways: Unionism in the U.S. and Other OECD Countries," *Industrial Relations* (Winter 1992), pp. 56–79, reprinted in M. Bognanno and M. Kleiner (eds.), *Labor Market Institutions and the Future Role of Unions* (London: Blackwell, 1992).
40. Katz, Loveman, and Blanchflower, "Comparison of Changes in the Structure of Wages."
41. Freeman, paper for Council on Foreign Relations.
42. Francine D. Blau and Lawrence M. Kahn, "International Differences in Male Wage Inequality: Institutions versus Market Forces," *Journal of Political Economy* 104, no. 4 (1996): 791–837.
43. Nichole M. Fortin and Thomas Lemieux, "Institutional Changes and Rising Wage Inequality," *American Economic Review* 86, no. 2 (May 1996), pp. 240–45; John E. DiNardo, Nichole M. Fortin, and Thomas Lemieux, "Labor Market Institutions and the Distribution of Wages, 1973–1992: A Semiparametric Approach," *Econometrica* 64, no. 5 (September 1996), pp. 1001–4.
44. A. J. Oswald, "Rent Sharing in the Labour Market," mimeo., University of Warwick, 1997.
45. For Europe, see David Blanchflower and Andrew Oswald, "Comment on House Prices," *Oxford Bulletin of Economics and Statistics* 51, no 2 (1989), pp. 137–43; and J. Van Reenan, "The Creation and Capture of Rents: Wages and Innovation in a Panel of U.K. Companies," *Quarterly Journal of Economics* 111, no. 1 (February 1996), pp. 195–226. For the United States and

Canada, see David G. Blanchflower, Andrew J. Oswald, and Peter Sanfey, "Wages, Profits, and Rent Sharing," *Quarterly Journal of Economics* 111, no. 1 (February 1996), pp. 227–51; L. N. Christofides and A. J. Oswald, "Real Wage Determination and Rent Sharing in Collective Bargaining Agreements," *Quarterly Journal of Economics* 107, no. 3 (August 1992), pp. 985–1002; and John M. Abowd and Thomas Lemieux, "The Effects of Product Market Competition on Collective Bargaining Agreements: The Case of Foreign Competition in Canada," *Quarterly Journal of Economics* 108, no. 4 (November 1993), pp. 983–1014.

46. Lawrence F. Katz and Larry Summers, "Interindustry Wage Differentials: Theory and Evidence," *Brookings Papers on Economic Activity: Microeconomics* (1989), pp. 209–75; Alan B. Krueger and Larry Summers, "Reflections on the Inter-Industry Wage Structure," in Kevin Lang and Jonathan S. Leonard (eds.), *Unemployment and the Structure of Labor Markets* (Oxford: Basil Blackwell, 1987); and Alan B. Krueger and Larry Summers, "Efficiency Wages and the Inter-Industry Wage Structure," *Econometrica* 56 (1988), pp. 259–93.

47. Adrian Wood, *North-South Trade, Employment, and Inequality* (Oxford: Oxford University Press, 1995).

48. See the following works by Robert C. Feenstra and Gordon H. Hanson: "Foreign Investment, Outsourcing, and Relative Wages," in Feenstra, Gene M. Grossman, and Douglas A. Irwin (eds.), *Political Economy of Trade Policy: Papers in Honor of Jagdish Bhagwati* (Cambridge, Mass.: MIT Press, 1996), pp. 89–128; and "Globalization, Outsourcing, and Wage Inequality," *American Economic Review* 86, no. 2 (May 1996), pp. 240–45.

49. Matthew J. Slaughter, "Production Transfer Within Multinational Enterprises and American Wages," *Journal of International Economics*, forthcoming.

50. George J. Borjas and Valerie A. Ramey, "Foreign Competition, Market Power, and Wage Inequality," *Quarterly Journal of Economics* 110, no. 4 (November 1995), pp. 1075–110.

51. Matthew J. Slaughter, "International Trade and Labor-Demand Elasticities," *Journal of International Economics* (forthcoming).

52. See, for example, Borjas, "Economic Benefits from Immigration," for calculations on the size of this aggregate gain.

4

Foreign Direct Investment and Good Jobs/Bad Jobs: The Impact of Outward Investment and Inward Investment on Jobs and Wages

THEODORE H. MORAN

AS PART of the widespread concern over the consequences of globalization, foreign direct investment, like trade, is often blamed for having an adverse impact on the distribution of income in advanced industrial economies. In the popular debate, there are two principal ways in which foreign direct investment might be responsible for a deterioration in wage structure, job structure, and distribution of income in countries that are both home and host to multinational corporations.

The first way is if outward investment were to "hollow out" the domestic economy, shifting good jobs abroad and leaving behind only a few low-wage, low-benefit employment opportunities in the home economy. This might be called the great-sucking-sound hypothesis. The second way is if inward investment were to capture large chunks of productive activity, disassembling/reassembling the resulting operations in a way that diverted high-wage, high-benefit jobs to the home countries of parent firms while consigning only a few low-wage, low-benefit jobs to the host economy. This might be called the siphoning-off-the-good-jobs hypothesis.

Under conditions of imperfect competition, which typically characterize foreign direct investment, neither hypothesis is, on its face, implausible. Each can be subjected to empirical scrutiny. Beneath the rhetoric and emotion that surround controversies about foreign direct investment there can be a genuine analytical debate.

This chapter uses the available evidence to test each hypothesis, focusing on circumstances in which parent firms exercise control over corporate operations in multiple countries (the definition of foreign direct investment). Foreign direct investment is distinct from portfolio investment that mutual funds or pension funds, for example, may make in the hope of participating passively in the appreciation of shares in overseas stock markets. It correlates very imperfectly with the broader category of "capital flows" (even though foreign investment movements do show up in balance-of-payments statistics), since the actual capital used to implement any given multinational corporate strategy may in fact be raised locally, or derived from a third country, rather than "shifted" from the country of the parent to the new site.

Outward Investment and the Debate About a "Great Sucking Sound"

The great-sucking-sound hypothesis contains a complicated mix of assertions (often imprecisely specified) about how outward investment might affect labor markets in the home country. It is useful to organize the analysis along three lines of inquiry: What is the impact of outward investment on job structure (the relative distribution between high-skill jobs and low-skill jobs)? What is the impact of outward investment on wage structure (the relative wages paid to high-skill jobs and low-skill jobs)? What is the impact of outward investment on the demand for labor and absolute level of wages paid to the least skilled workers in the home country?

These lines of inquiry overlap and merge with the more general issue of the relationship between trade and labor markets addressed in other chapters in this volume. They pose their own distinctive problems and have their own distinctive traditions of analysis that can be used to inform the contemporary debate.

Perhaps the most distinctive idea in the great-sucking-sound controversy is the contention that outward investment exports jobs rather than products—in other words, that outward investment sets up facilities to serve markets that otherwise could be supplied from the home country, and that outward investment substitutes for exports.

This has long been a worry of home countries, growing out of historical concerns about outward investment and the balance of payments. It has a direct bearing on the job structure of the home country: Since jobs in export industries pay 13 percent to 15 percent more than firms that do not export (in the United States, e.g.), provide 11 percent higher benefits, experience 20 percent faster employment growth, and are 9 percent less likely to go out of business, the job structure in the home country would clearly be worsened if outward investment substituted for exports.[1] On the other hand, the job structure in the home country clearly would be improved if outward investment actually enhanced the export performance of firms that moved some of their operations abroad.

The proponents of the outward-investment-exports-jobs-rather-than-products argument look at home-based firms establishing overseas operations and compare the consequent composition of home country economic activity with a favorable picture of what the domestic economy would look like if those operations were kept at home. Their key assumption (often implicit) is that such operations would survive, prosper, and contribute at least as much to the local economy if home-based firms were somehow retarded or prevented from moving abroad; domestic plants closed would remain open; domestic plants downsized would be maintained at the same size; and domestic plants not expanded could be expanded.

The opponents of this argument look at home-based firms establishing overseas operations and compare the consequent composition of home country economic activity with an unfavorable picture of what the domestic economy would look like if those operations were kept at home. Their key assumption (again, often implicit) is that such operations would not survive, prosper, or contribute as much to the local economy if home-based firms were somehow retarded or prevented from moving abroad; domestic plants open would have to be closed; domestic plants maintained at the same size would have to be downsized; and domestic plants expanded would have to be cut back.

In each case the point of contention is the counterfactual: What would happen to the domestic operations of the firms that want to move abroad if they were hindered in their attempts to do so? Would those domestic operations be just as dynamic, or even more so, if there were less foreign investment by the parent firms (because outward investment simply substitutes for local activity), or would those domestic operations be much less dynamic if there were less foreign investment by the parent firms (because outward investment complements local activity)?

In attempting to assess these counterfactual contentions with rigor, the analytic community begins by drawing a distinction that diverges substantially from popular perception, in a manner reminiscent of other discussions by members of the Council of Foreign Relations about the relationship between trade and employment.

What the great-sucking-sound debate is about is the kinds of jobs in any given economy—the distribution between good jobs and bad jobs (between the relative and absolute wage levels)—not about the overall number of jobs or about the aggregate level of employment, because the latter two are set by the actions of central bank monetary authorities (in the United States, the Federal Reserve) who aim to ensure the highest rate of economic growth and the fullest amount of employment consonant with low levels of inflation.[2]

The central bank monetary authorities may carry out their task relatively effectively, or ineffectively, and adjustment mechanisms may work well, or poorly, but except for short periods of time, outward investment, like trade, will not change the long-run aggregate demand for labor. Indeed if a burst of outward investment were to generate a momentary slump in the demand for labor (or if a burst of inward investment were to generate a momentary surge in the demand for labor), the central bank would be expected to react in a contrary fashion, to loosen or tighten monetary policy explicitly to offset such changes in the domestic labor market.

The question that requires attention, then, is what kind of jobs remain at home when domestic firms invest abroad in comparison to what kind of jobs would remain at home if those domestic firms were not to invest abroad.[3]

Using the analysis of the outward investment/export relationship to address the counterfactual to answer the question of what would have happened if something that did take place had not taken place, with the necessary degree of rigor, however, requires more subtlety than many of those involved in the debate suppose.

To appreciate the need for such analytic subtlety, it is instructive to assess perhaps the most ambitious recent effort to resolve the outward investment/export debate, undertaken by the Emergency Committee for American Trade (ECAT) in response to the debate about the North American Free Trade Agreement (NAFTA), entitled *Mainstay II: A New Account of the Critical Role of U.S. Multinational Companies in the U.S. Economy.*[4]

ECAT launched its research with the right question: How does the domestic performance of the U.S. multinational community (those that do invest abroad a lot) compare with other firms in the United States (those that do not invest abroad much if at all)?

The ECAT study found that "American companies with overseas investment have been waging a hard fight—and a successful one—to keep exports flowing from the United States," contributing an average net surplus of $83 billion annually to the U.S. balance of payments and accounting for 89 percent of U.S. economic growth. In fact, ECAT argued, the percentage of total shipments that were exported by multinational companies as a group has consistently been greater than "all other U.S. manufacturers."[5] Looking at industries with a high degree of globalization (foreign operations), multinational companies accounted for 84 percent of total exports by all firms in these industries, earning an aggregate trade surplus of $70 billion (1989) in contrast to an overall U.S. trade deficit of $30 billion in the same industries.

It is the ability to invest abroad, the ECAT study asserted, that has led to the multinational community's superior export performance; this contention is proved by the dismal performance of those firms that stay at home. If proposals to make investment abroad less easy/more difficult were adopted (e.g., by limiting the Foreign Tax Credit, eliminating deferral of taxes on overseas earnings, or disapproving NAFTA), ECAT concluded, the dynamic performance of the multinational community would be lost as its operations began to look more like the rest of the firms in the country. "The ... findings demonstrate that the simple contention that multinational companies are harming the U.S. economy by shifting jobs abroad and importing cheaper products into the United States does not bear up under scrutiny. Rather, the exact opposite is true. Investment abroad by multinational companies provides the platform for growth in exports and creates jobs in the United States."[6]

But what the ECAT study (and most of the popular efforts to defend the performance of international investors) misses is that export behavior and outward investment are *both* closely correlated with firm size, research and development (R&D) intensity, and advertising intensity, among other variables. Any rigorous analysis of the relationship between outward investment and export behavior requires holding such characteristics constant: comparing export performance of big U.S. firms that do invest abroad with those that do not, comparing export performance of R&D-intensive U.S. firms that do invest abroad with those that do not, comparing export performance of advertising-intensive U.S. firms that do invest abroad with those that do not, and so forth.

Thus, when ECAT shows U.S. multinational corporations (MNCs) to be exporting more as a percentage of sales than the average U.S. manufacturer, it is implicitly comparing General Electric's behavior with regional machine tool companies in the Midwest, United Technology's behavior with medium-size industrial equipment producers in the Southeast, DuPont's behavior with bulk chemical suppliers around the nation.[7] It would be extraordinary to find the smaller and less sophisticated firms to be equal or superior to General Electric, United Technology, and DuPont in penetrating international markets. It is not extraordinary to find the reverse.

To do justice to the great-sucking-sound debate, what is needed is to make comparisons that control for size, R&D intensity, advertising intensity (that compare apples with apples and oranges with oranges, so to speak), to assess how firms like GE, United Technology, and DuPont would behave if they kept more of their plants at home, and conversely, how the rest of the companies in counterpart industries would behave if they were given even more favorable conditions to move abroad.

Fortunately, a series of studies covering three decades of data for the United States, replicated for some other advanced industrial countries, have set the problem up in this rigorous fashion.[8]

Before summarizing the results, it is instructive to look at one of the early pioneering analytic efforts, by Thomas Horst, which was constructed to show more clearly than many of the subsequent statistical efforts what is going on "within" the sophisticated packages of correlations.[9]

Prior to running correlations, Horst divided his sample of firms by those characteristics that are likely to influence both export behavior and foreign investment behavior (size, R&D intensity, advertising intensity, etc.), and compared the export behavior (exports as a percentage of domestic shipments) of those that essentially stayed at home (the first quartile represents the least amount of foreign investment), those that had begun to move abroad more strongly (second quartile), those that were vigorously expanding overseas investment (third quartile), and those that were most thoroughly globalized in their operations (fourth quartile).

This analysis provides a direct look at the counterfactual, a direct answer to the question of what would happen if the firms stayed at home: Comparing the second quartile (or the third quartile or fourth quartile) with the first shows how companies similar to each other in all relevant aspects would be likely to perform if they did not invest overseas in comparison to those who did. This is as close as social science can come to answering the question: What if something that did happen were not to have happened? The approach is particularly valuable for offering a rough approximation of what changes in firm behavior occur at the margin.

What is striking in Horst's data is a finding he labeled the "threshold effect," that firms that undertook the establishment of overseas operations had a higher proportion of exports from the home-country market (and greater intensity of export-related jobs in their domestic operations) than did similar firms that decided to stay at home.

High-technology firms with little or no foreign investment had exports equal to 2.3 percent of their domestic shipments, whereas high-technology firms that had begun to establish a clear foreign presence had exports equal to 7.8 percent of their domestic shipments; even low-technology firms saw their exports jump from 1.3 percent to 3.0 percent of domestic shipments when they began to invest abroad. High-advertising firms with little or no foreign investment had exports equal to 1.0 percent of their domestic shipments, whereas high-advertising firms with a clear foreign presence had exports equal to 4.8 percent of their domestic shipments, and so on.

This threshold effect does not distinguish between offensive and defensive strategic rationales for undertaking the investment: offensive, so as to take advantage of new opportunities; defensive, so as to maintain sales in markets that can no longer be competitively serviced from home. Both offense and defense can generate exports by strengthening the firm's position in the international arena, increasing demand for the higher-skilled products, R&D output, and headquarters services supplied from home, in comparison to a firm that engages in neither offense nor defense.

Here we begin to see that this issue cannot correctly be viewed as one that pits home-country labor against multinational corporations.

Table 4–1 Export Performance of Particular Types of Industries by Foreign Investment Level (Exports as a Percentage of Domestic Shipments)

	I Least Amount or No Foreign Investment (%)	II Low Middle Range of Foreign Investment (%)	III High Middle Range of Foreign Investment (%)	IV Most Foreign Investment (%)
High Tech	2.3%	7.8%	9.7%	7.6%
Low Tech	1.3	3.0	2.5	3.5
High Advertising	1.0	2.8	2.4	4.6
Low Advertising	1.4	4.8	7.5	7.7
High Unionization	1.9	5.5	4.4	3.8
Low Unionization	1.3	3.2	7.0	7.8

Source: Adapted from C. Fred Bergsten, Thomas Horst, and Theodore H. Moran, *American Multinationals and American Interests* (Washington, D.C.: Brookings Institution, 1978), table 3-3, 81–82.

A pro-labor stance would be one that took advantage of this threshold effect, just as would a pro-MNC stance. Indeed, even from the point of view of organized labor in the home country, highly unionized companies that set up foreign operations have better domestic records in generating export-related jobs (5.5 percent of domestic shipments) than those that do not (1.9 percent of domestic shipments). For firms with low unionization that do and do not invest abroad, the export levels are 3.2 percent and 1.3 percent respectively.

To be sure, pro-labor proponents might want to argue on behalf of a tougher home-country negotiating posture on issues of trade and investment, as Pat Buchanan, Ross Perot, and Pat Choate have done, but "tougher" would have to mean in favor of greater liberalization for investment as well as trade, not less.[10] Similarly, those who argue in favor of community consent as a condition of factory closings, to retard "runaway plants," as Jesse Jackson has done in the United States and Hans Vredeling has done in the European Union, would want to include communities that would benefit from the consequences of outward investment as well as those that would not, a probably impossible organizational challenge.[11] As J. Bradford Jensen and Kenneth R. Troske point out in Chapter 5, plants that are expanding exports and those that are downsizing are likely to be different plants, even within the same industry, even within the same firm.

Overall, the stay-at-home option is simply not a viable strategy for those hoping to improve the access of workers to high-wage, high-benefit jobs in the home country. It should be recalled, however, that questions about relative wages and about absolute wage levels for the least skilled workers remain to be dealt with separately.

Beyond the threshold effect, Horst found that the relationship between greater levels of foreign direct investment and greater levels of exports was somewhat haphazard; at the least, there seemed to be a diminishing return in the relationship between outward investment and export performance. This led Horst and his coauthors to reject the call of multinational corporate companies that they actually be subsidized in their effort to expand operations internationally.[12]

Subsequent studies have not found such haphazardness in the impact of higher levels of foreign direct investment on export performance. Robert Lipsey and Herle Yahr Weiss have substantiated the positive relationship between outward investment and exports for all levels of investment. In an initial study, they showed that (after controlling for firm characteristics) the level of manufacturing activity in a given country by U.S. firms was positively associated with U.S. exports from the same industries to that country and negatively associated with exports by rival producers.[13] They also found that the presence of firms from foreign countries in a given country was negatively related to U.S. exports and positively related to foreign countries' exports. They concluded both that direct investment by U.S. firms in that country tended to increase U.S. exports and U.S. market shares and reduce those of rival producers, and that foreign-owned operations tended to raise their countries' exports and market shares and reduce those of U.S. firms. The counterfactual is the same as in Horst: Making domestic firms stay at home hurts the prospects for domestic workers to participate in higher-paying, higher-benefit, export-related jobs.

In a later study Lipsey and Weiss examined exports and foreign activity within individual U.S. firms to eliminate cultural bias that might simultaneously influence both U.S. investment and U.S. exports or the investment and exports of rivals from other countries.[14] They found that the higher the output of American firms in any given foreign area, the larger their exports from the United States to that area. Moreover, this relationship of complementarity between outward investment and domestic exports was strong not only for intermediate goods shipped for further processing but also for the exports of finished products by American firms. In short, the expansion of outward investment acts as a magnet for exports from the home country across regions and across kinds of products. Looking directly at the relationship between the multinationalization of corporate activities and wage levels in the parent corporation, Lipsey found that higher proportions of foreign activity in U.S. firms are associated with higher average compensation at home.[15]

Turning to similar studies done for outward investment from other home countries, Magnus Blomstrom, Birgitta Swedenborg, and others also have found a complementary relationship between outward investment on the part of Swedish multinationals and home-country exports and employment.[16] In an analysis of 458 of the world's largest multinational corporations of all nationalities, R. D. Pearce found a correlation between increases in foreign production and increases in exports from the parent's home, a correlation that was particularly strong for intrafirm exports in vertically integrated operations.[17]

Such a finding is confirmed by investigators such as Dennis Encarnation, who underscores the significance of opening Japan to foreign direct investment as a method of penetrating Japanese markets with U.S. exports.[18]

Finally, concerned that there might be a simultaneous determination of direct foreign investment and exports, such as level of income or size of market, Edward Graham has constructed a "gravity model" to see if there is a complementary relationship between foreign investment and exports once the analysis is corrected for the influence of per capita income in each host country market, total size of each host country market, and distance from the home to the host country.[19]

Using this methodology, Graham did find a complementarity between outward direct investment and exports of manufacturing products for both the United States and Japan. His study confirmed the opposite of the "hollowing out" or "deindustrialization" hypothesis: "as direct investment abroad expands, the affiliates of both U.S. and Japanese multinationals created by this investment acquire large appetites for goods produced in the home economies, and thus that expansion abroad is associated with increased, rather than decreased, export possibilities."[20]

These findings all suggest that there are more "good job" opportunities for workers in the home-country market with outward investment from that market than when there is no outward investment.

However, there is some more problematic news here, as well. Accompanying the favorable impact on job structure, outward investment is certain to increase demand for skilled labor to fill these good jobs, ceteris paribus, raising the premium paid to skilled workers beyond what it would otherwise already be and "worsening" inequality in the relative wage structure. That is, those who cannot take advantage of the better job opportunities are relatively worse off in comparison to those who can.

But proponents of the great sucking sound express a larger worry than this: namely, that outward investment not only changes the relative position of skilled and less skilled workers but damages the absolute position of the latter as well.

Economic theory supports this concern. The question is how large the absolute negative impact might be in practice.

The Stolper-Samuelson theorem demonstrates that changes in relative goods prices has a magnified effect on factor prices; that is, changes in the relative price for higher-skill–intensive goods will have an adverse absolute impact on the purchasing power of individuals who earn wages in lower-skill–intensive jobs.[21] Since outward investment expands the demand for exports, driving up their price and transferring resources to higher-skill–intensive activities, the standard of living of those with lower skills who do not participate in this process is likely to decline in absolute as well as in relative terms. Factor-price equalization considerations predict that imports of low-wage–intensive goods may put pressure on the wages of less skilled workers in the importing country. If outward investment were to expand imports of low-wage–intensive goods beyond what would be expected from trade processes alone, outward investment itself might be a culprit in causing declining earnings for less skilled workers in the home country.

There are no comprehensive measurements of how great the impact of outward investment might be on less skilled workers. But what evidence can be brought to bear to analyze the relationship suggests that the impact is not large, especially in relation to the effect of other changes going on in the home economy.

Attempts to assess changes in relative prices along Stolper-Samuelson lines have not yielded major results. Turning to factor-price equalization pressures on home wages via MNC-generated imports, Horst found that outward investment did not lead to higher than average imports; instead, imports grew more vigorously in industries characterized by low levels of outward investment from the United States. Graham, in contrast, found "weak evidence" of a positive relationship between outward direct investment from the United States and imports into the United States in the same sector, but such imports tended to originate with high-income/high-wage source countries, not low-wage countries. Still, greater demand for exports could be expected to draw home-country resources out of other sectors into the export sectors, perhaps leading to greater overall import penetration and consequent pressure on low-skill wages.

Of further concern, however, is that outward investment might increase the downward pressure on the wages of unskilled workers in the home country if the shift of production activities to low-wage countries ("outsourcing") were to drive down demand for low- or lesser-skilled production workers in the home country beyond what would occur if the outward investment did not take place.

Robert Lawrence and Matthew Slaughter provide some evidence that warrants skepticism on whether such an impact is occurring.[22] They have found that while employment in U.S. manufacturing MNCs in the developing countries has been growing (an increase of 5.9 percent between 1977 and 1989), the overall magnitude is surprisingly small, a mere 60,000 jobs. Moreover, of these 60,000 new jobs, only 4,000 were for production workers. Using production workers as the proxy for less skilled jobs and nonproduction workers the proxy for higher-skilled jobs, there is little evidence, they conclude, that U.S. multinationals are reducing the demand for the former by shifting large numbers of production worker jobs out of the U.S. market.

Instead, they argue that technological change is what is responsible for reducing the demand for unskilled workers worldwide, since there are parallel declines in the ratio of lower-paid production workers to higher-paid nonproduction workers in the U.S. manufacturing parents and in their affiliates in the developing countries, simultaneously. More broadly, they find that there has been a pervasive upward shift across industries in the U.S. home-country labor market in the ratio of skilled to nonskilled labor. If globalization were dictating the process, some sectors would be expected to be using the "cheaper" unskilled workers more intensively, but this has not been happening. Once again, the evidence fits better with a generalized bias toward use of more skilled labor caused by changes in technology.

Lawrence and Slaughter leave themselves open to the criticism that they do not take their analysis far enough. To hold outward investment responsible for "any" reduction in the demand for low-skilled labor in the home market, the counterfactual has to be addressed: What would happen to demand for low-skilled labor in the absence of the outward investment? This Lawrence and Slaughter fail to do. Multinational corporations have long categorized their operations as largely "defensive" in nature; that is, they would simply lose the ability to service markets for their products at home and abroad if they did not move production offshore. Foreign rivals would make the sales themselves, reducing the demand for lower-skilled labor in the home market as much (or as little) as the MNCs do. Earlier studies of outward investment from both the United Kingdom and the United States have emphasized the role of defensive investment. In seven of nine case studies from the United States, for example, Robert Stobaugh found that the parent companies had to choose between making an investment or giving up the chance to supply the market altogether; in the other two cases, the option of maintaining home-country–based production was likely to expire within a clearly defined time horizon.[23] To the extent that this "defensive investment" contention finds support in the data, trade per se, rather than multinational corporate "outsourcing," would be responsible for whatever changes took place in the demand for production workers and the consequent level of lower-skilled wages. The worst multinationals could be accused of is hastening the inevitable.

But, argue Robert Feenstra and Gordon Hanson, the analysis of Lawrence, Slaughter, and others has not fully captured the impact of outward investment on the labor market in the home country because these analysts have defined outsourcing too narrowly.[24]

Using a very expansive definition of "outsourcing" (all imported intermediate or final goods that are used in the production of, or sold under the brand name of, an American firm, plus the narrower category of imports by U.S. multinationals per se), Feenstra and Hanson find that such imports are positively and significantly correlated with the increase in the relative demand for nonproduction labor in the home country (between 1979 and 1990). That is, with the globalization of corporate activity, the demand for white-collar workers in the home country has increased, and, via the Stolper-Samuelson effects described earlier, the plight of less skilled workers may have worsened. (Oddly enough, their data show that what they call outsourcing is positively correlated with the change in the relative employment of nonproduction workers but weakly negatively correlated with the change in relative average annual earnings of nonproduction workers.) At the same time, they point out, the standard of living of unskilled workers in the home country need not necessarily be diminished in real terms since the increase in supply from host countries lowers the price of goods available through trade, which may be enough to offset any wage reduction.

Given the inclusiveness of their "outsourcing" definition, however, Feenstra and Hanson too are susceptible to the defensive investment criticism; namely, that the effect they observe would occur anyway (via "pure" trade) even if home-country firms did not engage in outward investment but merely bought goods and services from abroad.

Overall, outward investment has three impacts on the home-country labor market: First, it improves the job structure via an augmentation in the number of "good jobs" in the overall labor mix; second, it joins other forces in increasing the wage gap between higher- and lower-skilled labor by driving up demand for the former to fill these good jobs; third, it possibly contributes to some worsening in the standard of living of those lower-skilled individuals who are not equipped to take advantage of the new opportunities. In terms of magnitude, the impact of outward investment is almost certainly smaller than the impact of trade (which itself does not seem to be large), and much, much smaller than the impact of technological change.

Inward Direct Foreign Investment and the Domestic Structure of Jobs and Wages: The Siphoning-Off-the-Good-Jobs Hypothesis

The analysis of the impact of inward investment on a host economy has to begin with the same caveat as did the treatment of outward investment: The focus of attention must be the distribution of good jobs vs. bad jobs, and on the wages paid to each, not the total number of jobs per se (since, as indicated earlier, the latter is determined by macroeconomic policy, in particular the actions of the central bank to maintain steady noninflationary growth). A misfocus on the latter is a weakness of many studies that argue, for example, that foreign investment via acquisitions frequently begins by downsizing domestic operations, leading to job loss rather than job creation. To be sure, inward investment, like outward investment and like trade, can exacerbate adjustment problems, but inward investment will not determine the long-term number of jobs or level of employment. Instead of preoccupation with net job loss or net job gain, therefore, the focus should be on the contribution of inward investment to the productivity of domestic factors of production and the consequent impact on wages, on job structure, and on the consequent distribution of income.

The tension between a preoccupation with aggregate job loss and enhanced productivity of domestic factors of production, for example, permeates Norman J. Glickman and Douglas P. Woodward's study of foreign investment in the United States.[25] They painstakingly add up the number of jobs created in the mid-1980s in new foreign-owned plants and plant expansions (386,432 jobs gained) and subtract the number of jobs reduced in cutbacks and consolidations (442,295 jobs lost), to show a net loss of 55,863 jobs in the economy. This leads them to criticize inward direct investment in the United States (or, at least, to label it "less than meets the eye").[26] They liken foreign direct investment to Schumpeter's "creative destruction in action." At the same time, however, they look approvingly on foreigners for helping to restore the international competitiveness of industries they enter and firms they take over. Clearly there is a contradiction here, between praise for augmenting competitiveness on one hand and criticism for streamlining operations on the other. The way in which foreign investors meet these challenges, augmenting competitiveness and streamlining operations, in comparison to domestic firms that are attempting to meet the same challenges in the same industries is what will be important for domestic wages, job structure, and distribution of income.

At first glance, it might be useful to ask why there is any need to make such a comparison at all.

Under neoclassical assumptions of perfect competition, foreign direct investment should improve the distribution of income by adding to the supply of capital (thus lowering the returns to domestic owners of capital) and by increasing the demand for labor (thus raising the returns to both workers in the foreign firms and to workers in competing domestic firms), in comparison to a situation where foreign direct investment was not present.

But foreign direct investment does not take place under conditions of perfect competition.[27] Indeed, most theorists argue that it could not take place under such conditions (where barriers to entry such as control of technology or brand-name identification do not exist) since the local producer would always have a competitive advantage in terms of language, knowledge of local customs, proximity to market, and perhaps political influence. Empirically, foreign direct investment does take place in industries characterized by relatively high degrees of concentration. This complicates the analysis.

Even under less than perfect competition, it might still be supposed that to compete effectively in a market where language, custom, and perhaps political influences would logically tend to favor domestic producers, foreign entrants would have to carry with them some combination of technology, management, and capital that would give them an advantage in utilizing local factors of production more efficiently than indigenous firms in the sectors where they operate, or else they would not survive. Moreover, their operations might carry positive externalities, such as technology, management techniques, and production practices, that spill over into the host economy as domestic firms upgrade their own activities in the face of increased competition.

In general, therefore, the presumption would still be that inward foreign direct investment should improve local productivity and raise local wages in comparison to a situation in which no foreign investment were present.[28] But the analytic community would still have reason to check to see if the domestic subsidiaries of foreign firms differed in any systematic way from the behavior of local counterparts in the same industry.

Under conditions of imperfect competition, firms have more leeway about how they conduct their operations; they are not all driven to similar solutions in the deployment of capital, labor, and technology by market forces as the perfect competition model predicts. It is possible that foreign multinational corporations could discriminate between home and host economies in ways detrimental to the latter, favoring headquarters for the best jobs and research activities, for example, or, worse, taking over indigenous companies and rearranging operations so as to extinguish the relatively prized activities in the new host country.

In investigating this possibility, it is once again necessary to be rigorous in setting up the problem to compare the domestic activities of foreign firms with the domestic activities of similar indigenous firms to ensure that apples are compared with apples and oranges with oranges.

In undertaking such a study of foreign direct investment in the United States, Edward M. Graham and Paul R. Krugman found, for example, that both compensation and value added per worker actually were higher for affiliates of foreign firms than for the average U.S. firm.[29] But the difference was essentially due to the particular kinds of sectors where foreign direct investment in the United States is concentrated. When compared industry by industry, there was no systematic difference between domestic firms and foreign affiliates in compensation and value added per employee (a finding confirmed, in fact, by Glickman and Woodward).[30] These data, Graham and Krugman concluded, did not provide any support for the suspicion that foreign investors arrange their international operations to keep the good jobs or the high value-added activities at home.

Looking more closely at plant-level data, Mark E. Doms and J. Bradford Jensen have found that multinational corporations, whether foreign or domestic owned, are the most productive, most capital-intensive, highest-paying plants. They confirm that comparing foreign-owned plants to all domestic plants is similar to comparing apples and oranges. As between U.S.-based multinationals in the United States and the U.S. affiliates of foreign multinationals, the U.S. firms have the edge in productivity, size, capital intensity, and wages.[31]

The outcome for R&D expenditures is more complex. Graham and Krugman found that for all industries, company-funded R&D per worker was much higher for affiliates of foreign firms than for all U.S. firms, but such a comparison was quite probably biased by the concentration of foreign investment in particular types of industries. Looking at manufacturing alone, they still recorded (slightly) higher amounts of firm-funded R&D per worker in foreign affiliates in comparison to indigenous firms. Still, it would have been valuable to have comparisons broken down into electronics, chemicals, automobiles, and so on. Graham and Krugman nevertheless concluded that there was no sign of a "headquarters effect" that led foreign firms to undertake disproportionately large amounts of R&D in the parent country rather than in the United States.

Robert Lipsey, in contrast, found that for U.S. multinationals, the share of parent employment in R&D was more than twice that of affiliates in almost all major industry groups.[32] While Lipsey did not make an explicit comparison of foreign affiliates and indigenous counterparts in the U.S. economy, he concluded that higher skill levels within multinationals in general, especially those higher skill levels associated with R&D, probably were concentrated in the homelands of the parent companies.

Looking at nationality of foreign investors in the United States, Graham and Krugman found that affiliates from the United Kingdom (not, for example, from Japan) stood out. They tended to be less productive (have lower average product of labor), pay less well, and undertake less R&D than subsidiaries of other national origin. The Japanese ranked high in all of these comparative measures; German and French affiliates also showed up quite favorably. As for reliance on imports, foreign owned firms of all nationalities had a greater propensity to import than did their U.S. counterparts, with the Japanese subsidiaries substantially higher than others (almost three times the average of the rest), although this might have been partially due to the disproportionate "newness" of most Japanese investment.

Turning to the issue of union activity, Richard Freeman suggests that approximately one-fifth of the increase in inequality in the United States can be traced to the decline of unions.[33] The relationship between the decline of unions and inward foreign investment, however, is quite ambiguous. Glickman and Woodward, for example, have found that "labor climate" (their measurement of a combination of low unionization rates, right-to-work laws, and low strike activity) strongly influenced the location of foreign employment in the 1970s but that this "anti-union location bias" was reversed in the 1980s, with foreign firm employment growth positively associated with the rate of unionization in a state.[34]

Finally, several studies have shown that there might be a national security rationale for screening and perhaps blocking foreign investor takeovers of indigenous companies in "critical technology" or defense-related industries, but this rationale is much narrower than popular appeals to avoid dependence on foreign-controlled suppliers might suggest. A host country might be subject to delay, denial, blackmail, or political manipulation via its dependence on foreign-controlled suppliers only when the international industries where those suppliers are found are tightly concentrated. A genuine national security justification for blocking foreign acquisitions and subsidizing indigenous producers is quite unlikely to have a large impact on the structure of jobs in the host economy.[35]

Overall, there is no systematic evidence that inward investment siphons off the good jobs or worsens the distribution of employment opportunities in the host economy. The presumption remains that foreign direct investment enhances the competitiveness of the host economy, both directly and indirectly, through competitive pressures and externalities. Again, however, inward investment is likely to raise the demand for relatively skilled labor, in comparison to a situation with no inward investment, bidding up the wages of those who qualify.

Conclusions: Foreign Direct Investment and the Implicit Social Contract That Comes with the Globalization of Economic Activity

The preceding analysis suggests that foreign direct investment, like other elements in the globalization of trade, technology, and investment flows across borders, has a positive net benefit on the standard of living of both home and host economies. It appears likely to have a positive net impact on job structure, augmenting the number of workers in the better-off reaches of the job market, in comparison to a situation in which foreign investment does not take place, while at the same time it increases demand for skilled labor relative to unskilled labor. Measures to retard or stop the process of foreign direct investment are likely to worsen rather than improve both the overall social welfare and the welfare of most workers.

This fact suggests that public authorities in home and host countries, and the multilateral community at large will want to adopt policies toward both outward and inward investment that maximize the spread of foreign direct investment and minimize zero-sum struggles to capture and hold the benefits in any particular locale.

In the field of taxation, this implies capital export neutrality toward outward investment, following the principle that a multinational firm should pay the same total tax on foreign operations as it does on domestic operations (providing endorsement for a foreign tax credit but not for deferral); it implies national treatment for inward investment, following the principle that all investors in a given domestic market be treated in a nondiscriminatory fashion (subject to the narrow national security exception noted earlier).[36]

In the field of trade, this fact implies not just trade liberalization in general but specific attention aimed at reducing trade regulations whose primary purpose is to force investment, including high domestic content rules of origin in preferential trade areas, discriminatory antidumping rules, and other local content or export requirements.[37]

Still, foreign direct investment, like other elements in the globalization of trade, technology, and investment flows across borders, imposes substantial adjustment costs on particular members and particular communities in the society, and, at the end of the day, leaves some less well-off and some abandoned altogether.

In this context, the design of policy toward foreign direct investment, like the design of policy toward trade, necessarily requires acknowledging a broader social contract about public sector responsibility for coping with the stresses of globalization. This contract includes policies for adjustment assistance, for ongoing skill training, and for providing an ultimate safety net for those who are damaged by the globalization process itself and not through any special fault of their own (i.e., for those who, holding their own individual shortcomings constant, may end up absolutely worse off with the economic changes that accompany trade and foreign direct investment than they would be if trade and foreign direct investment were slowed or stopped).

This social contract carries an economic rationale for public action, that the entire society has an interest in ensuring that markets function effectively (labor markets are improved so that workers can move to where their skills are most needed, capital markets are improved so that individuals can find ways to finance skill enhancement, society is spared negative externalities such as crime or drug abuse) to minimize the drag that would otherwise retard the standard of living of the entire nation.

The social contract also has a political rationale for public action, that the winners should be willing to "buy off" the losers to ensure that public support for the process of globalization continues. (This rationale is strengthened by collective goods reasons to suspect that blocking efforts might be successful.)

Finally, the social contract has an ethical rationale for public action (usually associated in economic analysis with the search for Pareto optimality), that any given policy choice has to be justified not simply by demonstrating that the sum of goods and services in the society is greater with the policy than without but that none will be worse off and some will be better off if the policy is pursued (implying that compensation is paid from those who benefit to those who do not).

Lively debate about how to design public programs to improve the workings of markets and arrange for winners to compensate losers effectively and about how much of society's resources should be devoted to these tasks can be expected, but the debate must be conducted, in my view, in the context of such an implicit social contract, not, as is currently the fashion, as if once markets were allowed to work, no further political, social, or ethical considerations need to be explored or addressed.

Notes

1. J. David Richardson and Karin Rindal, *Why Exports Matter: More!* (Washington, D.C.: Institute for International Economics and National Association of Manufacturers, 1996). A requirement that outward investment substitute for or complement the export performance of the investing firms constitutes a particularly stringent test of the impact of outward investment on job structure since one outcome if firms kept their offshore operations at home might be that domestic demand continued to be serviced from domestic locales, maintaining the domestic job structure intact but leaving export performance unchanged; a second outcome might be that domestic operations simply contracted in the face of foreign competition, worsening the domestic job structure unless workers laid off found comparable jobs elsewhere but leaving export performance unaffected.

2. For a relatively arcane exception to this generalization, see note 28.

3. If perfectly efficient labor and capital markets are assumed, there is reason to argue that inward or outward investment would not alter the distribution of good jobs vs. bad jobs since the returns to each worker would be determined purely by his or her skill level. In reality, the predominant assumption is that foreign direct investment takes place in imperfectly competitive industries. In addition, as indicated in Richard B. Freeman's chapter in this volume, labor markets show many signs of inefficient function.

4. *Mainstay II: A New Account of the Critical Role of U.S. Multinational Companies in the U.S. Economy* (Washington, D.C.: Emergency Committee for American Trade, 1993).

5. Ibid., p. 19.

6. Ibid., p. 8.

7. The Emergency Committee for American Trade (ECAT) study (cited in note 4) takes a small step in the right direction by separating trade balances by industry (chart G, 18) and by degree of globalization (table A pp. 24, p. 38). But without controlling for size or R&D intensity, the ECAT use of data from the chemical industry (SIC 28), for example, still merely contrasts the relatively strong export record of DuPont with the much weaker export record of smaller, less sophisticated firms in the chemical sector.

8. The best early efforts to address this relationship include W. B. Reddaway, J. O. N. Perkins, S. J. Potter, and C. T. Potter, *Effects of U.K. Direct Investment Overseas* (London: Her Majesty's Publishing Office, 1967); Gary C. Hufbauer and F. M. Adler, "Overseas Manufacturing Investment and the Balance of Payments," *U.S. Treasury Department Tax Policy Research Study* no. 1 (Washington, D.C.: U.S. Government Printing Office, 1968); and R. H. Frank and Richard B. Freeman, *Distributional Consequences of Direct Foreign Investment* (New York: Academic Press, 1978).

9. C. Fred Bergsten, Thomas Horst, and Theodore H. Moran, *American Multinationals and American Interests* (Washington, D.C.: Brookings Institution, 1978), chaps. 3, 4, 6.

10. Ross Perot with Pat Choate, *Save Your Job, Save Our Country: Why NAFTA Must Be Stopped—Now!* (New York: Hyperion, 1993); Patrick Buchanan, "An American Economy for Americans," *Wall Street Journal*, July 5, 1996; Ross Perot, "Position Statement on International Trade" (November 1996).

11. It would be useful to examine what happened to the absolute levels of domestic shipments for those firms that moved some operations abroad in comparison to similar firms that did not, to discover what proportion of a given set of firms' jobs would simply be eliminated via competitive pressures if the parent firms stayed at home. The calculation of the impact of outward investment on distribution of good jobs/bad jobs in the home economy then would be the number of the better jobs created via enhanced exports minus the sum of (a) the number of lesser jobs to which

displaced workers moved when parent corporations set up new operations abroad minus (b) the number of lesser jobs to which workers would be displaced anyway if the corporations did not set up new operations abroad. The calculation of the impact of outward investment on relative wages would be a result of the increase in demand for high-skilled workers in comparison to the decrease in demand for low-skilled workers.

12. This meant endorsing capital export neutrality rather than competitive neutrality as the standard for U.S. tax policy and calling for the repeal of deferral and modification of the overall limitation on the foreign tax credit. The Horst analysis led them to support retention of the foreign tax credit itself, however.

13. Robert E. Lipsey and Herle Yahr Weiss, "Foreign Production and Exports in Manufacturing Industries," *Review of Economics and Statistics* 63, no. 4 (November 1981), pp. 488–94.

14. Robert E. Lipsey and Herle Yahr Weiss, "Foreign Production and Exports of Individual Firms," *Review of Economics and Statistics* 66, no. 2 (May 1984), pp. 304–8.

15. Robert E. Lipsey, "Outward Direct Investment and the U.S. Economy," *National Bureau of Economic Research (NBER) Reprint* no. 2020 (1995).

16. M. Blomstrom, R. E. Lipsey, and K. Kulchyck, "U.S. and Swedish Direct Investment and Exports," in Robert E. Baldwin (ed.), *Trade Policy Issues and Empirical Analysis* (Chicago: University of Chicago Press, for the National Bureau of Economic Research, 1988), pp. 259–97; and Birgitta Swedenborg, cited in Lipsey, "Outward Direct Investment."

17. R. D. Pearce, "Overseas Production and Exporting Performance: Some Further Investigations," *University of Reading Discussion Papers in International Investment and Business Studies* no. 135 (1990), cited in Edward M. Graham, "On the Relationships Among Direct Investment and International Trade in the Manufacturing Sector: Empirical Results for the United States and Japan," in Dennis Encarnation (ed.), *Does Ownership Matter: Japanese Multinationals in East Asia* (London: Oxford University Press, 1999).

18. Dennis Encarnation, "The Secret to Reversing Tokyo's Surpluses? Promote U.S. Direct Investment in Japan," *International Economy* 7, no. 3 (May–June 1993), pp. 43–48.

19. Graham, "On the Relationships Among Direct Investment and International Trade in the Manufacturing Sector."

20. Ibid., p. 18.

21. W. F. Stolper and P. A. Samuelson, "Protection and Real Wages," *Review of Economic Studies* 9 (November 1941), pp. 58–73.

22. Robert Z. Lawrence, "Trade, Multinationals, and Labor," *NBER Working Paper* no. 4836 (1994); Matthew J. Slaughter, "Multinational Corporations,

Outsourcing, and American Wage Divergence," *NBER Working Paper* no. 5253 (1995).

23. W. B. Reddaway et al., *Effects of U.K. Direct Investment Overseas* (Cambridge: Cambridge University Press, 1967); Robert B. Stobaugh et al., *Nine Investments Abroad and Their Impact at Home* (Cambridge, Mass.: Harvard University Press, Graduate School of Business Administration, 1976). For a discussion of "defensive investment," see Bergsten, Horst, and Moran, *American Multinationals*, chap. 3.

24. Robert C. Feenstra and Gordon H. Hanson, "Foreign Investment, Outsourcing and Relative Wages," in Robert C. Feenstra, Gene M. Grossman, and Douglas A. Irwin (eds.), *Political Economy of Trade Policy: Essays in Honor of Jagdish Bhagwati* (Cambridge, Mass.: MIT Press, 1996), pp. 89–127; Robert C. Feenstra and Gordon H. Hanson, "Globalization, Outsourcing, and Wage Inequality," *American Economic Review* 86, no. 2 (May 1996) (including errata page). The "others" mentioned in the text refer to Eli Berman, John Bound, and Zvi Griliches, "Changes in the Demand for Skilled Labor Within U.S. Manufacturing: Evidence from the Annual Survey of Manufacturers," *Quarterly Journal of Economics* 109, no. 2 (May 1994), pp. 367–398; Paul Krugman and Robert Z. Lawrence, "Trade, Jobs, and Wages," *Scientific American* (April 1994), pp. 44–49.

25. Norman J. Glickman and Douglas P. Woodward, *The New Competitors: How Foreign Investors Are Changing the U.S. Economy* (New York: Basic Books, 1989).

26. Ibid., pp. 134–35.

27. Richard E. Caves, *Multinational Enterprise and Economic Analysis* (Cambridge: Cambridge University Press, 1983); Claudio R. Frischtak and Richard S. Newfarmer, *Transnational Corporations: Market Structure and Industrial Performance* (New York: Routledge, 1996).

28. After having stated, and restated, that foreign investment, like trade, does not have the impact on the total number of jobs or overall employment levels in an economy that public debate attributes to it, it is necessary to point out an exception: If foreign investment, like trade, raises productivity, and hence wages, it might well increase the participation rate in the labor force, bringing in workers who would otherwise remain on the sidelines. In this context, foreign investment could lead to a greater total number of jobs and a higher long-term employment level than would be the case without it.

29. Edward M. Graham and Paul Krugman, *Foreign Direct Investment in the United States*, 3d ed. (Washington, D.C.: Institute for International Economics, 1995).

30. Glickman and Woodward, *The New Competitors*, p. 137.

31. Mark E. Doms and J. Bradford Jensen, "Comparing Wages, Skills, and Productivity Between Domestic and Foreign Owned Manufacturing Establishments in the United States," draft ms. (October 1996).

33. Lipsey, "Outward Direct Investment," p. 28.

34. Richard B. Freeman, *When Earnings Diverge: Causes, Consequences, and Cures for the New Inequality in the United States* (Washington, D.C.: National Policy Association, 1997), 32.

35. Glickman and Woodward, *The New Competitors,* pp. 209–15.

36. The calculus of how national security authorities might best respond to a proposed foreign acquisition of a "critical technology" or defense-related firm is quite complex. The interests of the host country might well not be best served by simply blocking the takeover. Cf. Theodore H. Moran, *American Economic Policy and National Security* (New York: Council on Foreign Relations, 1993); Graham and Krugman, *Foreign Direct Investment;* and Edward M. Graham and Michael E. Ebert, "Foreign Direct Investment and National Security: Fixing the Exon-Florio Process," *The World Economy* 14, no. 3 (September 1991), pp. 245–68.

37. Bergsten, Horst, and Moran, *American Multinationals;* Caves, *Multinational Enterprise;* Gary Hufbauer and Joanna van Rooij, *U.S. Taxation of International Income* (Washington, D.C.: Institute for International Economics, 1992), pp. 245–68.

38. Recent theoretical and empirical work has highlighted the sensitivity of multinational locational decisions to trade restraints. S. Lael Brainard, "A Simple Theory of Multinational Corporations and Trade with a Trade-off between Proximity and Concentration," *NBER Working Paper* no. 4269 (February 1993); S. Lael Brainard, "An Empirical Assessment of the Proximity-Concentration Tradeoff between Multinational Sales and Trade," *NBER Working Paper* no. 4580 (1995); James R. Markusen, "The Boundaries of Multinational Enterprises and the Theory of International Trade," *Journal of Economic Perspectives* 9, no. 2 (Spring 1995), pp. 169–89; Jeri Jensen-Moran, "Trade Battles as Investment Wars: The Coming Rules of Origin Debate," *Washington Quarterly* 19, no. 1 (Winter 1996), pp. 239–57.

5

Increasing Wage Dispersion in U.S. Manufacturing: Plant-Level Evidence on the Role of Trade and Technology

J. BRADFORD JENSEN AND KENNETH R. TROSKE

WHILE THERE is now widespread consensus among economists, policymakers, and the general public that wage dispersion has increased over the last 20 years, there is much less consensus on the cause of this increased dispersion.[1] Recent debate has focused on two competing hypotheses. The first holds that there has been a dramatic change in the types of technologies available to businesses and that this technical change has increased the relative demand for skilled workers. Since there has not been an equal increase in the supply of skilled workers, this skill-biased technological change has led to an increase in the relative wages of skilled workers. The second hypothesis holds that the last 20 years have seen a large increase in international competition, which has shifted U.S. production away from low-skill–intensive products to high-skill–intensive products. This in turn has led to a fall in the demand for as well as the wage of less skilled workers.

This chapter reviews the relatively new and growing body of research that uses plant-level data to examine these two primary explanations for the change in the structure of wages. Studies using plant-level data are valuable for three reasons. First, research on wage dispersion using worker data has found that a large part of the increase in dispersion has occurred among workers with the same identifiable characteristics.[2]

In other words, a large part of the increase in wage inequality is the result of increasing wage dispersion among workers with the same years of education or who work in the same industry. As is the case, it seems natural to turn to alternative data sources that contain other variables that could account for this increase in within-group dispersion of wages. Second, much of the research on these issues to date using information obtained from employers has been conducted using data at the four-digit Standard Industrial Classification (SIC) level or even more aggregate levels. Given that most of the change in wage dispersion has occurred within industries, it seems obvious that understanding the driving force behind these changes requires data that can capture within-industry changes. Finally, previous research has shown that even among plants within the same detailed industry there exists tremendous heterogeneity along a number of dimensions, such as technology use, exposure to international trade, wages, and workforce composition. Further, plants in the same industry also exhibit idiosyncratic outcomes along a number of dimensions, such as technology adoption, investment, productivity growth, and job flows. Aggregated data hide these differences. It may be this heterogeneity that accounts for the increase in within-group wage inequality.

Four main conclusions arise from this review. First, one of the main problems with studies that use either aggregate or microdata is that only relatively poor measures of trade, technology, or worker skill are available. The lack of good measures for these concepts ensures that reaching strong conclusions regarding the "cause" of the increased dispersion of wages will be very difficult.[3] Second, studies exploiting plant-level cross-sectional data find substantial heterogeneity among plants in the same four-digit industry in their use of technology, in their participation in export markets, and in the skill composition of their workforce. This research also has found that size, the use of skilled workers, the use of technology, and export performance are all highly correlated across plants. Due to these facts, it will be extremely challenging to identify a single source of the increase in wage dispersion. Third, studies exploiting plant-level longitudinal data find that there has been a dramatic increase in the demand for skilled workers between 1972 and 1988, with most of this increase occurring in recessionary periods. In addition, most of the increase in the nonproduction worker share of employment has occurred within plants in the same industry. No single observable variable or variables account for a majority of the secular increase in the demand for skilled workers or the cyclical component of the change. Finally, plant-level longitudinal studies have found that between-plant changes in relative wages, particularly shifts toward plants that export, have been the dominant source of the increasing relative wages of nonproduction workers.

As is frequently the case, this research seems to raise more questions than it answers. Therefore, we conclude by speculating on whether trade and technology actually may be proxies for some other unobserved change that is occurring at plants or firms, such as changes in the organization of firms. This discussion points to the need for more complete sources of microdata before we can begin to understand the true causes of increased dispersion.

Framework for Discussion

We focus on trade and technology as sources of the increasing wage dispersion, in part because these two hypotheses currently receive the most attention in the literature and in part because studies using microdata have been directed at these hypotheses. Other authors have considered the role of changes in the supply of skilled workers and changes in institutions (i.e., unions) as possible explanations for the increase in wage dispersion; almost all of these studies find that these alternative hypotheses account for little of the observed change in the structure of wages.[4]

In its simplest form, the argument that technology has caused the change in wage dispersion rests on the notion of "skill-biased" technical change. Skill-biased technical change improves the productivity of skilled workers relative to unskilled workers. This improved productivity in turn increases the demand for skilled workers, which, absent an increase in the supply of skilled workers, leads to an increase in their relative wages. The most commonly cited example of skill-biased technical change is the increased use of computers. In this example, plants invest in computers and simultaneously hire skilled technicians to run them and skilled engineers to use them.[5]

An alternative (and complementary) explanation is that increased foreign trade has contributed to increased wage dispersion. The argument is that since most of the increase in foreign trade consists of goods produced by low-skilled workers abroad, the demand for domestic goods produced by low-skilled workers has decreased. This situation has led domestic production to shift out of low-skill, import-competing industries, reducing the demand for and wages of less skilled workers. One frequently cited example here is the steel industry. Steel is primarily produced domestically using relatively low-skilled (but perhaps high-wage) workers. It is argued that imports of steel from low-skilled, low-wage, developing countries caused the price of steel to fall, which in turn reduced the relative demand for and wages of domestic steel workers.

To determine whether trade or technology caused the increase in wage dispersion, we need to identify contrasting testable implications that emerge from these alternative explanations. Researchers have focused on a few key differences between the two hypotheses.

IMPORTS, PRICES, AND WAGES

If trade has caused the increase in wage dispersion, there should be a negative correlation between imports from countries endowed with less skilled workers and the wages of less skilled workers in the United States. Further, the impact of imports should be identifiable in measures other than the wages of unskilled workers. That is, a negative correlation between some intervening variable, such as the price of import-competing goods, and changes in the wages of unskilled workers should be expected.

TECHNOLOGICAL CHANGE, PRODUCTIVITY, AND WAGES

If technological change has caused the increase in wage dispersion, there should be a positive correlation between technological change and changes in the wages of more skilled workers. Given that technological change is difficult to measure, a positive relationship between variables associated with technological change, such as investment (specifically investment in advanced capital, equipment, or computers), research and development expenditures, or productivity growth, and changes in wages might be expected.

"BETWEEN" VS. "WITHIN" SHIFTS IN EMPLOYMENT AND WAGES

Throughout this literature researchers have focused on a simple decomposition of changes in the skill distribution into "between" industry/plant and "within" industry/plant effects. Further, researchers have used this decomposition to interpret the possible causes of wage dispersion. In the simplest case, the technological change story suggests that much of the reallocation from unskilled to skilled workers will occur within individual plants. That is, individual plants will change the proportions of skilled and unskilled workers they employ in response to changes in their use of technology. In contrast, if trade is the cause of increased wage dispersion, then the reallocation toward skilled labor should occur mainly between industries. As industries that use relatively more unskilled workers shrink in response to import competition, the ratio of skilled to unskilled workers in the manufacturing sector will rise. Researchers have examined whether the change in the share of employment and wages reflects "within" plant (or industry) changes or "between" plant (or industry) changes as a way to assess the validity of these competing hypotheses.

While this "between vs. within" decomposition has received a lot of attention, it may be that trade and technology are interrelated, which would make this distinction meaningless. For example, if new technologies, such as computers, lower the fixed costs to a plant or firm of exporting output, then plants within industries that adopt new technologies (and increase their demand for skilled workers) also will be more likely to begin exporting. While this exporting would show up as a within effect, it is not clear whether the increase in the demand for skilled workers should be attributed solely to trade or technology.

Definitions and Methodologies

One difficulty with the debate over the effects of trade and technology on wages is that a number of concepts central to this debate, such as worker skill, trade, and technology, are difficult to define, difficult to measure, or both. Therefore, before reviewing the plant-level studies, it is useful first to discuss the various ways other researchers have measured these concepts and some of the problems with these measures.[6]

MEASURING WORKER SKILL

All of the studies examining increases in the relative demand for or the relative wages of skilled workers classify workers using one or more proxies for skill: education, work experience, or occupation. Most plant- or industry-level studies examining cross-sectional differences in technical change or trade use worker- or plant-level data to measure the average wages of college graduates relative to high school graduates, more experienced (older) workers relative to less experienced (younger) workers, or nonproduction workers relative to production workers. However, there is some concern whether these variables are good measures of the level or changes in the level of worker skill. This is particularly true for one of the more widely available (and therefore widely used) classifications, nonproduction vs. production workers.

The nonproduction worker group contains both very skilled workers, such as computer scientists, physicists, and chief executive officers, as well as less skilled workers, such as delivery workers, cafeteria workers, and bookkeepers. Evidence presented by Eli Berman, John Bound, and Zvi Griliches and Timothy Dunne, John Haltiwanger, and Kenneth Troske suggest that both cross-sectional and time-series variation in this measure is positively correlated with other observable measures of skill such as education, experience, and more detailed occupational differences.[7] However, this evidence is by no means definitive; clearly it would be preferable to have more accurate measures of worker skill.

MEASURING THE EFFECTS OF TRADE

The main tactic used to investigate the trade hypothesis has been to measure either cross-sectional or time-series variation in the level of imports into a country and then to compare this with cross-sectional or time-series variation in either the relative demand for or wages of less skilled workers.

A number of studies have measured trade as the ratio of imports to the total amount of goods produced in a country/industry/sector. For example, Steve Davis measures trade as the sum of imports and exports as a percentage of gross national product (GNP) and correlates cross-country variation in this measure with cross-country movements in the relative wages of less skilled workers.[8] He finds that increases in trade contribute to a *convergence* of wages within countries and concludes that some other unobserved factor must account for the *increase* in wage dispersion. Kevin Murphy and Finis Welch compare the time-series variation in the wages and employment of college graduates relative to high school graduates with time-series variation in the net imports of durable goods as a share of GNP.[9] They find that while changes in trade over this period were an important source of between-industry shifts in employment, most of the change occurs within industries. Therefore, Murphy and Welch conclude that some within-industry phenomenon, such as skill-biased technical change, must account for most of the change in the demand for skilled workers. Finally, George J. Borjas, Richard B. Freeman, and Lawrence Katz construct estimates of the quantity of unskilled labor embodied in net imports and compare movements in this variable with the wages of high school graduates relative to college graduates.[10] Borjas and his coauthors argue that this is a more accurate measure of the effective supply of unskilled workers in the economy. Using this measure, they find that trade accounts for over one-third of the 10 percent decline in the relative wages of unskilled workers.

Recently this work has been criticized by trade economists for using measures of trade that are not based on theory.[11] These more recent studies use the Stopler-Samuelson theorem to show that the "appropriate" measure of the effect of trade on wages should be changes in the terms of trade. Based on this reasoning, Ana Revenga constructs an index of the import prices for 38 three- and four-digit manufacturing industries and compares movements in this variable with changes in the employment and wages of unskilled workers in an industry.[12] She finds that changes in the terms of trade have resulted in a 2 percent decline in relative employment and a 4.5 percent to 7.5 percent decline in the relative wages of trade-intensive industries. Robert Z. Lawrence and Matthew J. Slaughter use the Bureau of Labor Statistics' export and import price indices, which are available for a handful of manufacturing industries in the 1980s, to compare relative price changes in these industries with movements in the relative wages of skilled workers.[13] They construct two measures of prices: actual market prices and market prices multiplied by total factor productivity in an industry (what they term the "effective price"). Regardless of the measure used, Lawrence and Slaughter find that trade has little to do with the slow growth in the average wages in U.S. manufacturing. Rather they find that the decrease in the relative wages of unskilled workers is the result of the slow productivity growth in the nontraded goods sectors.

Jeffrey Sachs and Howard Shatz criticize Lawrence and Slaughter on two counts.[14] First, they note that Lawrence and Slaughter have complete price data for only a few industries. In addition, Sachs and Shatz object to the inclusion of the computer industry when constructing effective prices. They show that the computer industry has accounted for an overwhelming majority of the productivity gains among durable goods industries. To avoid the downward price bias that results from including computers, Sachs and Shatz use price indices of domestic goods from the Bureau of Economic Analysis for all three-digit manufacturing industries for every year between 1980 and 1990. In addition, they effectively exclude the computer industry from their analysis. By so doing, Sachs and Shatz show that changes in the relative prices of skill-intensive goods due to increases in imports contributed to a 7.2 percent decline in the demand for production workers in the manufacturing sector.

Berman, Bound, and Griliches decompose the increase in the demand for skilled workers in the U.S. manufacturing industries into "between" and "within" components.[15] They use import and export shares to define subsectors within industries and examine how the demand for nonproduction workers has changed across import and export sectors, defense-related sectors, and the domestic consumption sector (industries that produced goods primarily consumed domestically). They find that the import and export sectors contribute small between-industry/sector changes, and they therefore conclude that trade has not played a large role in the increased demand for nonproduction workers.

Another way to gauge the impact of trade on increased wage dispersion is to examine plants that engage in foreign trade. Andrew B. Bernard and J. Bradford Jensen identify plants on the basis of whether they directly export goods and find that exporting plants figure prominently in the increase in demand for nonproduction workers and contribute significantly to the increased relative wages of these workers.[16] One shortcoming of this approach is that it does not account for changes in the wage structure due to increases in imports, which are thought to be an important factor in increasing wage dispersion.

MEASURING TECHNOLOGY
AND TECHNICAL CHANGE

Early in the debate over the causes of increased wage dispersion, efforts were made to account for this phenomenon using observed changes in trade and institutions, such as labor unions. When these variables failed to account for much of the change in the structure of wages, researchers were left to conclude that some unobservable factor, such as technical change, must be responsible. Obviously this is not an acceptable methodology, so more recently researchers have begun searching for more direct measures of technical change. Unfortunately, measuring technical change is fraught with difficulty.

One frequently used measure is the change in total factor productivity (TFP) at the sectoral level.[17] The problem with this measure is that it is essentially a residual from a regression of output on capital and labor. Obviously technical change is part of this residual, but so are a host of other factors, such as unmeasured change in the quality of inputs. Therefore, it is never clear what is producing the cross-sectional or time-series variation in TFP.[18] Clearly, it is desirable to have a more tangible measure of technical change.

One alternative has been to try to measure changes in the amount of research performed in a sector, implicitly assuming that the level of such activity is correlated with changes in technology. Examples of this type of measure are changes in the amount of research and development spending in an industry, the number of patents used in an industry, and the percentage of workers in a sector who are scientists and engineers.[19] While the evidence does suggest that levels of these measures are correlated with the skill of workers in an industry, it is not clear whether changes in these measures capture technical change in an industry. Most of the evidence on this issue consists of showing that the changes in these measures are correlated with changes in TFP. Therefore, this evidence suffers from the same criticism as the TFP measure.

A final way researchers have tried to measure technical changes is to measure changes in the type of capital used to produce output. Some of the ways researchers have measured changes in the type of capital include measures of investment in plant and equipment at the plant or industry level or the average age of capital used in an industry.[20] Both of these measures assume that newer capital embodies the current state of technology so that investment in new equipment is equivalent to technical change. Another measure is the stock of or investment in computer equipment.[21] The rationale for this measure is that the major innovation in recent years has been the movement of computers into the workplace. A final measure is the type of advanced technology capital used to produce output. This measure is constructed using data drawn from the U.S. Census Bureau's Survey of Manufacturing Technology (SMT), which was conducted in 1988 and 1993.[22] These surveys asked plant managers about their use of 17 different advanced production technologies. Their responses can be used to construct measures of the sophistication of the capital equipment used in a plant. The two major drawbacks of this measure and the computer investment measure are that they are available only for manufacturing industries and they are rather crude measures of the type of capital used in production.

One related measure of technical change that has been used recently is the amount, or changes in the amount, of high-tech capital used in an industry.[23] This measure is based on the Bureau of Economic Analysis (BEA) National Income and Product Accounts data. It usually consists of industry-level (measured at the two-digit level) investment in office machinery, communications equipment, instruments, and photocopy machines. The measure is popular because the BEA creates these numbers for a wide variety of industries, including nonmanufacturing industries. Unfortunately, these numbers are not directly collected through any survey, so the BEA must impute these numbers based on data that are collected. One piece of information the BEA uses to construct measures of investment by industry and by type of equipment is the occupational mix of workers employed in an industry.[24] Therefore, it seems inappropriate to use these data to examine the effects of technical change on changes in the skill of workers in an industry, since it is exactly this cross-sectional and time-series variation that the BEA is exploiting to impute these numbers in the first place.

One form of technical change that has not been examined empirically is changes in "organizational capital." By this we mean concepts such as total quality management, quality circles, just-in-time inventory, and outsourcing. Given the large amount of attention these concepts have received in recent years in the management literature as well as the popular press, they seem to be natural candidates for accounting for changes in the wage structure. These concepts have not been studied empirically because data on their use are lacking. Clearly more attention needs to be paid to collecting data that can measure these broader concepts of capital.

SUMMARY OF MEASUREMENT ISSUES

In addition to documenting the variety of ways that researchers have measured trade, technology, and worker skill, one goal of this section has been to point out the many problems inherent in measuring changes in those areas. Whether because it is unclear what is the appropriate measure to use (trade) or because the measures we have are not very precise (worker skill and technology), one thing is clear: No single measure is ideal. Given this, two conclusions emerge. First, no single study should be viewed as definitive. Instead, we should look for findings that are robust across various studies that use a variety of data sources and methodologies. Second, we clearly need to develop better data and measures. Until such time as we collect better data, any conclusions reached regarding the causes of increased dispersion in the wage structure will be, at best, tentative.

Why Microdata?

Given the difficulties in measuring skills, trade, and technology, why rely on plant-level data? Much of the research examining the role of technology and trade in accounting for increasing wage dispersion has relied on industry-level data, which is the most detailed data readily available. The analysis proceeds on the assumption that there is a "representative" firm or plant in the industry. In other words, firms or plants in a given industry are assumed to use similar inputs (purchased at similar prices), using similar methods of production, to produce similar products (sold at similar prices). In addition, all changes that occur in an industry are assumed to affect plants within the industry equally.

As mentioned earlier, one shortcoming of this approach is that much of the research using worker or plant-level data has found that most of the increase in the dispersion of wages has occurred within four-digit industries.[25] That is, increasing wage dispersion is the result of certain steel workers experiencing rising wages while other steel workers experience falling wages, and not the result of workers in certain industries experiencing falling wages while workers in other industries experience rising wages. Aggregate data hide these within-industry changes. A further difficulty with industry-level analysis is that almost all of the previous research using plant-level data has shown that the "representative firm" assumption is wrong. Plants, even those within the same four-digit industry, exhibit considerable heterogeneity both in their cross-sectional characteristics and in their behavior over time.[26]

For example, consider the within- and across-industry variation in productivity and capital intensity.[27] Table 5–1 presents the mean plant labor productivity for each two-digit industry in manufacturing. Considerable variation exists across industries. Petroleum is the most productive and capital-intensive industry while apparel is the least productive and least capital intensive. The average plant in petroleum is about 8.5 times as productive and 27 times as capital intensive as the average apparel plant. Table 5–2 presents measures of the variation of labor productivity and capital intensity within four-digit industries. It calculates the productivity or capital intensity of the plant at the 90th percentile relative to the plant in the 10th percentile for each four-digit industry.[28] Then the average of this ratio within each two-digit industry is presented. The table shows that there is considerable variation in these measures even within fairly detailed industries. In fact, for some industries, the 90/10 ratio of capital intensity or productivity within a four-digit industry is much greater than the ratio of the means at the two-digit level. For example, within petroleum, the 90th percentile plant is about 46 times more capital intensive than the 10th percentile plant. Even within capital-intensive industries, some plants are relatively labor intensive. Likewise, within low-productivity industries, some plants are relatively productive.

The assumption that there is a representative plant within an industry clearly does not hold. Even within detailed industries, some plants are large, some small; some are capital intensive, some labor intensive; some use mostly skilled workers, some mostly unskilled workers; some use technology intensively, others do not; some pay high wages, some do not.

Plants differ not only in their characteristics but also in their behavior over time. Some firms grow (even in declining industries) while others shrink (even in expanding industries). Haltiwanger shows that four-digit industry effects account for less than 10 percent of the time-series variation in employment growth, output growth, labor productivity growth, total factor productivity growth, and investment.[29] Plants

Table 5-1 Comparison of Two-Digit Industry Means, 1992

Industry Name	Two-Digit SIC Code	Mean Plant Capital Intensity ($000)	Mean Plant Labor Productivity ($000)
Food	20	70.76	263.94
Tobacco	21	71.84	310.25
Textiles	22	38.13	101.99
Apparel	23	7.22	65.46
Lumber and Wood	24	35.08	106.30
Furniture and Fixtures	25	16.15	82.69
Paper	26	78.26	163.82
Printing and Publishing	27	26.21	85.98
Chemicals	28	171.95	306.27
Petroleum	29	198.19	546.27
Rubber	30	42.40	114.68
Leather	31	11.30	81.49
Stone, Clay, and Glass	32	67.46	130.19
Primary Metal	33	66.62	158.40
Fabricated Metal	34	33.72	102.86
Industrial Machinery	35	36.21	95.53
Electronics	36	30.78	111.93
Transportation	37	35.96	127.02
Instruments	38	28.60	116.08
Miscellaneous	39	16.99	90.62

Note: Based on authors' calculations from the LRD. Capital intensity is the ratio of book value of capital to total employment in the plant. Labor productivity is defined as the value added per worker in the plant.

enter industries that are declining and plants exit industries that are growing.[30] Some plants experience improving productivity, others experience decreasing productivity. Again, the representative firm model is inadequate.

How are plant-level differences in performance reflected in aggregate changes in the economy? Consider a few different scenarios. Suppose labor productivity in every plant in an industry increased by 3 percent due to some exogenous shock (say, quality improvements in some input). This would appear as a 3 percent increase in aggregate industry productivity. Consider another possibility, where half the plants purchase new equipment and increase their productivity by 6 percent (assuming the plants were randomly assigned across the size distribution) while others make no investment and experience no productivity change. Again, at the industry level there would be a 3 percent

Table 5-2 Comparison of Within Four-Digit Industry Dispersion, 1992

Industry Name	Two-Digit SIC Code	Mean of Four-digit Industry Ratios of 90th/10th Capital Intensity	Mean of Four-digit Industry Ratios of 90th/10th Labor Productivity
Food	20	9.63	6.47
Tobacco	21	9.52	13.35
Textiles	22	9.01	4.52
Apparel	23	8.92	8.47
Lumber and Wood	24	8.70	4.11
Furniture and Fixtures	25	8.89	3.54
Paper	26	3.94	3.65
Printing and Publishing	27	8.58	4.05
Chemicals	28	15.08	6.55
Petroleum	29	46.70	7.34
Rubber	30	8.78	3.92
Leather	31	7.77	4.92
Stone, Clay, and Glass	32	9.88	3.43
Primary Metal	33	8.40	3.81
Fabricated Metal	34	7.18	3.43
Industrial Machinery	35	7.63	3.69
Electronics	36	10.02	3.90
Transportation	37	8.12	3.99
Instruments	38	9.03	3.77
Miscellaneous	39	8.55	3.57

Note: Based on authors' calculations from the LRD. Capital intensity is the ratio of book value of capital to total employment in the plant. Labor productivity is defined as the value added per worker in the plant.

increase in productivity. A third alternative is that, initially, half the plants in an industry were twice as productive as their rivals. If there is an exogenous shock to demand and the more productive plants gain market share (at the expense of their less productive rivals), there would again be an increase in average productivity. With industry-level data the three scenarios are observationally equivalent, although most people would agree that the underlying source of the productivity change in each case was different. Microdata are needed to distinguish between these scenarios.

Recent research using plant-level data sheds light on the sources of productivity growth and suggests that the reallocation of activity across plants with different characteristics (scenario 3) is an important source of aggregate changes. For a selected number of manufacturing industries, various authors find that the reallocation of output from less productive to more productive plants plays an important role in industry-level productivity growth.[31] Haltiwanger examines the entire manufacturing sector over the period from 1977 to 1987 and finds that some plants are increasing their productivity (scenario 2) but that shifts of output to higher-productivity plants (scenario 3) play a major role in industry-level productivity growth.[32] Haltiwanger also finds that the contribution of these various effects changes over time.

Most often the "representative" plant is not improving productivity. What is occurring is much more dynamic and complicated. The interaction of heterogeneous plant characteristics and idiosyncratic outcomes drives the aggregate changes. While the examples focus on changes in productivity, this heterogeneity extends to other performance measures. Clearly the impact of trade and technology differs according to the cross-plant distribution of attributes such as worker skill, size, and capital intensity. This suggests that the only way to develop a complete picture of the role of technology and trade in affecting the wage structure and the demand for skilled workers is through the use of plant-level data.

Cross-Sectional Evidence on Technology, Trade, Skills, and Wages

It is understood that plants are heterogeneous and that they experience idiosyncratic outcomes. To understand whether and how these two facts influence aggregate measures of the demand for and the wages of skilled workers, first it must be documented how plants differ in their wages, use of skilled workers, use of technology, and exposure to international trade. Then how plants differ in their behavior over time must be documented. Once the underlying characteristics of plants and how they behave over time are understood, the influence of heterogeneity and idiosyncratic outcomes on aggregate measures of the relative demand for and wages of skilled workers can be determined. We begin by describing some of the empirical regularities that emerge from cross-sectional microdata.

The primary source for the plant-level evidence discussed here and in the next section is the Longitudinal Research Database (LRD), which consists solely of manufacturing plants. Data in the LRD allow workers to be classified into only two groups, production and nonproduction workers. Therefore, the primary measure of worker skill is the nonproduction labor share, measured as either the ratio of the number of nonproduction workers to total employment (employment-share based) or the ratio of the wages paid to nonproduction workers to total wages paid to all workers (cost-share based). As mentioned earlier, there is some evidence to suggest that aggregate changes in the nonproduction labor share are correlated with changes in other observable measures of worker skill, such as education and a more detailed occupation. However, as there is no evidence of this relationship at the plant level, this may not be an adequate measure of skill.

TECHNOLOGY, SKILL MIX, AND WAGES

One of the main plant-level sources on technology use is the Census Bureau's 1988 and 1993 Survey of Manufacturing Technology (SMT). The SMT contains detailed information on the presence of 17 individual technologies (i.e., CAD/CAM, pick-and-place robots, etc.) in about 10,000 plants in SIC industries 34 to 38. Research using these data has identified a number of empirical regularities.

In a study that links the 1988 SMT to the 1987 Census of Manufactures (CM), Dunne and James Schmitz examine the relationship among plant size, technology use, nonproduction labor share, and the wage structure in manufacturing plants.[33] They find that large plants are more likely to use advanced technologies and are more likely to pay higher wages.[34] They also find that technology use is positively correlated with wages, for both production and nonproduction workers. Further, they find that plants that use more advanced technology employ more nonproduction workers. Dunne and Schmitz interpret these results as evidence of skill-technology complementarity and as being consistent with skill-biased technical change.

Mark Doms, Dunne, and Troske examine technology use and employment patterns using more detailed measures of the skills and wages of workers in manufacturing plants.[35] Because they have data on both worker and plant characteristics, they are able to conduct a more detailed examination of the relationship between skill and technology than previous studies, which relied exclusively on plant-level or worker-level data. These authors find that plants that use more advanced technology capital have a higher proportion of college-educated workers; technology use and the education of workers are positively correlated for both production and nonproduction workers; and the fraction of workers employed in scientific, engineering, managerial, and precision-craft occupations increases with the use of advanced technology. This represents further evidence in support of skill-technology complementarity and is again consistent with skill-biased technical change.

EXPORTING, SKILL MIX, AND WAGES

Measuring a plant's exposure to international trade is difficult. However, one dimension of trade exposure that is relatively easy to identify is whether a plant participates in export markets. Periodically prior to 1983, and in each year since, the Census Bureau has collected data on the amount of output that is directly exported from manufacturing plants in the CM and the Annual Survey of Manufactures (ASM). Using this information, Bernard and Jensen compare the wage and employment structure of exporting plants relative to nonexporting plants.[36] Their research shows that exporting plants are larger, more capital intensive, and more productive. Even controlling for other plant characteristics that are correlated with wages (i.e., size, capital intensity, and productivity), exporting is associated with higher wages for both production and nonproduction workers. Further, plants that export employ a higher proportion of nonproduction workers.

TECHNOLOGY VS. TRADE

The studies just described find that larger plants are more likely to use advanced technology and more likely to export. Is there an association between trade and technology use at the plant level? Bernard and Jensen and Jensen and Nathan Musick show that there is a positive correlation between exporting and technology use even after controlling for other plant characteristics.[37] Large plants are more likely to use advanced technologies, are more likely to export, are more capital intensive, are more productive, and pay higher wages. Which of these characteristics "cause" the others is far from clear. It may be that using advanced technologies or exporting "causes" plants to use more capital, employ more workers, and pay workers higher wages. Alternatively, it could be that larger, more capital-intensive, higher-wage plants are more likely to adopt advanced technologies or export because of economies of scale or because they employ more skilled workers.[38] Finally, it may be that plants run by more skilled managers (an unobserved attribute) grow faster; employ more skilled, higher-wage workers; are more likely to use new technologies; and are more likely to export output. Even with plant-level data it is difficult, if not impossible, to determine causality using cross-sectional data.

Time-Series Evidence on Technology, Trade, Skills, and Wages

As described, there is evidence of a positive relationship between a plant's use of technology, its participation in the export market, and the skill and wages of its workers. However, the aim is to find out how the plant-level demand for skilled workers and variance in wages has evolved over time to know whether these changes can be accounted for by plant-level changes in technology or trade. To begin, we present evidence on the time-series variation in the demand for skilled workers and the variance of wages. We then discuss whether these changes can be accounted for by changes in technology or trade.

CHANGES IN THE STRUCTURE OF WAGES
AND THE DEMAND FOR SKILLED WORKERS
IN U.S. MANUFACTURING

As has been extensively documented, the nonproduction labor share of U.S. manufacturing employment and wages has increased since 1970.[39] Moreover, the relative wages of nonproduction workers have increased in the 1980s. What is known about the timing of these changes?

The relative wage of nonproduction to production workers fell from 1.53 to 1.51 during the 1970s and then increased to 1.56 in 1987.[40] Figure 5-1 presents the time-series movements in the employment-share–based and cost-share–based nonproduction labor share variables. Two points bear mentioning. First, between 1972 and 1988, the cost-based nonproduction labor share has risen from 0.34 to 0.41, an increase of over 20 percent. This change has been interpreted as evidence of a substantial increase in the demand for skilled workers in U.S. manufacturing. Second, almost all of the change in the nonproduction labor share occurs in recessions, in particular the 1979 to 1982 recession. This fact has not been recognized in most previous work and stands as a puzzle for theoretical explanations of the changes in the skill mix.

The most obvious question to ask about the changes in the demand for and wages of skilled workers is, How did they occur? Did they reflect a shift in labor demand between plants, the entry or exit of plants, or a change in demand within plants? The simplest version of the trade hypothesis states that plants which produce skill-intensive products experienced an increase in demand relative to plants that

Figure 5–1   Nonproduction Labor Share in Manufacturing

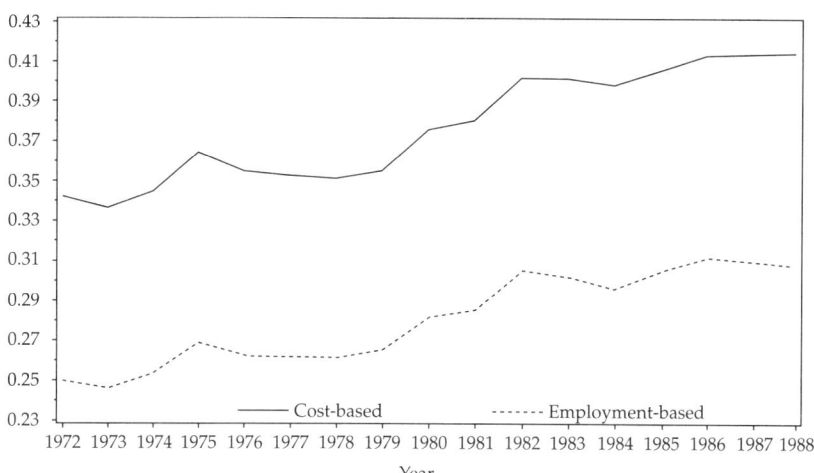

Source: Timothy Dunne, John Haltiwanger, and Kenneth R. Troske, "Technology and Jobs: Secular Change and Cyclical Dynamics," *Carnegie-Rochester Conference Series on Public Policy* 46 (1997), pp. 107–78.

produce less skill-intensive products. This in turn led to an increase in the aggregate level of skill in the economy, but the level of a skill in an individual plant remained the same. Thus, the increase in the aggregate level of skill was the result of a change in the allocation of employment *between* plants. In contrast, the simplest version of the skill-biased technical change hypothesis states that some plants adopted new technologies and as a result simultaneously increased their relative demand for skilled workers. Thus, the increase in the level of skill in the economy was the result of changes in the level of skill *within* plants. One way to examine whether technology or trade can account for the increase in the wage dispersion is to decompose the changes in the share of employment or wages of nonproduction workers into their "between" and "within" components. Two recent studies have utilized this methodology to examine plant-level changes in the demand for nonproduction workers.[41] The following formula is one example of how to decompose the year-to-year changes in the nonproduction labor share into its various components:

$$\Delta M_t = \sum_{continuers}(L_{it-1}/L_{t-1})\Delta M_{it} + \sum_{continuers}(M_{it-1} - M_{t-1})\Delta(L_{it}/L_t)$$
$$+ \sum_{continuers}\Delta(L_{it}/L_t)\Delta M_{it} + \sum_{entering\ plants}(L_{it}/L_t)(M_{it} - M_{t-1})$$
$$- \sum_{exiting\ plants}(L_{it-1}/L_{t-1})(M_{it-1} - M_{t-1}),$$

where M_t represents the aggregate nonproduction labor share in period t, M_{it} represents the nonproduction labor share among plants in group i in period t (continuing, entering, and exiting plants), L_t represents aggregate total employment in period t, and L_{it} represents total employment of plants in group i in period t.[42] The first term represents the within-plant change in the nonproduction labor share among continuing plants; the second represents the between-plant component among continuing plants; the third term is the covariance of the between and within effects; and the last two terms capture the contribution of net entry to changes in the nonproduction labor share.

Table 5–3 presents the results of this decomposition for the cost-based nonproduction labor share measure. The top panel uses data from the CM. The bottom panel is based on plants that are in the LRD in every year between 1972 and 1988.[43] The first thing to notice is that while both the between- and the within-plant components contribute to changes in the nonproduction labor share, the within component accounts for a larger share than the between component over the whole period and for each of the subperiods. Over the entire period, the within component accounts for 31 percent of the cost-share–based measure, while the between component accounts for 26 percent. Over the period from 1977 to 1982 when most of the changes occur, the within component accounts for 46 percent of the change in the nonproduction labor share while the between component accounts for 42 percent of the change.

Interpreting the contribution of net entry is difficult. Net entry accounts for a substantial fraction of the long-run change in the nonproduction labor share (37 percent) and as much as 33 percent of the change in the subperiods. This is because entering plants contain a very small fraction of employment in any given intercensal period (about 12 percent), but this share grows quite dramatically for plants that survive over the entire period (to 30 percent). Dunne, Haltiwanger, and Troske show that most of the net entry occurs within industries and that entering plants are more skill intensive than exiting plants (but less skill intensive than existing plants).[44] These results can be interpreted to mean that because net entry is a within-industry phenomenon, it is similar to within-plant changes. Alternatively, since the

Table 5–3 Decomposition of Nonproduction Labor Share Changes, 1972–1988 (Cost Share Based)

Sample Used	Total	Within	Between	Covariance	Net Entry
Census of Manufactures					
1972–87	.0708	.0219	.0186	.0042	.0261
1972–77	.0083	.0066	.0000	.0009	.0008
1977–82	.0494	.0229	.0207	.0000	.0058
1982–87	.0130	.0045	.0007	.0034	.0044
Balanced Panel of Continuing Plants					
Annual Average					
for 1972–88	.0038	.0025	.0015	–.0003	N.A.

Note: Based on authors' calculations from the LRD.

shift is from less-skill-intensive exiting plants to more-skill-intensive entering plants, it could be interpreted as a between-plant phenomenon. Therefore, while net entry plays an important role in the changing wage structure, it is difficult to categorize it using the between/within dichotomy. This is another reason why that dichotomy may act to obscure important relationships.

Next we turn to decomposing the year-to-year changes in the nonproduction labor share. Figure 5–2 plots the time-series movements in the nonproduction labor share and its three components. Because this decomposition can be performed only using continuing plants, there is no net entry component. Focusing on the cost-based measure in the bottom panel of this figure, it is again evident that while both the between and within components are important, the latter accounts for a slightly larger fraction of the overall change and more closely tracks the year-to-year variation in the nonproduction labor share.

Bernard and Jensen find that while within-plant changes account for the bulk of the change in the employment-based nonproduction labor share, the increase in the relative wage of nonproduction workers is due primarily to shifts between plants.[45] Focusing on the period from 1979 to 1987 and using a different decomposition method, they find that for a sample of continuing plants, the within component accounts for 55 percent of the change in employment-based nonproduction labor share. However, they also find that, for the cost-share–based nonproduction labor share, the between component accounts for 59 percent of the increase. Bernard and Jensen note that while the cost-based and employment-based nonproduction labor shares are both increasing, the former is increasing faster. Because nonproduction workers are

Figure 5–2 Decomposing Changes in Nonproduction Share

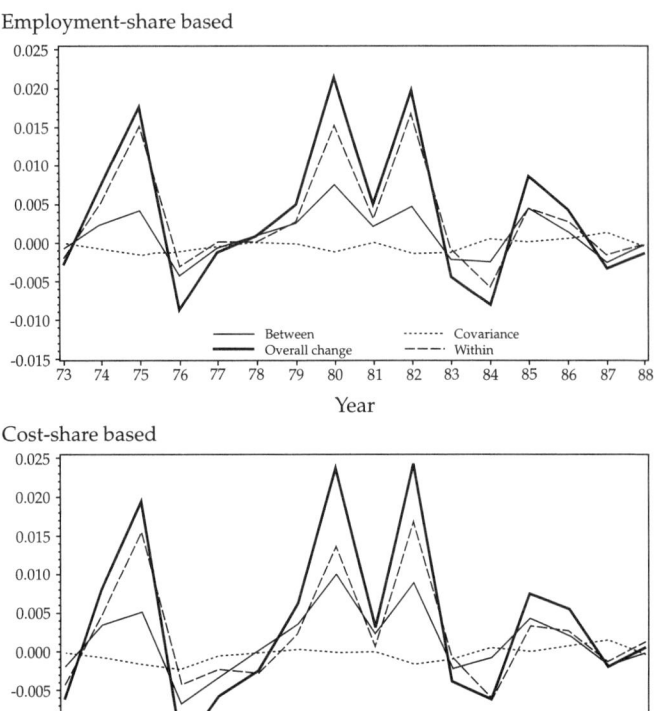

Source: LRD balanced panel

paid higher wages than production workers, as the employment-based nonproduction labor share increases, the cost-based nonproduction labor share will rise faster (even without a change in the relative wages of nonproduction workers). If relative wages are increasing (as they did over this period), the cost-based share will grow even faster. Bernard and Jensen construct a measure of this "wage gap" and decompose it into within and between components. They find that, even at the industry level, the between-industry component accounts for 59 percent of the increase in the relative wages of nonproduction workers. For the sample of continuing plants between 1980 and 1987, the between-plant component accounts for 82 percent of the increase in the wage gap. Thus, while there is evidence that plants and industries increased the share of nonproduction workers in their labor mix, between-industry and between-plant movements contributed significantly to the increase in relative wages for nonproduction workers.

The finding that within-plant changes account for most of the change in the employment-based nonproduction labor share, while between-plant changes account for most of the cost-based nonproduction labor share, is something of a puzzle. One possible explanation is the fact that most of the increase in wage dispersion has occurred within groups of workers. In particular, the wages of the most skilled nonproduction workers increased relative to the wages of the less skilled nonproduction workers. Given that this was the case, increases in the demand for goods among plants that employ the most highly paid nonproduction workers could account for most of the aggregate increase in the relative wages of nonproduction workers, while increases in the relative demand for nonproduction workers within plants could account for most of the aggregate increase in the relative number of nonproduction workers.

Turning now to changes in the structure of wages, Davis and Haltiwanger, using data from the March Current Population Survey (CPS) files between 1975 and 1988, show that changes in the dispersion of manufacturing worker wages are similar to the observed changes among all workers.[46] In addition, using data from the LRD combined with the CPS, Davis and Haltiwanger show that most of the increase in wage inequality for both production and nonproduction workers is the result of rising between-plant dispersion of wages, suggesting that the cross-plant distribution of skilled workers is becoming more segregated.

THE ROLE OF TECHNOLOGY

Next we review the plant-level evidence on the role of technology in affecting the demand for and wages of skilled workers. Dunne, Haltiwanger, and Troske have conducted a series of exercises examining whether changes in technology can account for the within-plant changes in the demand for skilled workers.[47] They use three measures of technical change: plant-level investment in new equipment, changes in the stock of research-and-development (R&D) capital in a plant's firm, and (for a subset of plants in their data) whether the plant adopts any new information-based technologies or production-based technologies. Their results show that while observable measures of technical change account for a significant fraction of the secular increase in the within-plant component of the nonproduction labor share, unobservable factors account for a majority of the increase in the demand for skilled workers, and changes in unobservable factors account for almost all of the cyclical variation in the demand for skilled workers.

Doms, Dunne, and Troske, using data from the LRD matched to data from the 1988 and 1993 SMT, also attempt to account for within-plant changes in the demand for skilled workers using the detailed information on plant-level adoption of new technologies.[48] Their results show that plant-level adoption of new technologies is uncorrelated with plant-level changes in the demand for skilled workers. Instead, it appears that plants that already employ more skilled workers are more likely to adopt new technologies. These results stand in sharp contrast to the results of studies using industry-level data, which find a positive correlation between technical change and changes in the demand for skilled workers.[49]

The source of these different findings appears to be the different measures of technical change the authors use. The industry-level studies use investment in new computer equipment as the proxy for technical change, whereas Doms, Dunne, and Troske measure technical change as the adoption of new production-based technologies, such as robots, automated guided vehicle-control systems, and numerically controlled machines.[50] When those authors repeat their analysis using plant-level data on computer investment, they find that this variable is positively correlated with plant-level changes in the nonproduction labor share. However, they also find that investment in computers is not correlated with changes in the skill of either production or nonproduction workers.

Bernard and Jensen examine the role of technology in increasing the demand for and wages of nonproduction workers, focusing on changes in firms' R&D-to-sales ratio, computer investment, and new equipment investment.[51] They find that changes in technology are positively associated with within-plant increases in the nonproduction worker share of employment. However, as noted earlier, between-plant movements appear to be the source of increased wage dispersion, and changes in technology do not appear to be associated with between-plant movements of employment or wages.

One related issue concerns the relationship between technology use and the growth and survival of plants. Doms, Dunne, and Mark Roberts examine these relationships using data on plants in the LRD, again matched to data from the 1988 SMT, and find that plants that are more technologically advanced have higher growth rates and are less likely to fail.[52] These results, in conjunction with the results in Doms, Dunne, and Troske showing that more technologically advanced plants employ more skilled workers, lend further support to the hypothesis that recent technical change has been skill-biased.[53]

THE ROLE OF TRADE

Davis and Haltiwanger combine plant-level data on wages and other characteristics with industry-level data on trade to examine whether changes in trade can account for the between-plant changes in the wages of production and nonproduction workers.[54] They construct two different measures of trade: the import penetration ratio at the four-digit level and the share of output in a four-digit industry that is exported. Davis and Haltiwanger then compare the cross-sectional variation in these measures with cross-sectional variation in the average wages of production and nonproduction workers. Their basic result is that changes in these trade variables account for very little of the increase in the between-plant variance in wages for either of these groups of workers. Instead, the majority of these changes are accounted for by initial plant size and changes in unobservable factors. Davis and Haltiwanger conclude that this unobservable change is technical change and, therefore, that technical change accounts for a majority of the between-plant increase in the dispersion of wages.

Bernard and Jensen recognize and explicitly control for the heterogeneity in exposure to trade within four-digit industries and examine changes in employment and wages at plants that export.[55] Even within four-digit industries, exporters have different characteristics from non-exporters: They pay higher wages, use nonproduction workers more intensively, and are more capital intensive. Because of these differences, shifts in activity across these plants can affect relative wages. In regression analysis examining the role of exporting and technology in the between and within movements of employment and wages, they find that changes in technology are positively associated with within-plant increases in nonproduction workers. However, it is changes in demand across plants, particularly shifts in employment to plants that export, that account for changes in the relative wages of nonproduction workers.[56] While this study does not present a complete picture of the role of trade on domestic labor markets because it does not have data on imports, the authors conclude that their results do indicate that between-plant movements of employment and wages to exporters play a significant role in the increasing relative wages of nonproduction workers.

Summary and Conclusion

Plant-level data from the manufacturing sector provide a number of key insights into the relationships among wages, skill mix, technology, and trade. First, there is considerable heterogeneity along all of these dimensions, even within narrowly defined industries. Thus, for many types of research questions, industry-level data are clearly inappropriate. Nevertheless, a number of empirical regularities can be observed. Plants that use more high-technology equipment are more likely to employ skilled workers and pay higher wages. Plants that export are more likely to employ nonproduction workers and also pay higher wages. Further, larger plants are more likely to use advanced technology capital and are more likely to export. Even after controlling for size, exporting and technology use are positively correlated. The relationships among these variables makes it difficult to determine whether any can be said to "cause" export status or technology use.

The time-series evidence shows that there was a marked increase in the demand for skilled workers between 1972 and 1988 and also a marked increase in the dispersion of wages among workers over this same period. Most of this increase in wage dispersion appears to be the result of an increase in the between-plant dispersion of wages. The evidence shows that most of the increase in the demand for skilled workers has occurred in recessionary periods and in particular in the period from 1979 to 1982. Most of the increase in the nonproduction worker share of employment is due to within-plant changes. It appears that while changes in technology can account for some of the secular within-plant increase in the demand for skilled workers, unobserved factors account for most of the changes. The increase in the relative wages of nonproduction workers seems to be due to changes between plants, specifically, shifts of employment and wages to plants that export. However, industry-level measures of change in overall trade account for very little of the between-plant increase in the dispersion of wages. None of these explanations accounts for the distinct cyclical pattern in the demand for skilled workers.

So what is going on? One possibility is that changes in the demand for skilled workers, the use of technology, and the export status of plants reflect some other change that is occurring at the plant or firm. For example, computer use is often considered to be a measure of technical change, but it could also reflect broader shifts in the organization of production or in the nature of the product plants produce. One of the primary functions of a computer is to help workers manage and use information more efficiently. Computers may allow firms to decentralize production and distribution of goods and perhaps lower the fixed costs of exporting. Computers may contribute to improved quality of products or increased variety of products, allowing firms to sell in more markets. They also may allow firms to move some parts of their production outside of the firm. If these reorganizations entail opportunity costs due to lost output, it seems quite likely that firms will want to make these changes in recessionary periods when demand is low.[57] This fact could explain why the observed changes in the structure of employment and wages occur in recessionary periods and why neither trade nor technology alone can fully account for the observed changes in the dispersion of wages.

To make further progress in identifying the sources of increasing wage dispersion, a better understanding of the underlying relationships among technology, the composition of the workforce, and a firm's marketing and export strategy is needed. The evidence presented in this chapter underscores the need for plant-level data. However, currently available microdata are limited in several respects. First, these data are available only for plants in manufacturing industries. Thus, they miss changes occurring in other important industries such as health care, finance, insurance and real estate, telecommunications, and software, all of which have experienced profound changes in recent years. Second, these data contain only indirect measures of worker skill, technology, and trade. Obviously, since these concepts are central to the debate of the causes of increasing wage dispersion, it is important to be able to measure them accurately. Related to this is the need for matched worker-plant data. Because of the heterogeneity of both workers and plants, the interaction of plant characteristics and the demand for workers with particular characteristics needs to be observed. Finally, these data contain almost no measures of other kinds of plant- or firm-level changes that may be equally important, such as changes in organizational capital.

One question that has arisen lately is, Must the causes of the increased wage dispersion be known in order to "solve" the problem? One possible answer is, no. Policy tools are available to decrease wage dispersion: A variety of income reallocation and social welfare programs exist to transfer income from rich to poor. However, these do not come without risks, potentially at the cost of the creation of new employment opportunities. As several European countries demonstrate, decreased wage dispersion is at least correlated with higher levels of unemployment.

A second policy tool would be to provide "lower-skilled" workers with more "skill." Even if it could be agreed that this is the correct response, developing and implementing such a policy would be difficult. The cause of the increase in wage dispersion is unknown, and much of that increase has occurred among workers with similar characteristics. Workers with the same education experienced increased wage dispersion. Thus, it would be difficult to identify whom to direct subsidies toward and what "skills" should be subsidized. Given the lack of success in establishing the effectiveness of job training programs, it is hard to imagine that this type of subsidy program would be effective.

We feel that the most appropriate policy response is to invest in better measurement tools, in this case better plant-level and worker-level data, so that researchers can better understand and respond to increasing wage inequality.

Notes

We would like to thank Karen Parker and James Tybout for helpful comments. Opinions expressed in this chapter are those of the authors and do not necessarily reflect official positions of the Bureau of the Census.

1. Richard B. Freeman, "When Earnings Diverge: Causes, Consequences, and Cures for the New Inequality in the U.S.," mimeo., Council on Foreign Relations Study Group on Trade and Wages, 1996.
2. Steve J. Davis and John Haltiwanger, "Wage Dispersion Between and Within U.S. Manufacturing Plants, 1963–1986," *Brookings Papers on Economic Activity: Microeconomics* (1991): 115–200; Chinhui Juhn, Kevin M. Murphy, and Brooks Pierce, "Wage Inequality and the Rise in the Return to Skill," *Journal of Political Economy* 101 (1993): 410–42; and Lawrence F. Katz and Kevin Murphy, "Changes in Relative Wages, 1963–1987: Supply and Demand Factors," *Quarterly Journal of Economics* 107, no. 1 (February 1992): 1–34.
3. The fact that only relatively poor measures of worker skill are available may be one reason why most of the increase in wage dispersion occurs within skill groups.
4. Davis and Haltiwanger, "Wage Dispersion"; John Bound and George Johnson, "Changes in the Structure of Wages in the 1980s: An Evaluation of Alternative Explanations," *American Economic Review* 82, no. 3 (June 1992): 371–92; Katz and Murphy, "Changes in Relative Wages."
5. For a discussion of how technical change could affect the skill composition of a plant's workforce, see Mark Doms, Timothy Dunne, and Kenneth R. Troske, "Workers, Wages, and Technology," *Quarterly Journal of Economics* 112, no. 1 (February 1997): 253–90.
6. This review is not meant to be exhaustive but is meant to highlight different measurement methodologies that have been employed.
7. Eli Berman, John Bound, and Zvi Griliches, "Changes in the Demand for Skilled Labor Within U.S. Manufacturing Industries: Evidence from the Annual Survey of Manufacturing," *Quarterly Journal of Economics* 109, no. 2 (May 1994): 367–98; Timothy Dunne, John Haltiwanger, and Kenneth R. Troske, "Technology and Jobs: Secular Change and Cyclical Dynamics," *Carnegie-Rochester Conference Series on Public Policy* 46 (1997): 107–78.

8. Steve J. Davis, "Cross-Country Patterns of Change in Relative Wages," in Oliver Blanchard and Stanley Fischer (eds.), *National Bureau of Economic Research* [NBER] *Macroeconomics Annual* (Cambridge, Mass.: MIT Press, 1992), pp. 239–92.

9. Kevin Murphy and Finis Welch, "The Structure of Wages," *Quarterly Journal of Economics* 107, no. 1 (February 1992): 285–326.

10. George J. Borjas, Richard B. Freeman, and Lawrence Katz, "On the Labor Market Impacts of Immigration and Trade," in George J. Borjas and Richard B. Freeman (eds.), *Immigration and the Work Force: Economic Consequences for the United States and Source Areas* (Chicago: University of Chicago Press, 1992), pp. 213–44.

11. Robert Z. Lawrence and Matthew J. Slaughter, "International Trade and American Wages in the 1980s," *Brookings Papers on Economic Activity: Microeconomics* (1993): 115–80; Jeffrey Sachs and Howard Shatz, "Trade and Jobs in U.S. Manufacturing," *Brookings Papers on Economic Activity* 1 (1994): 1–84. However, see the the paper by Paul Krugman for a discussion of why these may be the correct measures. Krugman, "Technology, Trade, and Factor Prices," *NBER Working Paper* no. 5355 (November 1995).

12. Ana L. Revenga, "Exporting Jobs: The Impact of Import Competition on Employment and Wages in U.S. Manufacturing," *Quarterly Journal of Economics* 107, no. 1 (February 1992): 255–84.

13. Lawrence and Slaughter, "International Trade and American Wages."

14. Sacks and Shatz, "Trade and Jobs"; Lawrence and Slaughter, "International Trade and American Wages."

15. Berman, Bound, and Griliches, "Changes in the Demand for Skilled Labor."

16. Andrew B. Bernard and J. Bradford Jensen, "Exporters, Skill Upgrading, and the Wage Gap," *Journal of International Economics* 42 (February 1997): 3–31.

17. Steven G. Allen, "Technology and the Wage Structure," *NBER Working Paper* no. 5534 (April 1996); Ann P. Bartel and Frank R. Lichtenberg, "The Comparative Advantage of Educated Workers in Implementing New Technology," *Review of Economics and Statistics* 69, no. 1 (February 1987): 1–11; Lawrence and Slaughter, "International Trade and American Wages."

18. One thing to keep in mind is that, even if the largest component of cross-sectional differences in total factor productivity (TFP) is cross-sectional differences in technology, it still may not be the case that a majority of the time-series variation in TFP reflects technical change.

19. Allen, "Technology and the Wage Structure"; Ann P. Bartel and Nachum Sicherman, "Technical Change and Wages: An Interindustry Analysis," *Journal of Political Economy* 107 (April 1999): 285–325; and George J. Borjas and Valerie A. Ramey, "Time–Series Evidence on the Sources of Trends in Wage Inequality," *American Economic Review* 84, no. 2 (May 1994): 10–16.

20. David Autor, Lawrence Katz, and Alan Krueger, "Computing Inequality: Have Computers Changed the Labor Market?" *Quarterly Journal of Economics* 113, no. 4 (November 1998): 1169–1213. Berman, Bound, and Griliches, "Changes in the Demand for Skilled Labor"; Bernard and Jensen, "Exporters, Skill Upgrading, and the Wage Gap"; and Dunne, Haltiwanger, and Troske, "Technology and Jobs."

21. David Autor, Lawrence Katz, and Alan Krueger, "Computing Inequality: Have Computers Changed the Labor Market?" *NBER Working Paper* no. 5956 (March 1997); Berman, Bound, and Griliches, "Changes in the Demand for Skilled Labor"; Bartel and Sicherman, "Technical Change and Wages"; and Bernard and Jensen, "Exporters, Skill Upgrading, and the Wage Gap."

22. Bernard and Jensen, "Exporters, Skill Upgrading, and the Wage Gap"; Mark Doms, Timothy Dunne, and Mark Roberts, "The Role of Technology Use in the Survival and Growth of Manufacturing Plants," *International Journal of Industrial Organization* 13, no. 4 (December 1995): 523–42; Doms, Dunne, and Troske, "Workers, Wages, and Technology"; Timothy Dunne, "Patterns of Technology Usage in U.S. Manufacturing Plants," *RAND Journal of Economics* 25 (1994): 488–99; Dunne, Haltiwanger, and Troske, "Technology and Jobs."

23. Allen, "Technology and the Wage Structure"; Autor, Katz, and Krueger, "Computing Inequality," *Quarterly Journal of Economics*; and Ernst Berndt, Catherine Morrison, and Larry Rosenblum, "High Tech Capital Formation and Labor Composition in U.S. Manufacturing Industries: An Exploratory Analysis," *NBER Working Paper* no. 4010 (March 1992).

24. Gerald Silverstein, "New Structures and Equipment by Using Industry, 1977," *Survey of Current Business* (November 1989): 26–35.

25. For a review of this literature, see Frank Levy and Richard J. Murname, "U.S. Earnings Levels and Earnings Inequality: A Review of Recent Trends and Proposed Explanations," *Journal of Economic Literature* 30, no. 3 (September 1992): 1333–81.

26. Heterogeneity persists even when plants are classified along other observable dimensions, such as region, age, or size.

27. These are examples of some of the characteristics over which plants vary. For further examples, see J. Bradford Jensen and Robert McGuckin, "Firm Performance and Evolution: Empirical Regularities in the U.S. Microdata," *Industrial and Corporate Change* special issue, vol. 6, no. 1 (1997): 25–47.

28. We already have excluded the 1st and 99th percentiles for each four-digit SIC prior to calculating the 90th and 10th percentiles.

29. John Haltiwanger, "Measuring and Analyzing Aggregate Fluctuations: The Importance of Building from Microeconomic Evidence," mimeo., University of Maryland, 1996.

30. Steven J. Davis, John C. Haltiwanger, and Scott Schuh, *Job Creation and Destruction* (Cambridge, Mass.: MIT Press, 1996).

31. Martin Baily, Charles Hulten, and David Campbell, "Productivity Dynamics in Manufacturing Plants," *Brookings Papers on Economic Activity: Microeconomics* (1992): 187–249; Eric Bartelsman and Phoebus Dhrymes, "Productivity Dynamics in U.S. Manufacturing Plants, 1972–86," *Finance and Economic Discussion Series* no. 94-1, Board of Governors, Federal Reserve, 1994; and Steven Olley and Ariel Pakes, "The Dynamics of Productivity in the Telecommunications Industry," *Econometrica* 64, no. 6 (November 1996): 1263–97.

32. Haltiwanger, "Measuring and Analyzing Aggregate Fluctuations."

33. Timothy Dunne and James Schmitz Jr., "Wages, Employment Structure and Employer Size–Wage Premia: Their Relationship to Advanced-Technology Usage at U.S. Manufacturing Establishments," *Economica* 62, no. 245 (February 1995): 89–107.

34. In a study using the 1988 Survey of Manufacturing Technology (SMT), Dunne finds that technology use is positively correlated with plant size. He also finds that plants of multiunit firms and plants engaged in defense-related production are more likely to use advanced technologies. Dunne, "Patterns of Technology Usage."

35. Doms, Dunne, and Troske, in "Workers, Wages, and Technology," use data from the 1988 SMT, the 1987 Census of Manufactures (CM), and the 1990 Decennial Census long form (the WECD). For more information, see Kenneth R. Troske, "The Worker-Establishment Characteristics Data," *Center for Economic Studies Discussion Paper* 95-10 (Washington, D.C.: U.S. Bureau of the Census, 1995).

36. Andrew B. Bernard and J. Bradford Jensen, "Exporters, Jobs, and Wages in U.S. Manufacturing: 1976–1987," *Brookings Papers on Economic Activity: Microeconomics* (1995): 67–119.

37. Bernard and Jensen, "Exporters, Skill Upgrading, and the Wage Gap"; J. Bradford Jensen and Nathan Musick, "Trade, Technology, and Plant Performance," *Working Papers on Industrial and Economic Performance,* ESA/OPD 96-4 (Washington, D.C.: U.S. Department of Commerce, 1996).

38. For an examination of the differences between exporters and nonexporters, see Andrew B. Bernard and J. Bradford Jensen, "Exceptional Exporter Performance: Cause, Effect, or Both," mimeo., Center for Economic Studies, 1996.

39. Autor, Katz, and Krueger, "Computing Inequality," *Quarterly Journal of Economics*; Berman, Bound, and Griliches, "Changes in the Demand for Skilled Labor"; Dunne, Haltiwanger, and Troske, "Technology and Jobs"; Claudia Goldin and Lawrence F. Katz, "The Origins of Capital-Skill Complementarity," *NBER Working Paper* no. 5657 (1996).

40. Bernard and Jensen, "Exporters, Skill Upgrading, and the Wage Gap."

41. Ibid.; Dunne, Haltiwanger, and Troske, "Technology and Jobs."

42. This decomposition is identical to that of Dunne, Haltiwanger, and Troske, "Technology and Jobs," and is similar to that used in Berman,

Bound, and Griliches, "Changes in the Demand for Skilled Labor," and in Bernard and Jensen, "Exporters, Skill Upgrading, and the Wage Gap."

43. See Dunne, Haltiwanger, and Troske, "Technology and Jobs," for a discussion of how these data sets are constructed.

44. Ibid.

45. Bernard and Jensen, "Exporters, Skill Upgrading, and the Wage Gap."

46. Davis and Haltiwanger, "Wage Dispersion Between and Within U.S. Manufacturing Plants."

47. Dunne, Haltiwanger, and Troske, "Technology and Jobs."

48. Doms, Dunne, and Troske, "Workers, Wages, and Technology."

49. Autor, Katz, and Krueger, "Computing Inequality," *Quarterly Journal of Economics*; Berman, Bound, and Griliches, "Changes in the Demand for Skilled Labor."

50. Doms, Dunne, and Troske, "Workers, Wages, and Technology."

51. Bernard and Jensen, "Exporters, Skill Upgrading, and the Wage Gap."

52. Doms, Dunne, and Roberts, "Role of Technology Use."

53. Doms, Dunne, and Troske, "Workers, Wages, and Technology."

54. Davis and Haltiwanger, "Wage Dispersion Between and Within U.S. Manufacturing Plants."

55. Bernard and Jensen, "Exporters, Skill Upgrading, and the Wage Gap."

56. There is some question as to what is measured by a plant's export status or by changes in that status. At a very simple level, changes in export status merely indicate that there has been a change in where a plant sells its products. Bernard and Jensen (in "Exceptional Exporter Performance") present evidence that plants that export are already different from nonexporters three or four years prior to exporting. However, given the recent research that shows that plants must incur substantial fixed costs when they begin to export their products, changes in the export status of a plant do appear to be correlated with some change in a plant. See Andrew B. Bernard and J. Bradford Jensen, "Why Some Firms Export," mimeo., Center for Economic Studies, 1996; and Mark Roberts and James Tybout, "An Empirical Model of Sunk Costs and the Decision to Export," mimeo., Pennsylvania State University, 1994. One possibility is that export status is a proxy for some unmeasured product characteristic.

57. For further discussion of this issue, see Russell Cooper and John Haltiwanger, "The Macroeconomic Implications of Machine Replacement: Theory and Evidence," *American Economic Review* 83 (1993): 360–82; Russell Cooper, John Haltiwanger, and Laura Power, "Machine Replacement and the Business Cycle: Lumps and Bumps," *NBER Working Paper* no. 5260 (September 1995); and Robert E. Hall, "Labor Demand, Labor Supply, and Employment Volatility," *NBER Macroeconomics Annual* no. 6 (1991): 17–47.

6

The Impact of Immigration on the U.S. Labor Market

Steven A. Camarota and Mark Krikorian

Over the last 30 years, socioeconomic and political factors, especially in the developing world, have caused 20 million people to leave their homelands and immigrate legally to the United States. Additionally, the Immigration and Naturalization Service (INS) estimates that the number of illegal immigrants living in the country grows by about 275,000 each year and now numbers 5 million. This influx has caused the foreign-born share of the population to increase from 4.8 percent in 1970 to 9.3 percent by 1996, and it is projected to reach 10 percent by the end of the decade. While this is less than the 14.7 percent in 1910, the 24.5 million immigrants currently residing in the country make up almost twice the number recorded earlier in this century.[1] Large-scale migration of this kind would have important implications for the social, political, and economic situation in any society, and the United States is no exception. While other areas are clearly also important, here we focus on the labor market consequences of immigration.

This analysis is divided into four parts: In the first, we briefly explain immigration policy since 1965 and provide some historical background. In the second part we discuss conceptual and analytical issues surrounding the labor market implications of immigration. In the third part we review the literature on immigration and the labor market as well as report the findings of our own research that appears in the July 1997 issue of *Social Science Quarterly*. In the final part we discuss the various options open to policymakers to deal with labor market issues arising from immigration.

American Immigration Policy

Figure 6–1 provides a graphical representation of the number of immigrants entering between 1820 and 1996.[2] It indicates that there has been a good deal of variation since the early 1800s. It also shows that when illegal immigration is counted, the number of immigrants entering the country is roughly equal to the great wave of migration that occurred in the early part of this century. Figure 6–2 reports the foreign-born percentage of the U.S. population between 1850 and 2000. A variety of factors account for the variations in immigrant flows. Among them are the economic, political, and social conditions in sending countries—the so-called push factors contributing to international migration to the United States. On the other side of the equation are what can be referred to as "pull" factors, such as the socioeconomic conditions existing in the United States, especially the economic opportunities available to immigrants. Both the push and pull factors provide the context in which American immigration policy is formulated and operates. Some combination of push and pull

Figure 6–1 U.S. Immigration, 1820–1996

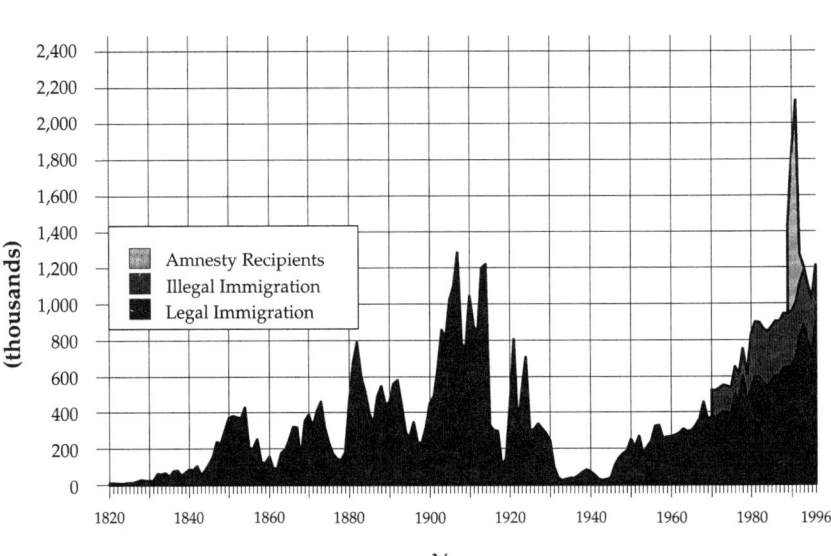

Source: Generated from official INS numbers found in U.S. Immigration and Naturalization Service, *Statistical Yearbook of the Immigration and Naturalization Service, 1996* (Washington, D.C.: U.S. Government Printing Office, 1997).

Figure 6–2 Percent Foreign Born in the United States, 1850–2000

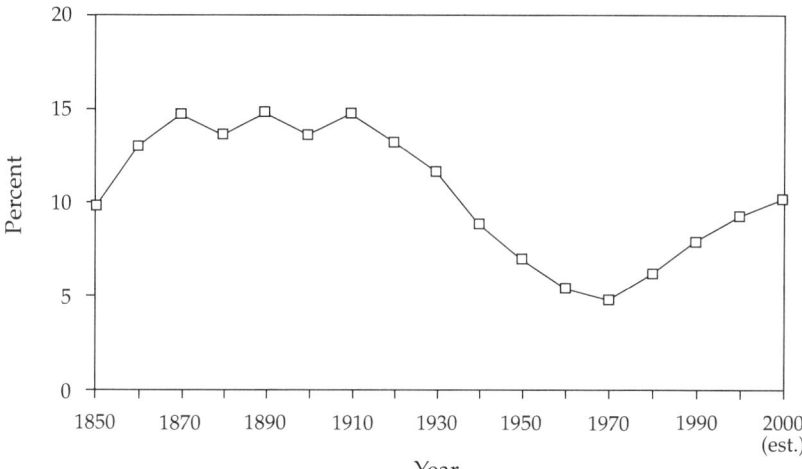

Source: Generated from official Census Bureau figures. *Historical Statistics of the United States, Colonial Times to 1970, Bicentennial Edition* (Washington, D.C.: Department of Commerce, 1975), and *Statistical Abstract of the United States, 1996* (Washington, D.C.: U.S. Department of Commerce, 1996).

factors along with American immigration policy is responsible for the variation in immigration since 1850.

The basic structure of current immigration policy was set forth in the Immigration and Nationality Act of 1965, often referred to as the Hart-Celler Immigration Act. That act fundamentally changed the admission system, and, while it did not immediately cause a dramatic jump in immigration, it did lay much of the groundwork for the current high level of legal and perhaps illegal immigration.

Before 1965 immigration policy was based on the national origins quota system established in 1924. That system was designed to curtail immigration from eastern and southern Europe, from which most of the immigrants had been coming prior to its enactment. It did, however, leave immigration from the Western Hemisphere unrestricted. The 1924 legislation reduced immigration by allocating visas based on the ethnic makeup of the United States at the time of the 1890 census. Thus 42 percent of the visas were allocated to Great Britain. Pressure to change the system in 1965 was due not only to the ethnic bias in the law but also because only 61 percent of the system's quota visas were issued and yet tens of thousands of people who sought to come to the United States were unable to do so. Most of those who wished to immigrate were from countries that had been allocated few visas under the 1924 system.[3]

The 1965 act sought to alleviate these problems by allocating visas based primarily on family relationships. The law also established for the first time a limit of 120,000 on the number of immigrants who could come from the Western Hemisphere and placed a limit of 170,000 on the Eastern Hemisphere.[4] Humanitarian immigrants and the immediate relatives of U.S. citizens were exempted from these limits. At the time, it was thought that these changes would cause immigration to rise only slightly.[5]

The most important changes to immigration law since 1965 have been the Refugee Act of 1980, the Immigration Reform and Control Act of 1986 (IRCA), the Immigration Act of 1990, and the Illegal Immigration Reform and Immigrant Responsibility Act of 1996. The Refugee Act of 1980 created a systematic procedure for setting the number of refugees each year, their admission criteria and their resettlement. The 1986 act provided for the legalization of 2.7 million illegal aliens, required employers to verify that all new employees are eligible to work in the United States, and enacted fines for those employers who knowingly hire illegal aliens. It also created the first "visa lottery." The Immigration Act of 1990 increased the limit on the total number of immigrants who could enter each year from 290,000 to 675,000, expanded the number of employment-based visas to 140,000, and increased the visa lottery, now called diversity visas, to 55,000.[6] The Illegal Immigration Reform and Immigrant Responsibility Act of 1996 tightened up procedures for asylum, increased funding for border patrol efforts, increased the penalty for alien smuggling and document fraud, and established slightly higher income standards for sponsors of family immigrants.[7]

VISA CATEGORIES

Immigration law is extremely complex, and space does not permit a comprehensive description of the myriad of laws, administrative decisions, executive orders, standard operating procedures, and court rulings that make up the details of immigration policy. Therefore, the following descriptions are meant to provide some basic background only.

While all of the visa categories have undergone some modifications since 1965, the four basic categories created at that time remain. First, there is family-based immigration, the largest single category of admission in every year since 1965. The parents, spouses, and unmarried minor children (under 21) of U.S. citizens are eligible to come to the United States exempt from any per-country limit as well as the old hemispheric limits or current worldwide limit. This category accounts for roughly half of family-based immigration in most years. Additionally, the 1965 act allowed citizens to bring in their siblings and adult children (married and unmarried) under a second category called "family preference" immigration. Legal permanent residents (noncitizens) also are allowed to bring in their spouses and minor children under these provisions. Family preference immigration was counted against both the hemispheric limits when they were in force and currently is counted against the worldwide limit.[8] It is also subject to a per-country limit of 7 percent of total preference visas. Because of the per-country limits and worldwide limit, there continues to be a long waiting list in many countries for family preference immigrants. The family categories account for 65 to 70 percent of legal immigration in most years.

The second largest category of legal immigration in most years is humanitarian. Since 1951, as a result of treaty obligations, U.S. law has defined people as refugees or asylees if they are outside of their country of nationality and are unable or unwilling to return to that country because they either have been "persecuted" or have "a well-founded fear of persecution" because of their "race, religion, nationality, membership in a particular social group or political opinion." Refugees are persons brought to the United States for resettlement because they are found to meet these criteria. In addition to refugees, some individuals claim asylum at the port of entry or after they have been in the country for some time—legally or illegally. Those seeking asylum must meet the same criteria as refugees. Humanitarian immigration accounts for about 15 percent of legal immigration in most years.

Similar in size to humanitarian immigration is employment-based immigration. These immigrants are granted visas because they are thought to have some very broadly defined abilities that would substantially benefit the United States or have a job offer from an employer in the United States. Employment-based immigration, including accompanying family members, represents about 12 percent of legal immigration in most years.

The fourth and smallest category is diversity immigration. The 1965 act allocated a small number of visas for those individuals who had no humanitarian, employment, or family eligibility to apply as "nonpreference immigrants." Waiting lists grew to be many years long under this system. As an alternative approach, the 1986 Immigration Reform and Control Act created a lottery system. Prospective immigrants mailed in postcards, and visas were issued to those who were randomly selected. The 1990 Immigration Act expanded the list of countries and increased the total number of visas available to 55,000 with a 3,850 per-country limit. Diversity immigration accounts for about 6 percent of total legal immigration.

In addition to these four categories, the Immigration Reform and Control Act of 1986 offered amnesty to illegal aliens who could show that they had resided continuously in the United States for a certain number of years. A total of 2.7 million illegal aliens took advantage of this legislation by 1994. Those immigrants who legalized were found to be predominately Mexican and low skilled, with 74 percent lacking a high school degree and only about 5 percent having a college diploma.[9]

Finally, there are illegal aliens, sometimes referred to as illegal immigrants or undocumented immigrants. In most years since 1970, the number of new illegal immigrants is thought to be larger than any category of legal immigration with the exception of family based. The INS estimates that as of October 1996 there were 5 million illegal aliens living in the country and that 420,000 illegal aliens join the long-term illegal population each year. This number is offset by deaths, out-migration, and those who adjust to legal status, so that the increase in the illegal population is 275,000 annually.

One of the most striking features of American immigration policy is the fact that only a very small proportion of immigrants currently residing in the United States were admitted because they are thought to provide economic benefits to the country. This is very different from other immigrant-receiving countries, such as Canada or Australia, which have selection criteria that strongly favor skilled immigrants. This does not mean that immigrants are not a benefit to the U.S. economy; however, it does mean that at present, our immigration policy is not designed with economic benefits as an explicit objective.

Conceptual and Analytical Issues for the U.S. Labor Market

The most important issue surrounding the impact of immigration on the labor market is its potential to have an adverse effect on the opportunities available to native-born workers. One way to think about the consequences of immigration for the labor market is to imagine an immigration policy that admits immigrants with exactly the same skills as natives. Thus, the distribution of immigrants across occupations would mirror that of natives, as would their qualifications. Let us also assume that this immigrant influx is accompanied by a corresponding increase in factors of production so that the immigrants have the same tools, capital, infrastructure, and so on to work with as natives. Under this hypothetical scenario, we would expect to see no effect on the labor market opportunities available to natives in the receiving country. Thus the impact of immigration depends on both the human capital attributes of immigrants relative to natives and the ability of capital formation to keep pace with immigrant inflows.

At present, we know very little about the effect of immigration on capital stocks.[10] In the 1990s, 35 percent of the 1.1 percent annual increase in the size of the U.S. population is directly attributable to the arrival of immigrants. This means that in order to prevent a significant change in the capital-labor ratio, the U.S. economy must increase it capital stock 50 percent faster than it would have to without immigration. This is a substantial increase and may be sufficient to create capital dilution effects. If capital stocks cannot be replenished fast enough, then wages may fall and unemployment may rise. At present, no body of research indicates whether this kind of growth in the supply of labor is outstripping the country's ability to replenish its capital stock. Stagnant or falling wages for some categories of workers over the last two decades may indicate that immigration is having such an effect; however, there is no strong evidence of this. And there are many potential explanations for falling wages other than immigrant-induced changes in the capital-labor ratio.

Unlike capital formation in response to immigration, a good deal is known about the labor market characteristics of immigrants. Table 6–1 provides information about the attributes of immigrants and natives in the workforce. The table indicates that immigrants are concentrated at the ends of the labor market, with fewer in the middle skill and wage categories. For example, 34 percent of immigrants who came in the 1980s have no high school education, and for those who came in the 1990s, 39 percent are high school dropouts. In comparison, only 10 percent of natives in the labor market lack a high school degree. At the high end of the labor market, 26 percent of immigrants have completed college, making them only slightly less likely than natives to have at least a four-year college degree.

Across the earnings deciles, we find a similar distribution of immigrants. One-fifth of immigrants are employed in the bottom earnings deciles, and one-third are in the bottom fifth of the earnings distribution. The data also show that immigrants who arrived before 1980 have an earnings distribution similar to that of natives.[12] This fact suggests significant economic progress for immigrants over time. However, as the educational data indicate, a larger proportion of recent immigrants have low levels of educational attainment compared to earlier immigrants. This fact may hinder the social mobility of post-1980 immigrants.

Table 6–1 Labor Market Characteristics of Immigrants and Natives, 1996

	Natives	All Immigrants	Pre-1980s Immigrants	1980s Immigrants	1990s Immigrants
High school dropouts	10%	32%	26%	34%	39%
High school only	35	23	24	23	23
Some college	29	20	24	18	14
College graduates	27	26	26	25	25
Earnings Decile:					
1	11%	20%	14%	22%	29%
2	8	13	9	15	16
3	9	12	9	14	12
4	11	9	9	10	8
5	11	10	11	9	8
6	9	7	8	9	5
7	11	9	10	7	5
8	10	7	10	8	7
9	11	7	10	5	4
10	10	7	10	6	6
Average earnings last year	$35,339	$30,903	$36,995	$26,235	$16,495
Average age of those in workforce	39.8	38.8	44.4	36.1	32.7
25- to 64-year olds who worked last year	82%	75%	78%	77%	64%

Notes: Analysis confined to nonstudents 16 and over in the workforce.
Totals do not equal 100 percent because of rounding.
Source: Authors' tabulations from March 1996 *Current Population Survey.*

As a result of their skill distribution, immigrants have increased the supply of some categories of workers more than others. Table 6–2 contains information on the proportion of each educational category and earnings decile that is composed of immigrants. It indicates that while immigrants comprise 11 percent of the workforce, they make up 29 percent of those in the labor market without a high school degree. In contrast, they comprise 16 percent of those with a high school diploma and some college and 11 percent of those with a college degree. We see a similar distribution in the earnings deciles, with immigrants representing 17 percent of those in the bottom fifth of the labor market. Based on the distribution of immigrants across earnings deciles found in Tables 6–1 and 6–2, it is clear that immigration has skewed the income distribution toward the bottom of the labor market by increasing the number of workers in the lowest-paying jobs. This means that there is a more uneven distribution of income in the country and some reduction in per capita gross domestic product (GDP) as a direct result of immigration. However, it does not mean that immigration has nec-

Table 6–2 Percentage of Each Educational Category and Decile That Was Immigrant (1996)

	Percent
High school dropouts	29
High school degree	8
Some college	8
College degrees	11
Total workforce	11
Earnings Decile:	
1	18
2	16
3	13
4	10
5	10
6	8
7	9
8	7
9	7
10	7

Notes: Analysis confined to nonstudents 16 and over in the workforce. Totals do not always equal 100% because of rounding.
Source: Authors' tabulations from March 1996 *Current Population Survey*.

essarily reduced the wages of natives, nor does it mean that immigration has lowered the per capita GDP of natives. It simply means that because immigrants are poorer than natives, the average earnings and per capita GDP in the United States is lower when immigrants are counted. This is cause for concern only to the extent that disparity in income may contribute to social disharmony or other forms of instability that are deemed undesirable. There may also be reason for concern if it takes two or three generations for the descendants of today's immigrants to reach economic parity with natives. Immigration policy could set the stage for sizable ethnic differentials in economic outcomes that could have important socioeconomic and political implication for decades to come.

Table 6–3 provides historical data on immigrants and natives drawn from the 1970, 1980, and 1990 censuses.[12] It indicates that there has been a decline in the economic position of recent immigrants relative to that of natives over the last three censuses. In 1970 the average annual earnings of recent male immigrants was 81 percent that of natives; by 1990 that figure had declined to 65 percent. The decline in relative earnings is closely tied to the decline in the educational attainment of immigrants relative to that of natives. As the table shows, the percentage of immigrants who lack a high school degree has declined for both immigrants and natives; however, because the decline has been more dramatic for natives, the percentage of immigrants who have few years of schooling is significantly greater. The decline in relative immigrant educational attainment has not been confined to the bottom of the labor market. In 1970 recent immigrants were almost twice as likely as natives to have a college degree. As Table 6–1 has shown, by 1996 roughly the same proportion of recent immigrants and natives had completed college. As a result of these changes, recent immigrants have fallen farther behind natives.

Basic economic theory would predict that a significant increase in the supply of less skilled labor brought about by immigration to the United States would reduce the wage rates and employment opportunities available for those workers with few skills. However, the reality of immigration is not nearly so straightforward. Immigrants do not simply increase the size of the workforce; through their consumption of goods and services, their entrepreneurship, and the capital they bring with them, immigrants also increase the demand for labor. While wages may decline for those workers who compete with immigrants, they may rise for those natives who have skills that complement immigrant labor. Lower prices for labor may also spur investment and business activity, and consumers benefit if the prices for some goods and services

Table 6–3 Socioeconomic Characteristics of Recent Immigrants and Natives, 1970–1990 (in 1995 $)

Nativity and Gender	Annual Earnings			1970		1980		1990	
	1970	1980	1990	Less than HS	College Graduate	Less than HS	College Graduate	Less than HS	College Graduate
Native males	$37,212	$37,591	$37,551	40.2%	15.0%	22.7%	22.9%	14.4%	26.3%
Recent male immigrants	$30,156	$27,107	$24,318	46.0	27.7	37.5	29.6	36.2	30.5
Native females	$14,899	$16,805	$20,196	40.7	9.0	26.0	14.3	16.7	20.4
Recent female immigrants	$13,894	$14,606	$15,157	52.8	13.0	42.2	19.3	37.4	24.1

Note: The analysis is confined to only persons 25 years of age and older at the time of the survey. For the earnings data, recent arrivals are defined as foreign-born persons who arrived in the ten years preceding the census. For educational data, recent arrivals are those who entered within five years of the census.

Source: The New Americans: Economic, Demographic and Fiscal Effects of Immigration (Washington, D.C.: National Academy Press, 1997).

decline. However, because immigrants are so concentrated at the lower end of the earnings distribution, they account for a relatively small portion of the labor market incomes. It is estimated that in 1994, immigrant labor accounted for only about 4.9 percent of the average American household's consumption expenditures, with higher-income households consuming significantly more immigrant-provided goods and services than those households with lower incomes.[13] Overall, while there may be a significant effect on the prices of a few particular products, immigrant labor accounts for too small a portion of total economic output to have a large effect on aggregate prices.

In many ways the effects of immigration on the economy are similar to those of free trade. The primary benefit from both trade and immigration is that both allow the receiving country to specialize in producing those things that it does well. Both trade and immigration also allow the receiving country to consume products that it would not otherwise have access to. The freer the trading regime a country operates in, the less impact there will be from immigration; alternatively, the more immigration there is, the less need there will be for trade. As with trade, there may be aggregate gains as well as both "winners" and "losers." In the case of immigration, the losers are likely to be the working poor and those with few skills, such as long-term welfare recipients looking for work. These workers are the most negatively affected by immigration because they tend to be employed in those segments of the labor market where immigrants are most heavily concentrated. The winners are those in the middle and upper classes, whose skills will tend to complement those of immigrants, consumers, and the owners of capital, who may realize higher rates of return on their investments as demand for capital rises.

While many advocates argue for high immigration on the grounds that it imparts economic benefits to receiving societies similar to trade, there are also important differences between trade and immigration. Immigration, unlike trade, alters the supply of labor permanently (as long as the immigrant remains), not just in the year that a product is imported. With trade, for instance, a country can reduce imports when its economy slips into recession. By importing workers this flexibility is lost. Additionally, by coming to the United States, immigrants become eligible for certain benefits that do not have to be paid for if they stay at home. For example, if a low-wage worker who heads a large family picks strawberries in Mexico, Americans can have access to the product of his labor by simply importing strawberries. If he comes here and does the same work, he and his family will have access to taxpayer-provided public services. And his low income makes it very unlikely that he will pay enough in taxes to cover his consumption of these services.[14] This means that because immigrants consume public services, the large-scale migration of immigrants who have very low earnings actually can reduce the standard of living in the receiving country in a way that simply importing products produced by low-wage workers will not.[15] Finally, immigration is distinct from trade because unlike simply importing goods, immigrants are human beings and not mere factors in production. They are entitled to be treated in certain ways, and they have certain rights. And as people, they can have a profound influence on the cultural, political, demographic, and environmental situation in the receiving country. This makes immigration very different from simply importing inanimate objects.

To summarize, the impact of immigration on the labor market depends on three variables: the human capital attributes of immigrants, capital formation in response to immigration, and the effect of immigrants on the demand for labor. There are reasons to believe that immigration will have both positive and negative effects on the economy of the receiving country, although these effects will not be evenly distributed throughout the society. From a theoretical standpoint, it is very difficult to say how large an impact immigration will have even in the case of the dramatic increase in the supply of less skilled workers brought about by immigration. Based on economic theory, some reduction in wages for the less skilled workers would be expected, since this is the segment of the labor market where immigrants are concentrated. But, as is the case with many public policy questions, economic theory is far better at predicting that there will be more or less of something than it is at predicting how much more or less. Ultimately, the effect of immigration can be determined empirically only by careful study of the available data.

Literature Review and a New Model

Much of the research on the labor market has focused on whether immigration reduces labor market opportunities for natives and for immigrants. Trying to determine the consequences of immigration is not as easy as might be thought. With the exception of the census, most surveys used to examine the labor market did not ask questions about country of birth on a regular basis until the 1990s. This makes comparing the current high level of immigration with earlier periods of low immigration difficult. Moreover, as is the case with many societal phenomena, research on the impact of immigration is by its nature counterfactual. There is no way to be sure what wages or employment patterns would have been without immigration.

There is no question that wages for some workers in the United States have stagnated or declined at the same time as immigrants have grown as a proportion of the workforce. This is especially true for high school dropouts and those with only a high school degree. The real wages (adjusting for inflation) of these workers have declined by between 15 and 30 percent since the late 1970s.[16] The decline has hit male high school dropouts and younger workers the hardest.[17] Many authors believe that the poor labor market prospects less skilled workers face have greatly contributed to the creation of an underclass.[18] The fact that labor market opportunities for less skilled workers have declined at the same time as immigration has increased does not necessarily mean that immigration has contributed to this problem. Research on this question has come to contradictory conclusions: older studies have found little or no evidence that immigration harmed natives while newer studies have come to the opposite conclusion.

Earlier research concluded that immigration does not have a significant negative impact on the labor market performance of natives.[19] The basic methodology employed by these studies is to compare labor market outcomes in cities of differing immigrant composition. Each metropolitan area is treated as a discrete labor market so that comparisons can be made in unemployment, wages, or workforce participation. This type of research is referred to as a cross-market or spatial analysis. It is based on the assumption that any effect of immigration will be confined to the cities where immigrants reside. In general, this approach finds only small effects on the wages and employment opportunities available to natives from immigration.

Beginning in 1993, however, the findings of the research began to change. Borjas, Freeman, and Katz have examined increases in the effective or relative supply of labor attributable to immigration between 1980 and 1996.[20] By treating the entire country as one labor market, they found that immigration reduced the wages of high school dropouts nationally by increasing the supply of this type of labor. Their basic methodology is to estimate the educational distribution of immigrants using census and Current Population Survey data and compare it to that of natives. They then estimate the increase in the supply of workers in one skill category relative to other skill categories brought about by immigration. An increase in the relative supply of one type of worker is assumed to lower wages for those natives in competition with immigrants. In contrast, those who tend not to be in competition with immigrants will see their wages rise. The estimated effects from immigration using this method are based on an existing body of literature, developed independent of immigration, that has attempted to calculate what a change in the relative number of skilled to unskilled workers implies for the wages of both types of workers. This method is called the factor-proportions approach. To illustrate how this method works, consider the following example: Assume that in a hypothetical economy there are only two types of workers—supervisors and unskilled laborers. Also assume that immigrants enter the economy and double the number of laborers. While the increase in the supply of laborers will reduce wages for native-born laborers, it will also increase the wages of supervisors because there will be an increase in demand for supervisory personnel. The wages of supervisors will also rise because they will be in charge of more laborers and therefore are being worked more intensively. And it is the reduction in wages for laborers that provides some of the money so that supervisors can be paid more. Using this basic approach, Borjas and coauthors estimate that one-third of the decline in wages for high school dropouts in the 1980s and early 1990s was a direct result of immigration. Using a similar approach and relying on a comparison of the 1980 and 1990 censuses, Jaeger has confirmed these findings.[21] He also found that immigrant and native dropouts are almost perfect substitutes for one another in the labor market. In other words, they hold the same type of jobs and compete directly with each other.

Immigration also has been found to contribute to the increase in income inequality. Topel found that immigration was responsible for a large portion of the growth in earnings inequality in the western part of the United States.[22] Partridge, Rickman, and Levernier conducted a panel study of the 48 contiguous states from 1960 to 1990.[23] They found that the level of income inequality increases in high-immigrant states and also concluded that immigration seems to be driving down wages for those at the bottom of the economic scale, thereby increasing the gap between rich and poor. Their work indicates that it is not simply that an influx of relatively low-skilled immigrants increases the size of the low-wage population. Instead, they concluded that immigration is also making low-income natives poorer.

The particular effect of immigration on the wages of minorities has received some attention. Native-born blacks are thought to be especially vulnerable to immigrant competition partly because they are concentrated in less skilled, lower-paying occupations and partly because some employers may view new immigrants as more reliable.[24] Kposowa looked at change over time in the income of minority families as well as unemployment rates among minorities over the period from 1940 to 1980.[25] She found both that family income fell and unemployment rose for native-born racial minorities as the number of immigrants increased. She concludes that probably the low skill level of racial minorities exposes them to the harmful effects of immigration. These findings contradict earlier cross-city comparisons by Borjas and Enchautegui, which concluded that immigration did not reduce the labor market opportunities available to minorities.[26]

Problems with Existing Literature

There are a number of problems with much of the literature in this field. First, studies of immigration often aggregate data in a way that makes it very difficult to determine the effects of immigration on particular subcategories of workers or segments of the labor market. Looking at the wages of all workers in each city may mask the consequences of immigration in a particular sector or in sectors of the local economy.

The second and most serious problem with much of the previous research stems from the spatial approach utilized by many researchers. This problem is especially pronounced in the older studies, which generally examined immigration by comparing cities at one point in time. The assumption that the labor markets of metropolitan areas are unconnected from each other is highly questionable. In a hypothetical absence of immigration, many native-born, less skilled workers might have improved their labor market position by migrating to areas that did, in fact, experience high levels of foreign immigration. Not only would this internal migration have improved the job prospects of those who moved; it also would have improved the prospects of those left behind by reducing the supply of labor. Further, those natives harmed by immigration may leave high-immigrant areas to avoid competition with immigrants. If natives adjust their migration patterns because of foreign immigration, then this would preserve equilibrium in wages and unemployment between metropolitan areas.

Throughout American history laborers have moved to different parts of the country to better their job prospects.[27] Most of the research on the migration of blacks from the South in the early part of this century has emphasized the importance of labor market conditions in the North as the primary factor contributing to migration.[28] Kuznets argues that the primary reason blacks had not gone north earlier was the presence of immigrants.[29] He concludes that it is no coincidence that large-scale migration from the South did not occur until after the number of immigrants from Europe decreased.

Recent demographic studies indicate that immigrants have a significant impact on the internal migration patterns of native-born workers.

Card concluded that the Mariel boatlift, which increased the population of Miami by 7 percent in only a few months, had a negligible effect on the city's size because it reduced the number of native-born workers who came to the city.[30] Separate studies conducted by demographers Filer and Frey have found that as the concentration of immigrants increases in a state or metropolitan area, the net out-migration of native-born workers increases.[31] The work of all these authors indicates that spatial studies may have failed to pick up significant effects of immigration because they do not control for the response of native-born workers.

The huge volume of goods and services exchanged between cities all across the country creates pressure toward factor price equalization even when there is no migration between them. For example, newly arrived immigrants who take jobs in light manufacturing in a high-immigrant cities such as Los Angeles come into direct and immediate competition with natives doing the same work in a low-immigrant city like Pittsburgh. Like internal migration, intercity trade will defuse the impact of immigration from high-immigrant areas to the rest of the country. Finally, the mobility of capital should play some role in preserving wage equilibrium between cities. Any immigrant-induced reduction in wages should result in an influx of capital seeking to take advantage of this situation. Thus the mobility of labor, goods, and capital makes it very difficult to determine the impact of immigration by comparing cities. It seems far more likely that any effect of immigration on the labor market is not confined just to high-immigrant areas but instead is national in scope.

The factor-proportions approach of Borjas and coauthors and Jaeger avoids the problems of the spatial approach by examining increases in the supply of unskilled labor nationally.[32] However, the validity of their conclusions rests entirely on the underlying assumption of the model they use. Since there is no way to measure what wages would have been in the United States without immigrants, there is no way to verify that the estimated changes in wages in response to immigration are correct. Thus this approach is entirely dependent on how accurately the existing literature reflects actual changes in wages due to shifts in the relative supply of labor caused by immigration. The factor-proportions approach assumes that any relative increase in the supply of unskilled labor must reduce the wages of unskilled natives. Thus a negative effect on lower-skilled natives always follows—the question simply is the size of the effect.

The time-series approach utilized by some recent studies also suffers from significant problems. Looking at change over time in order to discern trends in labor market outcomes caused by immigration raises the problem that any uncontrolled-for trend that happens to coincide with immigration may be falsely attributed to its effects. For example, when trying to explain the decline in wages for less skilled workers or the rise of income inequality, there is no established or widely accepted way to observe and measure "skill-biased technological change," even though this is likely to be a very important factor in explaining the decline in wages for low-skilled workers.[33]

The Center for Immigration Studies has undertaken research that attempts to avoid many of the problems in the existing literature. Instead of comparing cities, this new approach compares occupations in an attempt to determine the effect of immigration on wages nationally and examines the relationship between the immigrant composition of a native worker's occupation and his or her weekly wages. The primary advantage of this approach is that it examines wages nationally and thus avoids the problems associated with spatial studies. The possibility of omitted variables is reduced because the study is cross-sectional and does not look for change over time. This approach also has not assumed a negative effect from any immigrant-induced increase in the relative supply of labor. And unlike the factor-proportions approach, comparing the actual wages of natives who have immigrants in their occupation with those who do not allows the data to "speak" freely.

Methodology

The June 1991 *Current Population Survey* (CPS) provides the data for the analysis.[34] To account for the presence of illegal aliens, this study uses the formulation of Borjas, Freeman, and Katz.[35] The immigration variable is created by calculating the percentage of foreign-born persons in each of the Census Bureau's occupational categories.[36] This variable will be used in a log-linear regression to evaluate the amount of variation in individual and aggregate logged weekly wages that is due to variations in the immigrant composition of each individual's occupation. The immigrant variable also is used to measure the effect of immigration on the average wage of each occupation.

In addition to the percentage of immigrants in each individual's occupation, four other occupational-level control variables are included in the model: the percentage of men in each individual's occupation, the average years of schooling for persons in each individual's occupation, the percent unionization in the occupation, and the average age of persons in each individual's occupation.[37] All persons in the same occupation have the same value assigned to them for these four variables. These occupational-level control variables are included because it is well established by previous research that they have a large impact on individual wages. These variables capture the occupational-level effects other than the percent immigrant variable.

There are six individual-level variables in the model: the individual's employment status, age, sex, union membership, education level, and minority status. As with the aggregate-level control variables, these individual-level variables are included because it is well established that they all have an important effect on wages.[38]

Formally, the model takes the following shape:

$$W_i = a + b_1(PM_i) + b_2(AE_i) + b_3(PU_i) + b_4(AO_i) + b_5(PI_i) + b_6(FP_i)$$
$$+ b_7(A_i) + b_8(S_i) + b_9(U_i) + b_{10}(E_i) + b_{11}(M_i) + b_{12}(SEI_i) + e,$$

where W equals the log of individual weekly wages (natives only); PM equals the percent male in each individual's occupation; AE equals average education level of persons in each individual's occupation; PU equals percent unionization of one's occupation; AO equals average age of each individual's occupation; PI equals the percentage of immigrants in each individual's occupation; FP equals full- or part-time worker; A equals individual's age; S equals individual's sex; U equals individual's union membership; E equals individual's education level; M equals minority status; SEI equals state earnings inflation index; and e equals the error term.

There are a number of reasons to believe that the effect of immigration varies across occupations. Borjas, Freeman, and Katz as well as Jaeger found that immigrants held down wages for only high school dropouts.[39] The high concentration of immigrants in occupations that require few years of schooling means that it is in this segment of the labor market that immigrants are most likely to exert a downward pressure on wages. Additionally, workers in the lowest-skilled occupations have experienced the most significant decline in wages, which implies that demand is already weak in this segment of the labor market. Therefore, a second regression is performed using the same variables as in the first with the addition of an interactive term that is the product of average occupational education and the percentage of immigrants in the occupation. The purpose of the interactive model is to determine if the effect of immigrants is dependent on the skill level of an individual's occupation. A third individual-level regression is conducted with only low-skilled workers (those with only a high school degree or less) in order to examine the possible relationship between immigration and the poor labor market performance of these workers. In addition to the three individual-level regressions, two aggregate-level regressions are conducted with occupations as the unit of analysis and average weekly wages as the dependent variable. These regressions are conducted to add further support to the model.

Findings

Table 6–4 provides descriptive statistics for all the variables in the equation. Table 6–5 reports correlations among all the variables.[40] Table 6–6 contains the results of the individual regressions. The dependent variable is the natural log of weekly wages for *natives only*. The first column gives the coefficients for the noninteractive model. The second column reports coefficients for the interactive model. The third column reports

Table 6–4 Descriptive Statistics for Native-Born Workers

Variable	Mean	Standard Deviation
All natives ($n = 12{,}967$)		
% Male	52.30	30.87
Average education	2.68	.76
% unionized	15.71	14.41
Average age	37.68	3.85
% immigrant	9.51	5.32
Interactive term	32.67	15.38
Full or part time	.81	.39
Age	37.25	13.03
Sex	.51	.50
Union	.16	.36
Education level	2.68	1.17
Minority	.15	.35
State earnings inflation	98.62	14.70
Log weekly earnings	5.82	.78
Low-skilled natives ($n = 6{,}567$)		
% male	55.02	32.37
Average education	2.32	.51
% unionized	16.35	13.63
Average age	36.87	4.00
% immigrant	10.63	6.00
Full or part time	.77	.42
Age	37.64	14.16
Sex	.51	.50
Union	.17	.37
Minority	.18	.38
State earnings inflation	97.46	14.46
Log weekly earnings	5.60	.76

Table 6–5 Correlations for Variables in the Equation

	Log of Weekly Earnings	% Male	Average Education	% Unionized	Average Age	% Immigrant	Interactive Term	Full or Part-time	Age	Sex	Union Member
Log of weekly earnings	—	.25**	.42**	.12**	.42**	-.22**	.05**	.61**	.22**	.26**	.20**
% male	.25**	—	-.12**	.22**	.09**	.13**	.12**	.20**	.01	.62**	.09**
Average education	.42**	-.12**	—	.02*	.50**	-.41**	.17**	.17**	.13**	-.08**	.01
% unionized	.12**	.22**	.02*	—	.20**	-.11**	-.17**	.10**	.09**	.15**	.40**
Average age	.42**	.09**	.50**	.20**	—	-.25**	.01	.26**	.30**	.05**	.08**
% immigrant	-.22**	.13**	-.41**	-.11**	-.25**	—	.78**	-.13**	-.05**	.08**	-.04**
Interactive term	.05**	.12**	.17**	-.17**	.01	.78**	—	-.017*	.01	.06**	-.07**
Full or part time	.61**	.20**	.17**	.10**	.26**	-.13**	-.02*	—	.08**	.19**	.18**
Age	.22**	.01	.13**	.09**	.29**	-.05**	.01	.08**	—	.00	.13**
Sex	.26**	.62**	-.08**	.15**	.05**	.08**	.06**	.19**	.00	—	.09**
Union member	.20**	.09**	.01	.40**	.08**	-.04**	-.07**	.12**	.13**	.09**	—
Education level	.41**	-.08**	.64**	.01	.32**	-.26**	.11**	.16**	.05**	.01	.02*
Minority	-.06**	-.04**	-.10**	.04**	-.04**	.06**	.00	.00	-.02**	-.04**	.05**
State earnings inflation	.15**	-.03**	.12**	-.02*	.06**	-.06**	.02*	.00	.02**	-.01	.13**

Note: Statistical significance (1-tailed): **p < .01; *p < .05.

Table 6–6 Regression Coefficients and Standard Errors for Log of Individual Weekly Wages

	Noninteractive Coefficient (SE)	Interactive Coefficient (SE)	Low-Skilled Coefficient (SE)
Occupational-level Variables			
% Male	.0030 (.00019)	.0026 (.00019)	.0021 (.27466)
Average education	.1600 (.00876)	.0584 (.01420)	.1849 (.01674)
% unionized	−.0022 (.00035)	−.0015 (.00035)	−.0012 (.00056)
Average age	.0197 (.00144)	.0209 (.00144)	.0188 (.00192)
% immigrant	−.0051 (.00093)	−.0290 (.00279)	−.0066 (.00124)
Interactive term	—	.0112 (.00123)	—
Individual-level Variables			
Full or part time	.9323 (.0120)	.9286 (.01201)	.9738 (.01600)
Age	.0065 (.00036)	.0065 (.00036)	.0052 (.00047)
Sex	.1703 (.01133)	.1708 (.01129)	.1639 (.01716)
Union	.2099 (.01352)	.2104 (.01348)	.2840 (.01846)
Education level	.1263 (.00495)	.1274 (.00493)	—
Minority	−.0413 (.01260)	−.0376 (.01257)	−.0499 (.01661)
State wage inflation	.0051 (.00031)	.0050 (.05987)	.0043 (.00044)
Constant	2.6198 (.05548)	2.828 (.00006)	2.926 (.07712)
Adjusted R^2	.5883	.5909	.5529
Standard error	(.5020)	(.5004)	(.5059)
N, observations	12,967	12,967	6,567

Note: All variables are significant at the .01 level.

coefficients for a regression with only low-skilled workers. All three regressions indicate that immigrants affect wages, although the effect varies across occupations.

All of the variables in all of the models are statistically significant at the .01 level and behave as expected with the exception of the percent unionization variable.[41] Because the dependent variable is the log of weekly wages, the coefficients can be interpreted as simple percentages. Thus the slope of −.0051 for the immigrant variable in the first regression means that controlling for all other factors, a 1 percent increase in the immigrant composition of an individual's occupation reduces a worker's weekly wage by about 0.5 of 1 percent relative to the wages of a worker with no immigrants in the occupation. Since native-born workers are in occupations that are 9.5 percent immigrant on average, the typical worker is experiencing a reduction in wages of about 4.9 percent as a result of immigration.

The relationship between immigrants and wages is more complex than that represented by the first model in Table 6–6. The coefficients on the interactive term and the immigrant variable in the second regression indicate that the effect of immigrants on wages is dependent on the average education level of the occupation. The range for the slope of the immigrant variable is as follows: At the bottom end of the range is an occupation with an average education level of 1.6. This value multiplied by the .0112 interactive term is .018. The immigrant variable's slope in the interactive equation is −.029; therefore, in the lowest-skilled occupation, the effect of immigration on wages is −.011. The high range for the occupational education variable is 4.9. This value multiplied by the interactive term slope is .055. The sum of the immigration variable and the interactive term in the highest-skilled occupation is .026. Therefore, the slope of the immigrant variable ranges in value from −.011 to .026. This indicates that at the highest skill level, immigrants increase wages, while in the lowest-skilled occupations, they depress wages. We will deal with the higher-skilled occupations shortly; first, let us turn to lower-skilled occupations.

If we examine the 23 percent of natives employed in those jobs that on average are done by workers with only a high school degree or less (henceforth referred to as low-skilled occupations), we get the following results: The product of the interactive slope and the average education level of 2 is .022. The sum of this figure and the immigrant variable is −.007. This means that in low-skill occupations, a 1 percent increase in the immigrant composition of an occupation reduces wages by at least 0.7 percent. Since these occupations are on average 15 percent immigrant, a rough estimate of the impact of immigration on natives in these occupations reveals a 10.5 percent reduction in wages compared to a worker with the same individual and occupational attributes except with no immigrants in the occupation. This comes to $32.24 a week for a group of workers who made only $307 a week in 1991.

While the second regression does indicate that immigrants have a negative effect on workers in low-skilled occupations, only 40 percent of native-born low-skilled workers are employed in such jobs, and low-skilled workers comprise 80 percent of native-born workers in these occupations. The question remains: Has immigration played any role in the labor market difficulties of low-skilled workers in general? The answer, based on the third column in Table 6–6, which reports the effects of immigration on only native-born low-skilled workers, appears to be yes. The regression coefficient for the immigrant variable is $-.0066$ and is slightly larger than that of the immigrant variable in the first regression. On average, the weekly wages of low-skilled workers were $341 a week in 1991. A 0.66 percent reduction in weekly wages for these workers is $2.25. Low-skilled workers are in occupations that are on average 10.6 percent immigrant. Thus, holding all other variables constant, the average low-skilled worker's wages were reduced by $23.86 a week in 1991, or by 7 percent.

When taken together, the findings in Table 6–6 suggest that immigrants depress wages by reducing the pay rates of workers in low-skilled occupations. Because so many low-skilled workers are in low-skilled occupations, immigrants contribute to the relative decline in wages for low-skilled workers generally. The fact that in higher-skilled occupations immigrants do not depress wages and may increase them indicates that it is a worker's occupation and not the skill level per se that makes him or her vulnerable to the effects of immigrant competition. While the model itself is biased toward producing occupational-level effects because the immigrant variable is assigned by occupation, the six individual-level variables, along with the wage inflation variable, create significant differences in the characteristics of individuals in the same occupation. Additionally, the results make intuitive sense. The likely avenue by which immigrants affect native-born wages is by occupation or in groups of occupations in which there is a good deal of movement between them.

In addition to the implication these results have for workers in low-skilled occupations generally, they also suggest that the effects of immigration may be disproportionally concentrated in some racial and ethnic groups. In the sample, 21.5 percent of native-born whites reported being employed in the bottom third of lowest-skilled occupations. In contrast, 33.6 percent of native-born minorities are employed in low-skilled occupations.[42] This means that in the sample, minorities are 56 percent more likely to be in those occupations adversely affected by immigration. Immigration's disproportional effect on minorities may be cause for concern. It also suggests that reforming immigration policy may be particularly helpful to low-skilled minority workers.

We have focused primarily on natives in low-skilled occupations for a number of reasons. First, as has already been pointed out, it is low-skilled workers who have experienced the most difficult time in the labor market. Determining whether immigration has contributed to this phenomenon is clearly an important question for policymakers and social scientists. Second, only about 7 percent of the workers in the top one-third of the most skilled occupations are immigrants. In contrast, about 15 percent of the workers in low-skilled occupations are immigrants. Therefore, it is in the low-skilled occupations that immigrants have the greatest impact.

There is reason to believe that the positive coefficients for the immigrant variable in higher-skilled occupations may not mean that immigrants cause higher wages in these occupations. Very likely distinct labor market forces are at work at the opposite ends of the labor market. Low-skilled immigrants often come to the United States because they face bleak prospects in their home country. They are, in effect, pushed into the United States by conditions at home. In contrast, immigrants with high skill levels may be pulled to the United States by the possibility of better wages. In every country skilled persons enjoy a higher standard of living than do unskilled persons. A significant wage differential between the United States and their home country is required to lure immigrant professionals to this country. Therefore, the highest percentage of immigrants would be expected in those occupations in which the wages are highest, although information about earnings differentials is not included in this study. In other words, the higher paying the occupation, the greater the chance that there will be a large wage differential between the United States and the rest of the world. The large number of immigrants in such high-skilled occupations as medicine and engineering attests to this phenomenon. These conditions would produce a situation in which immigrants are in the highest-paying occupations but do not cause higher wages.

The different sign of the coefficient for the percent immigration variable at the opposite ends of the labor market also may be due to different conditions prevailing at those opposite ends. The decline in wages for less skilled workers is powerful evidence that less skilled labor is not in short supply. Additionally, the proportion of the workforce employed in occupations that require few years of schooling has fallen in every decade in the postwar period. The opposite is true in higher-skilled occupations; there has been steady and continual growth in the number of jobs requiring skilled workers. This means that in higher-skilled occupations, immigrant labor may be more easily absorbed into an ever-expanding pool of jobs, while in low-skilled occupations, immigrants and natives are competing for an ever-dwindling supply of jobs.

Of course, it is possible that high-skilled immigrants do increase wages for natives. Immigrant professionals may possess skills that they transfer to natives in the same occupation. This would make natives more productive and thus might increase their wages. However, at the bottom end of the labor market, this is much less likely to be true. Immigrant agricultural workers or dishwashers are unlikely to possess specialized skills that their native-born counterparts lack. Thus competition is the primary effect low-skilled immigrants have on natives in the same occupation. Also, if immigrants do increase wages for those at the top of the labor market, only about 25 percent of the workforce is employed in those occupations that would benefit significantly from immigration, and that 25 percent of the workforce is least in need of a pay increase.

One potential problem with the approach utilized herein is that comparisons are made for individuals across occupations. If the variables in the analysis fail to tap those "occupational"-level effects that have a downward effect on wages, these untapped effects might confound the findings with regard to the immigrant variable in lower-skilled occupations. In other words, immigrants may be concentrated in jobs that do not pay very well. If this were the case, then it would appear as if the percentage of immigrants in an occupation depressed wages (since this variable is simply the aggregate of immigrants in an occupation), but in fact they would not cause the lower wages. While this line of argument seems plausible, it is not consistent with the available information.

If some omitted occupational-level variable is confounding the results, then the immigrant variable should be highly negatively correlated with weekly wages. However, the −.22 correlation found in Table 6–5 for these two variables suggests that immigrants are spread throughout the workforce. Additionally, a ranking of the ten occupations with the lowest average weekly wage reveals that only three are among the ten highest in immigrant composition. Thus it would not appear that immigrants are simply concentrated in the lowest-paying jobs. Previous research also indicates that both legal and illegal immigrants tend to hold jobs commensurate with natives with the same skills and of the same ethnic origin only a few years after arriving.[43] Most important, a regression using the data from this study reveals statistically insignificant results for being immigrant. This confirms the previous findings that reveal that, by itself, being foreign-born is not a significant handicap in the labor market. If being an immigrant does not consign one to working in low-paying jobs, it is difficult to imagine that the percent immigrant variable reflects selection bias.

Table 6–7 also indicates that most of the occupational-level effects are accounted for by the four occupation control variables. In the table the unit of analysis is the occupation, with the log of average weekly wages as the dependent variable. The first regression includes only the four occupational-level control variables. The large R squared and small standard error lend strong support to the argument that these occupational-level control variables capture the occupational-level effects other than the percentage of immigrants. The second regression in the table includes the immigration variable, which is significant and indicates that the results of the individual-level regressions are *not* simply caused by a few low-paying high-immigrant occupations, because each occupation in the table is treated as a single observation.

A second potential limitation of the national cross-occupation approach used here is that the effect of immigration is estimated by comparing the wages of natives employed in occupations with differ-

Table 6–7   Regression Coefficients and Standard Errors for Log of Average Occupational Weekly Wages

Independent Occupational-Level Variables	Control Model Coefficient (Standard Error)	Full Model Coefficient (Standard Error)
% Male	.0074	.0072
	(.5705)	(.5551)
Average education	.4259	.3914
	(.0250)	(.0259)
% unionized	.0046	.0040
	(.0011)	(.0011)
Average age	.0204	.0212
	(.0045)	(.0043)
% immigrant	—	−.0092
		(.0025)
Adjusted R^2	.7513	.7665
Standard error	(.2310)	(.2238)
N, observations	204	204

Note: All variables are significant at the .01 level.

ent percentages of immigrants. It is possible that immigrants employed outside of low-skilled occupations have also increased demand for low-skilled native labor. This could offset, at least in part, the wage reduction experienced by natives in low-skilled occupations due to immigrant competition.[44] However, since immigration has increased the supply of low-skilled workers much more than that of higher-skilled workers (see Table 6–2), it is unlikely that they could have increased demand enough to completely offset the increase in the supply of labor in low-skilled occupations. Further, as a relative measure, the findings remain valid: The more immigrants in a low-skilled occupation, the lower the wages of natives in that occupation.

The primary advantage of the approach utilized here is that it does not suffer from the problems associated with cross-city comparisons. Also, it does not assume that an increase in the supply of less skilled labor via immigration necessarily reduces wages. The model can and does find both positive and negative effects of immigration.

Because this study is cross-sectional, it does not directly answer the question of whether immigration contributed to the decline in earnings for low-skilled workers over the last 25 years. However, the findings do indicate that as the percentage of immigrants increased in low-skilled occupations, there was a corresponding decline in wages for natives in these occupations. This research also suggests that immigration should be properly understood as a national issue and not simply a phenomenon affecting high-immigrant states.

Policy Recommendations

The components of an ideal immigration policy depend on a wide variety of considerations. The priorities and goals to be served by immigration must be decided first. Are economic considerations to be given primacy, or should humanitarian considerations be the focus of immigration policy? Does the United States wish to continue making family relationships the primary criteria for admission, and, if so, does this include brothers and sisters or only spouses and minor children? On the question of illegal immigration, most seem to agree that more can and should be done to reduce it. However, there is much less agreement on how best to accomplish this goal, and at what cost. Finally, the question of what, if any, obligation exists to low-skilled workers already here who are likely to be harmed by the immigration of more low-skilled workers must be decided. While newer research in this field indicates that immigration increases the wage disparity between skilled and low-skilled workers and may also depress real wages for those with few years of schooling, it does not tell us whether we should care about this situation.

In addition to economic factors, environmental and cultural considerations concerning immigration may have little to do directly with the economy. Some see the increased racial, ethnic, and cultural diversity resulting from immigration as contributing to the quality of life in the United States.[45] Others argue that it will Balkanize the country and increase social conflict.[46] On the environmental side, Census Bureau projections place the size of the U.S. population in 2050 at around 393 million if current immigration continues and 319 million with zero net immigration.[47] Some environmentalists worry about this rate of population growth. There is also the question of what role public opinion should play in policy formulation. On one hand, when polled, large majorities of Americans of every racial and ethnic group have repeatedly responded that both legal and illegal immigration should be reduced. On the other hand, the issue does not seem very salient for those living outside of high-immigration areas, and the general public remains uninformed about immigration policy. Finally, there is the question of the country's national tradition of accepting immigrants. Those calling for reductions in immigrants tend to minimize the importance of immigration in the nation's past. Alternatively, acknowledging that immigration is an integral part of American history provides little meaningful guidance as to the number of immigrants to admit each year or the selection criteria to be used in the 1990s.

The fact that immigration policy may be harmful to low-skilled workers does not by itself tell us what, if anything, should be done about immigration. The next sections summarize possible policy responses to the problems immigration creates for low-skilled natives and also discuss their relative advantages and disadvantages. Broadly defined, the possible policy responses to this situation fit into three separate categories: do nothing; take action other than changing immigration policy; change immigration policy. These categories need not be mutually exclusive; it may be that some combination of them offers the best solution.

TAKE NO ACTION

The most straightforward and simple response is to leave the status quo in place. The primary advantage of taking no action to deal with the problems created by immigration for low-skilled workers is that it requires no new spending. Increases in funding for income support programs or efforts to better control illegal immigration are likely to cost billions. Leaving things as they are avoids these expenditures. A second advantage of taking no action is that the costs of new government efforts may tend to dissipate the positive effects of immigration for consumers and those workers with skills that complement those of immigrants. A third advantage is that by taking no action, no new problems will be created by our efforts to correct the harm done by immigration. For example, if we reduce legal immigration, we may dramatically increase pressure for illegal immigration. For a variety of reasons this may be a significantly worse state of affairs than currently exists. A fourth advantage to inaction is that it would avoid a time-consuming and what some may consider a distracting national debate over immigration policy or over new programs designed to mitigate its harmful effects. To some extent, time and energy devoted to solving the problems created by immigration cannot be used to solve other pressing national problems.

The primary argument against taking no action stems from the fact that the federal government sets the level of legal immigration and also allocates funding to combat illegal immigration. Thus Washington can be seen as directly responsible for the consequences of immigration. This makes immigration very different from those factors that have reduced wages for low-skilled workers. Economic globalization, skill-biased technological change, and the entry of women into the workforce may have all contributed to the decline of wages for workers with few skills. However, immigration is different because Congress cannot legislate a pause in the expansion of human knowledge or instruct women to exit the workforce or stop the Japanese from setting up factories in Malaysia—but it can reduce the number of low-skilled workers coming into the country each year. Thus not only did Congress create the problem, it has the power to stop it or at least prevent further deterioration. The obligation of the federal government to cut immigration or spend more to deal with its consequences stems, at least in part, from the central role government action has played in creating and perpetuating the problem.

An argument for some governmental response also can be made based on the self-interest of those not adversely affected by immigrant competition. The severe economic difficulty in the labor market experienced by those with few years of schooling must have played some role in the emergence of the underclass over the last 30 years. Cuts in low-skilled immigration or other efforts to increase the earnings potential of those with few skills probably would be helpful in improving this situation, a result beneficial not only to the recipients of such efforts but also to the society generally. Of course, making an argument that the government ought to do something about the negative consequences of immigration does not necessarily mean that immigration policy should change. There are a number of other possible solutions to this situation.

TAKE ACTION OTHER THAN CHANGING IMMIGRATION POLICY

To deal with the wage-suppression effects of immigration, income support programs such as the Earned Income Tax Credit could be expanded both in scope or in the amount they pay out to recipients. Since research indicates that the negative effect of immigration on wages is confined to those at the bottom of the labor market, the most effective response would be one that increases the overall size of the credit as opposed to increasing the number of persons covered by the program. Another possibility might be to raise the minimum wage. While this would create some disemployment effects, it would improve the wages of low-skilled workers in the occupations negatively affected by immigration.[48] Other policies also might be helpful, such as allowing more of the working poor to use noncash assistance programs such as food stamps, public housing, or Medicaid. While allowing the working poor greater access to these programs would not increase their wages, large enough benefits could conceivably offset the harmful effects of immigrant competition.

Besides increasing income support and other noncash assistance programs, helping natives avoid job competition with immigrants might also lessen the impact of immigration. Job retraining programs designed to increase the skill level of those in adversely affected occupations might reduce the number of natives harmed by immigration. Retraining efforts might include vocational education and increased funding for adults who wish to go to college. Efforts of this kind could be targeted specifically at workers with few years of schooling and those in occupations with the highest concentration of immigrants. The primary advantage to these options is that they deal with the negative effects of immigration on low-skilled workers without cutting immigration. Thus these solutions would avoid a lengthy national debate over immigration policy and preserve many of the benefits from immigration. Yet there are significant drawbacks to trying to deal with the problems caused by immigration while leaving immigration policy intact.

The most obvious disadvantage to increasing government spending to deal with immigration is the cost. Even a modest increase of, say, 10 percent in the Earned Income Tax Credit would add roughly $4 billion to the program. Thus, if there are economic benefits from immigration, devoting more tax dollars to income support programs or job retraining would reduce or eliminate them. Of course, any noneconomic benefits from immigration that may exist would remain even in the face of new spending. Additionally, given the current skepticism of the public and policymakers concerning antipoverty programs, it is very unlikely that the country will undertake any new large-scale efforts to assist the working poor in the current political environment. It is also worth noting that increased spending may only get the working poor back to where they would have been without immigration. This points to an underlying dilemma of immigration as it pertains to low-skilled natives: Any new effort to uplift the working poor may only bring them back to the same point they would have been at if low-skilled immigration had simply been curtailed.

CHANGING IMMIGRATION POLICY

None of the research cited here indicates that the current level of immigration is too high. The labor market literature indicates only that the number of immigrants with few years of schooling needs to be reduced if we are concerned about the effect on the wages of natives. The overall number of immigrants could remain at the current level or could even be increased. If immigration policy were redesigned to limit the impact on low-skilled natives, it would involve changes in the selection criteria for legal immigrants and significantly stepped-up efforts to reduce illegal immigration. Let us consider changes to legal immigration first.

The primary change to legal immigration policy would be to reorient it so as to give much greater emphasis to the skill level of newly arriving immigrants. Recognizing the need to reduce low-skilled immigration, the U.S. Commission on Immigration Reform has suggested limiting family immigration to the spouses, minor children, and parents of citizens and the spouses and minor children of Lawful Permanent Residents (LPRs).[49] This would eliminate the preferences now in the law for siblings and adult children of citizens and adult children of LPRs. A strong case also can be made for eliminating the preference for spouses and children of noncitizens, since these provisions apply to family members acquired after the alien has received a green card, but before he or she has become a citizen.[50] Defining family immigration in this way would reduce family-based immigrants to about 350,000 per year, based on the fiscal year 1996 level, and the number would likely fall to 200,000 or less after a few years.

For employment-based immigration, the most important obvious change that is needed is to drop the 10,000 visas for unskilled workers.

It is very difficult to justify unskilled immigration given the decline in wages for unskilled labor generally in the United States. This category also encourages illegal immigration because it offers unskilled illegal aliens the hope that they will find an employer who eventually will petition to bring them in legally. While the number of illegal aliens who actually are able to take advantage of this situation is small, it does offer the hope of legal status to many illegals.

The commission also has suggested eliminating the diversity lottery. Since diversity immigrants represent only about 7 percent of the legal immigrant flow, its direct effect on low-skilled occupations is likely to be small. The primary drawback to the lottery is that immigrants are admitted based on luck, not their likely benefit to the economy. If we wish to continue the lottery, then perhaps eligibility should be limited to only those individuals who can verify that they have at least a college degree.

Restricting family immigration to only the spouses, minor children, and parents of citizens, ending unskilled employment-based immigration, and eliminating or modifying the Diversity Lottery would cut the flow of low-skilled immigration significantly. Cutting illegal immigration would also be a necessary prerequisite to reducing low-skilled immigration.[51] Recently released INS estimates indicate that the long-term illegal population is 5 million and this number is thought to grow by 275,000 annually. An estimated 80 to 90 percent of these immigrants have no more than a high school degree, and they make up the lowest-skilled flow of immigrants.

There is widespread agreement that cutting illegal aliens off from jobs offers the best hope of reducing illegal immigration. Since 1986 it has been unlawful to employ illegal aliens. However, to date "worksite" enforcement efforts have been ineffective. A number of steps would have to be implemented to make worksite enforcement more effective. First, a national computerized system that allows employers to verify that persons are legally entitled to work in the United States should be implemented. Besides helping honest employers determine the eligibility of prospective employees, such a system would make it more difficult for employers who knowingly hire illegal aliens to argue that they were unaware of an employee's illegal status. Second, the INS would need to dramatically increase the number of man-hours devoted to worksite enforcement efforts. At present, the INS devotes the equivalent of 300 agents working year round on worksite enforcement in an effort to track down approximately 3 to 4 million illegal aliens who hold jobs in the United States. Congress has repeatedly failed to increase funding for worksite enforcement, even though the INS continues to ask for more agents. Without stepped-up funding, there will continue to be little incentive for employers to comply with the law.

While of less importance than worksite enforcement efforts, more could also be done to control the border. Despite increases in funding over the last few years, efforts along the border remain inadequate. Even with the additional 5,000 agents authorized by Congress in 1996 to be hired over the next five years, there will still be more New York City transit police than INS agents patrolling the border at any one time. A real effort to control the border with Mexico would require perhaps 20,000 agents and the development of a system of formidable fences and barriers in those areas that are used extensively for illegal crossings.

The changes in legal immigration policy just outlined would go a long way in reducing illegal immigration, because the current system of family-based immigration creates a strong incentive to come illegally. At the present time, there are approximately 4 million people qualified for immigration to the United States who are waiting their turn to receive the limited number of visas available each year in the various family categories. Such a system encourages those who have been selected but have to wait simply to come to the United States and settle illegally in anticipation of the day they are granted visas. Moreover, this problem has been made worse by a provision in the law that allows illegal aliens on immigration waiting lists to acquire legal status without first returning to their home countries. Based on numbers complied by the INS, it is estimated that 25 percent of the green cards issued in 1996 were to persons already residing in the United States illegally.[52] Eliminating the sibling and adult children categories would help to alleviate this situation by doing away with the long waiting lists.

These legal immigration proposals would undoubtedly reduce the overall number of legal immigrants arriving each year. Such a reduction in the flow of legal immigrants might be helpful in reducing the level of illegal immigration. Controlling illegal immigration becomes much more difficult as long as there are large communities of recent immigrants in the United States. Recent immigrants serve as magnets for illegal immigration, providing housing, jobs, and entry to America for illegals from the same country. It is no coincidence that the top immigrant-sending countries are also the top countries in sending illegal immigrants to the United States. Thus a cut in legal immigration would disrupt the networks that have developed that facilitate illegal immigrations. This is likely to make it easier to control illegal immigration in the long run. In the short term, however, cuts in legal immigration would create greater pressure for illegal immigration, as many realize that the only way to come to the United States is by illegal means. Therefore, before making large-scale cuts in legal immigration, first it would be necessary to put in place the illegal immigration control policies just outlined.

These changes in legal and illegal immigration policy would restore immigration levels to their historical average of about 300,000 to 400,000 annually. Even with these changes, the United States would continue to accept two to three times as many immigrants as any other country. However, the flow of immigrants would be more skilled and more diverse than it currently is. If the nation wishes to accept more immigrants, it could increase the number of visas in the employment-based categories from 140,000 to whatever number is thought to be desirable. At the present time not all of the 140,000 employment visas are used. It is doubtful that the cuts in family-based immigration suggested would substantially increase the number of persons seeking to enter the country in the employment-based immigration category, because most of those who would become ineligible for family-based visas would not qualify in the employment categories. Thus, very likely, any attempt to increase the skill level of newly arriving immigrants would reduce the overall level of immigration. If a reduction in the overall level of immigration is thought to be undesirable, then the number of visas in the employment-based categories could be increased and a greater effort could be made to recruit more skilled immigrants from abroad.

One disadvantage of cutting low-skilled immigration would be that fewer people could share in the prosperity provided by the American economy. Some argue that as a rich country, the United States has an obligation to allow in as many immigrants as possible even if some Americans are harmed by this process.[53] There can be no doubt that most immigrants improve their standard of living significantly by coming here: otherwise they would not have come. Most Americans, however, seem to feel that primary consideration should always be given to the well-being of their fellow Americans rather than to the interests of foreigners. Even if helping the world's poor was made a higher priority, it is still unclear what immigration policy should be pursued. First, even if the United States were to accept many times the number of poor and low-skilled immigrants than it now does, the proportion of the world's poor that could be helped in this way would remain infinitesimally small. Moreover, taking industrious and enterprising people away from developing countries may slow the pace of economic development in those parts of the world most in need of such people. It also may allow corrupt and oppressive regimes to persist as would-be reformers simply leave the country. Finally, if assisting the poor of the world is an important objective, then taxing the wealthy in the United States and sending the money abroad is always an option. Not only could such a policy reach more people by assisting the development of entire countries, it would avoid harming low-skilled workers in the United States. Therefore, even if alleviating world poverty is an important objective, it is doubtful that immigration policy is an effective or fair means of achieving this goal.

From the perspective of the American political system, the primary disadvantage to reducing low-skilled immigration is the cost. While cutting legal immigration would involve no new fiscal costs, any real effort to control illegal immigration would be very expensive. In fiscal year 1997 the INS budget was $3.3 billion. If most of the policies listed to control illegal immigration were implemented, the INS's budget would expand significantly. However, even a doubling of its budget would still mean that less than 0.5 of 1 percent of federal expenditures were devoted to securing the nation's borders and improving the plight of the most disadvantaged Americans. Given the importance of these goals, this level of expenditure seems justified. If there is no desire to take the necessary steps to change immigration policy, then Congress should at least consider new income transfer programs and other measures to deal with the consequences of immigration for less skilled natives. Given the discretionary nature of immigration policy, to do neither would suggest a disregard for the plight of the most vulnerable and disadvantaged Americans.

Notes

1. This figure is for all persons who identified themselves as having been born outside of the United States at the time of the March 1996 *Current Population Survey*. It includes legal permanent residents, illegal aliens, and those granted temporary visas for such purposes as work and study.

2. In Figure 6–1 the net increase in the number of illegal immigrants is estimated to be 150,000 annually from 1970 to 1979 and 275,000 for the period 1980 to 1996.

3. Vernon M. Briggs Jr., *Mass Immigration and the National Interest* (New York: M. E. Sharpe, 1996), 109–10.

4. In 1978 the two hemispheric limits were combined into one worldwide limit of 290,000.

5. The sponsor of the bill, Representative Emanuel Celler (D-N.Y.), told his fellow representatives, "There will not be, comparatively, many Asians or Africans entering this country" as a result of the new law. In a letter to the editor of the *New York Times* on August 24, 1964, Attorney General Robert Kennedy stated that the changes being considered in immigration law

"would increase the amount of authorized immigration by only a fraction." Senator Edward Kennedy (D-Mass.), a member of the immigration subcommittee, reassured his colleagues that "under the proposed bill, the present level of immigration remains substantially the same." U.S. Senate, Subcommittee on Immigration and Naturalization of the Committee on the Judiciary, Washington, D.C., February 10, 1965, 1–3.

6. Unlike the 1965 and 1986 acts, this new limit did factor in the number falling into the category of immediate relatives of U.S. citizens when establishing annual limits on the other categories.

7. The 1996 act also made some changes in the welfare eligibility requirement for immigrants.

8. When immigrants are issued visas in any of the family categories, their spouses and minor children are also given visas. For example, if a U.S. citizen sponsors her brother, who is married with two children, four visas are issued: one for the brother, one for the brother's wife, and one for each child. This means that the brothers and sisters category can include not only siblings but in-laws and nieces and nephews. All of these visas are counted against the per-country and worldwide limits. Family preference immigration is primarily what creates a continual stream of immigrants (referred to as chain migration) as in-laws bring in their family members.

9. Shirley J. Smith, Roger G. Kramer, and Audrey Singer, *Characteristics and Labor Market Behavior of the Legalized Population Five Years Following Legalization* (Washington, D.C.: U.S. Department of Labor, 1996), 14–17.

10. Immigrants may affect capital stocks in a number of different ways. First, immigrants may bring capital with them. They also may make the United States a more attractive place to invest by increasing the skills base of the U.S. workforce or by stimulating investment by providing a conduit for foreigners looking to invest in the United States. Conversely, immigrants also may make the United States a less attractive place to invest by becoming a net drain on the public coffers. This may reduce the quality of public services in the country, increase the tax burden on businesses, or some combination of both. Immigrant remittances sent to their home countries also may represent a reduction in the supply of capital available domestically.

11. This is partly to be expected because immigrants in the workforce who arrived before 1980 are now older than the average native in the workforce. This increase in experience should translate into higher earnings. It is also likely that less successful immigrants are more likely to return home after finding that they cannot make it in the United States. Return migration makes it possible that observed differences in earnings might be due to selection bias.

12. Differences between the figures in Tables 6–2 and 6–3 are due to sampling variations, the year of the surveys, and the slightly different population examined.

13. It is estimated that immigrant labor accounted for $557 of consumption expenditures for the average household in the lowest income decile in 1994. In contrast, the average household in the top income decile consumed $2,809 worth of immigrant-provided goods and services. See James Smith and Conny Edmonston, *The New Americans: Economic, Demographic and Fiscal Effects of Immigration* (Washington, D.C.: National Academy Press, 1997).

14. According to an emerging body of evidence, immigrants are a net fiscal drain on public coffers, at least at the present time. A recent study of the state of New Jersey found that immigrant families paid less in taxes and used more in services than native households. Deborah L. Garvey and Thomas J. Espenshade, "State and Local Fiscal Impacts of New Jersey's Immigrant and Native Households, in Thomas J. Espenshade (ed.), *Keys to Successful Immigration: The Implications of the New Jersey Experience* (Washington, D.C.: Urban Institute Press, 1997), 139–72. This was found to be true even though the skills and earnings of New Jersey's immigrants are significantly higher than those of immigrants nationally. After surveying the recent research in the field, Smith and Edmonston concluded that the net annual fiscal burden imposed on native households nationally by all immigrant-headed households ranges from –$14.77 to –$20.16 billion. Further, they estimate that the negative fiscal impact of immigration is substantially greater than any net benefit to natives that is likely to result from having immigrants in the labor market even under the most optimistic scenarios. Smith and Edmonston, "The New Americans," 6–28. Research by Steven A. Camarota indicates that the negative fiscal impact of immigration on public coffers from immigration is entirely the result of the 60 percent of immigrant households headed by persons with only a high school degree or less. Steven A. Camarota, "Public Services Used and Taxes Paid by Immigrants in the United States," paper presented at the Annual Meeting of the American Sociological Association, 1997.

15. For a more detailed discussion of why the migration of immigrants with few years of schooling and low earnings potential can reduce the aggregate well-being of natives once fiscal costs are counted, see Barry R. Chiswick, "The Economic Consequences of Immigration: Application to the United States and Japan 1997," in Myron Weiner and Tadashi Hanami (eds.), *Temporary Workers or Future Citizens: Japanese and U.S. Migration Policies* (New York: New York University Press, 1998), 177–208.

16. McKinley L. Blackburn, David E. Bloom, and Richard B. Freeman, "The Declining Economic Position of Less Skilled American Men," in Gary Butless (ed.), *A Future of Lousy Jobs: The Changing Structure of U.S. Wages* (Washington, D.C.: Brookings Institution, 1990), 227.

17. Frank Levy and Richard J. Murnane, "U.S. Earnings Levels and Earnings Inequality: A Review of Recent Trends and Proposed Explanations," *Journal of Economic Literature* 30, no. 3 (September 1992), 1334.

18. Blackburn, Bloom, and Freeman, "Declining Economic Position of Less Skilled American Men"; Joel A. Devine and James D. Wright, *The Greatest of Evils: Urban Poverty and the American Underclass* (New York: Aldine De Gruyter, 1993); David T. Ellwood, *Poor Support* (New York: Basic Books, 1988); and William J. Wilson, *The Truly Disadvantaged: The Inner City, the Underclass, and Public Policy* (Chicago: University of Chicago Press, 1987).

19. Joseph G. Altonji and David Card, "The Effects of Immigration on the Labor Market Outcomes of Less-skilled Natives," in John M. Abowd and Richard B. Freeman (eds.), *Immigration, Trade and Labor* (Chicago: University of Chicago Press, 1991); Frank D. Bean, B. Lindsay Lowell, and John Taylor, "Undocumented Mexican Immigrants and the Earnings of Other Workers in the United States," *Demography* 25, no. 1 (1988), 201–34; George J. Borjas, "The Substitutability of Black, Hispanic and White Labor," *Economic Inquiry* 21, no. 1 (January 1983), 93–106; George J. Borjas, "The Impact of Immigrants on the Earnings of the Native-Born," in W. M. Briggs and M. Tienda (eds.), *Immigration: Issues and Policies* (Salt Lake City, Utah: Olympus, 1984); Kristin F. Butcher and David Card, "Immigration and Wages: Evidence from the 1980s," *American Economic Review* 81, no. 2 (May 1991), 292–6; Gregory DeFreitas and Adriana Marshall, "Immigration and Wage Growth in U.S. Manufacturing in the 1970s," *Proceedings of the 36th Annual Meeting of the Industrial Relations Research Association* (Madison, Wisc.: IRRA, 1983); Thomas Muller and Thomas Espanshade, *The Fourth Wave: California's Newest Immigrants* (Washington, D.C.: Urban Institute Press, 1985).

20. George Borjas, Richard B. Freeman, and Lawrence F. Katz, "On the Labor Market Effects of Immigration and Trade," in George Borjas and Richard B. Freeman (eds.), *Immigration and the Work Force* (Chicago: University of Chicago Press, 1993), 213–44; George J. Borjas, Richard B. Freeman, and Lawrence F. Katz, "How Much Do Immigration and Trade Affect Labor Market Outcome?" *Brookings Papers on Economic Activity* 1 (Washington, D.C.: Brookings Institution Press, 1997).

21. David A. Jaeger, "Skill Differences and the Effect of Immigration on the Wages of Natives," *Bureau of Labor Statistics Working Paper* 274 (1996).

22. Robert H. Topel, "Regional Labor Markets and the Determinants of Wage Inequality," *American Economic Review* 84, no. 2 (May 1994), 17–22.

23. Mark D. Partridge, Dan S. Rickman, and William Levernier, "Trends in U.S. Income Inequality: Evidence from a Panel of States," *Quarterly Review of Economics and Finance* 36, no. 1 (Spring 1996), 17–18.

24. In addition to anecdotal evidence, public opinion surveys continue to find that nonblack Americans see blacks as lazier and less intelligent than themselves. A recent study of the Harlem labor market by Katherine Newman and Chauncy Lennon found a clear preference on the part of employers to hire immigrants over native-born blacks. The study found that although immigrants were only 11 percent of the job candidates in the

sample, they represented 26 percent of those hired. Moreover, 41 percent of the low-wage immigrants in the sample were able to find employment within one year, in contrast to only 14 percent of native-born blacks. The authors conclude that immigrants fare better in the low-wage labor market because employers see them as more desirable employees than native-born blacks. Newman and Lennon, "Finding Work in the Inner City: How Hard Is It Now? How Hard Will It Be for AFDC Recipients?" *Russell Sage Foundation Working Paper* 76 (1995).

25. Augustine J. Kposowa, "The Impact of Immigration on Unemployment and Earnings Among Racial Minorities in the United States," *Racial and Ethnic Studies* 18, no. 3 (July 1995), 605.

26. George Borjas, "Immigrants, Minorities, and Labor Market Competition," *Industrial and Labor Relations Review* 40, no. 3 (April 1987), 382–92.

27. Elliot Brownlee, *The Dynamics of Ascent, A History of the American Economy* (New York: M. E. Sharpe, 1979).

28. Neil Fligstein, *Going North: Migration of Blacks and Whites from the South* (New York: Academic Press, 1981); Daniel M. Johnson and Rex R. Campbell, *Black Migration in America: A Social Demographic History* (Durham, N.C.: Duke University Press, 1981).

29. Simon Kuznets, "Two Centuries of Economic Growth: Reflection on U.S. Experience," *American Economic Review* 67, no. 1 (March 1977), 4.

30. David Card, "The Impact of the Mariel Boatlift on the Miami Labor Market," *Industrial and Labor Relations Review* 43, no. 2 (January 1990), 245–57.

31. Randall K. Filer, "The Effect of Immigrant Arrivals on Migratory Patterns of Native Workers," in Borjas and Freeman (eds.), *Immigration and the Work Force*, 245–67; William H. Frey, "Immigration, Domestic Migration, and Demographic Balkanization in America: New Evidence for the 1990s," *Population and Development Review* 22, no. 4 (December 1996), 741–63; and William H. Frey, *Race, Class and Poverty Polarization of U.S. Metro Areas: Findings from the 1990 Census* (Ann Arbor, Mich.: Population Studies Center, 1993).

32. Borjas, Freeman, and Katz, "On the Labor Market Effects of Immigration and Trade," and "How Much Do Immigration and Trade Affect Labor Market Outcomes?"; Jaeger, "Skill Differences and the Effect of Immigration."

33. Economists use this term to mean that the technology used in the workplace increasingly required more educated workers.

34. To get a more accurate picture of the immigrant population, it is necessary to use the sample weights in the Current Population Survey (CPS). Sample weights are assigned to all persons in the survey based on what the Census Bureau believes is the actual distribution of persons in the country. Using the sample weights increases some demographic groups while

decreasing others and is especially important in estimating the percentage of immigrants in each occupation because immigrants tend to be undercounted. Significance tests in the analysis reflect sample weights.

35. Borjas, Freeman, and Katz, "On the Labor Market Effects of Immigration and Trade." This analysis uses weighted averages to increase the number of foreign-born persons in the workforce by 6 percent. The 6 percent increase in the immigration population is divided .75 between Mexican and .25 non-Mexican immigrants. This is based on the authors' assumption that 75 percent of the uncounted illegal immigrant population in the workforce is Mexican and 25 percent is non-Mexican.

36. The Census Bureau classifies occupations at three different levels of detail, resulting in 13, 46, and 504 occupations. While the first two levels do not seem sufficiently detailed to get a good representation of the variation in immigrants across occupations, 504 is too large because there are only 70,002 adult workers in the CPS, and they are not evenly distributed. Therefore, the 504 occupations have been combined into 204 occupations. Occupations have been combined only with others that are very similar and in the same category at the next level up in detail. For example, light and heavy truck drivers have been combined into one truck driver category, as have all secondary-school teachers, who had been classified by subject. The findings appear robust, with alternative coding schemes yielding similar results.

37. There is a good deal of research to indicate that years of education should not be treated as a simple interval ratio level variable. The attainment of a diploma confers significant earning potential on individuals. See Dale Belman and John S. Heywood, "Sheepskin Effects in the Return to Education: An Examination of Women and Minorities," *Review of Economics and Statistics* 73, no. 4 (November 1991), 720–4; and Thomas Hungerford and Gary Solon, "Sheepskin Effects in the Returns to Education," *Review of Economics and Statistics* 69, no. 1 (February 1987), 175–7. Therefore, individual education level has been coded so that dropouts equal 1, high school graduates 2, those with some college 3, those with a four-year degree 4, and those with more education 5. Once this is done, average years of schooling are calculated for each occupation and are carried out to two decimal points. However, coding education in its original 0 to 18 range does not significantly alter the results.

38. With the exception of age and education, all the individual-level variables are dummies. Age is used because it is the only experience-related variable in the CPS. Individual education level is calculated on a 1-to-5 scale in the same manner as the average education variable. The dummy variables are coded as follows: 0 for part-time worker and 1 for full-time worker; 0 for female and 1 for male; 0 for nonunion worker and 1 for union member; 0 for white and 1 for minority. In addition to the six individual-level variables, a wage inflation variable is included in the equation to control for

variations in individual earnings that are due to the difference in pay rates in each state. This variable is created by assigning a value to each respondent that reflects the state's per capita income as a percentage of national per capita income.

39. Borjas, Freeman, and Katz, "On the Labor Market Effects of Immigration and Trade," and "How Much Do Immigration and Trade Affect Labor Market Outcomes?"; Jaeger, "Skill Differences and the Effect of Immigration."

40. Correlations are included because the occupational-level control variables are derived from the individual-level variables, and therefore the possibility of multicolinearity exists. While most of the correlations are statistically significant due to the large size of the sample, there does not appear to be any problem with multicolinearity. The only exception is the high correlation between percent immigrant and the interactive term. This is expected since the interactive term is the product of the immigrant variable and the occupational-level education variable.

41. While the negative coefficient for the percent union variable may be counterintuitive, it is consistent with previous research. Work by Richard B. Freeman and James L. Medoff ("The Impact of the Percentage Organized on Union and Nonunion Wages," *Review of Economics and Statistics* 63, no. 4 [November 1981], 561–72) and Sherwin Rosen ("Unionism and the Occupational Wage Structure in the United States," *Economic Review* 11 [1970], 269–86) indicates that in highly unionized occupations, the wages of nonunion members are often lowered. Since the model controls for being a union member, the percent union variable primarily measures the effect of unionization on nonunion workers. A possible explanation for this result is that union wage gains increase the supply of workers in the nonunionized segment of an occupation by making employers reluctant to hire union workers and by creating an incentive to shed union workers.

42. By far the largest native-born minority groups are blacks and Hispanics. In the survey, 36 percent of native-born blacks and 29.7 percent of native-born Hispanics were employed in low-skilled occupations.

43. Andrew Gill and Stewart Long, "Is There an Immigration Status Wage Differential Between Legal and Undocumented Workers? Evidence from the Los Angeles Garment Industry," *Social Science Quarterly* 70, no. 1 (March 1989), 164–73; Jaeger, "Skill Differences and the Effect of Immigration."

44. This argument is partly dependent on what plausible counterfactual comparison is used when determining the effect of immigration on wages. For example, if immigrants in low-skilled occupations reduce the wages of natives in the same occupation by, say, 10 percent and if immigrants in higher-skilled occupations increase demand and thus wages in low-skill occupations by the same amount, then the effect of all immigrants on wages could be regarded as zero. However, if the counterfactual comparison is made between a labor market with both skilled and unskilled immigrants and one with *only* skilled immigrants, then low-skilled immi-

grants could be regarded as having reduced the wages of natives in low-skilled occupations by 10 percent compared to what they would have been if there had been no low-skilled immigration. In other words, skilled immigrants would have increased wages in low-skilled occupations by 10 percent had it not been for low-skilled immigrants who eliminated this positive effect. It is certainly possible that the United States could have an immigration policy that admits only skilled immigrants. Many other countries have such policies, and the suggestion is often made in the United States.

45. John Isbister, *The Immigration Debate: Remaking America* (West Hartford, Conn.: Kumarian Press, 1996).

46. Peter Brimelow, *Alien Nation: Common Sense About America's Immigration Disaster* (New York: Random House, 1995).

47. *Population Projections of the United States by Age, Sex, Race and Hispanic Origin: 1995 to 2050,* Report P25-1130 (Washington, D.C.: U.S. Government Printing Office, 1996).

48. Increasing the minimum wage while continuing the current level of low-skilled immigration may have significant drawbacks. A relatively open-ended labor market for low-skilled labor coupled with a significant increase in the minimum wage probably will increase unemployment among low-skilled workers. If low-skilled immigration is reduced first, then any increase in unemployment resulting from a higher minimum wage might be offset by the gains for those who retain their jobs. However, without a change in immigration policy, raising the minimum wage could substantially increase unemployment among workers with few years of schooling, a group already suffering from rates of unemployment well above the national average.

49. United States Commission on Immigration Reform, *Interim Report to Congress* (Washington, D.C.: U.S. Government Printing Office, 1994).

50. Currently there is a large backlog of persons waiting to enter in the spouses and minor children LPR category. The vast majority of these individuals are the family members of IRCA amnesty beneficiaries. It seems unwise to continue to separate these families. Therefore, we suggest grandfathering in those already on the waiting list. However, no future applications would be taken for the spouses and minor children of LPRs.

51. We estimate that between 30 and 40 percent of those immigrants with only a high school degree or less are here illegally, based on the work of Borjas, Freeman, and Katz, "On the Labor Market Effects of Immigration and Trade," and of Smith, Kramer, and Singer, *Characteristics and Labor Market Behavior.*

52. Jessica Vaughan, "Laundering Their Status: One-Fourth of 1996 Immigrants Are Former Illegals," *Immigration Review* 29 (Summer 1997), 10–11.

53. Isbister, *The Immigration Debate.*

7

What Can We Do? Remedies for Reducing Inequality

Lisa M. Lynch

RESEARCH on earnings behavior in the United States has presented indisputable evidence on the problem of inequality. In fact, 1996 was the third consecutive year in which there was no year-to-year change in inequality despite the fact that the nation is well into its longest peacetime recovery in the post–World War II era. Americans have gone from a society that was "growing together" between 1950 and 1979 to one that has been "growing apart" since then. At the same time, the evidence on earnings inequality has been puzzling. Much of the level and growth in inequality is within groups rather than across groups.[1] This chapter discusses the relative effectiveness of investments in education and training vs. other strategies in ameliorating some of the trends in inequality.

A Quick Review of the Problem

In the debate on the relative importance of trade vs. technological change as the main reason for increased inequality, it is important to note that some of these sources of change are not unique to the United States. Many other countries have experienced these same changes without a corresponding increase in inequality. This finding suggests that there are other institutions or factors at play that ameliorate the effect these changes have on the distribution of wages. This chapter argues that education and training systems are an important part of these institutional differences.

As Blanchflower and Slaughter discuss in Chapter 3, there are three basic explanations for the differences across countries in inequality shifts in relative demand for skilled labor, shifts in relative supply of skilled labor, and changes in labor market institutions (e.g., union power, real value of the minimum wage). So one explanation of the variance in the degree of inequality across countries in spite of similar technological and trade shocks is that the relative supply of skilled workers in some countries has been better able to keep up with the changes in the relative demand for skilled workers than in the United States. Nickell and Bell examine this issue for Germany, Britain, and the United States.[2] They argue that the German educational system produces a much more compressed distribution of human capital than the U.S. system. As shown in Table 7–1, the variation in mathematics ability is much smaller in Germany than in the United States. There are about three times as many employees with zero or minimal reading and math skills in the United States as there are in Germany. In Germany basic educational standards are set for all students to attain, and students know that their performance will be a critical factor in the probability that they attend university or obtain a good apprenticeship. In other words, the educational system sets high minimum standards for all and there are incentives in place for everyone, not just for those going on in higher education, to do well in school. More generally, comparing the variation in skills and the changes in wage inequality across countries, it can be seen that those countries that have higher variation in skills also experienced more inequality growth between 1979 and 1990.

Table 7–1 Employees at Various Literacy Levels and Changes in Male Inequality, 1979–1990

Country	Math Level				Change in Inequality (Males)
	Very High 4/5	Medium 3	Low 2	Minimal 1	
United States	27.1%	32.5%	24.5%	15.9%	+.28%
Germany	27.6	45.2	22.9	4.3	−.06
Canada	27.6	36.0	25.0	11.4	+.13
Netherlands	24.8	48.0	21.2	6.0	.00
Sweden	38.1	39.8	17.4	4.7	.00

Sources: OECD, *Literacy, Economy and Society: Results from the International Adult Literacy Survey, 1995* (revised data) (Paris: OECD, 1994); and Richard B. Freeman and Lawrence F. Katz, eds., *Differences and Changes in Wage Structures* (Chicago: University of Chicago Press and National Bureau of Economic Research, 1995).

When youths complete their schooling in Germany, as many as three-quarters continue on in apprenticeship training. This school-to-work transition results in a very different level of skills attainment for new entrants in the labor market in Germany than in the United States, especially for those in the bottom half of the ability distribution. For example, Buechtemann, Schupp, and Sclof followed two cohorts of youths leaving compulsory schooling in Germany and the United States in 1978/1979.[3] They found that 12 years later, 80 percent of the German youths had attained a vocational training certificate or university degree after leaving school while only 54 percent of their U.S. counterparts had done so. Nickell and Bell conclude that a school system that sets and achieves a high level of performance for those in the bottom half of the ability range combined with a comprehensive post–school leaving vocational training system can help minimize many of the negative consequences of a relative demand shift away from the unskilled.[4]

Figure 7–1 describes cross-country differences in the probability of obtaining post-school, firm-provided training. There again significant differences across countries in the probability that workers will acquire human capital after school can be seen. These cross-country differences in the accumulation of human capital and the quality of skills attainment, especially for those in the bottom half of the ability distribution, may go some way in explaining differences in inequality across countries and within the United States over time.

Figure 7–1 Percentage of Workers Receiving Firm-Provided Training

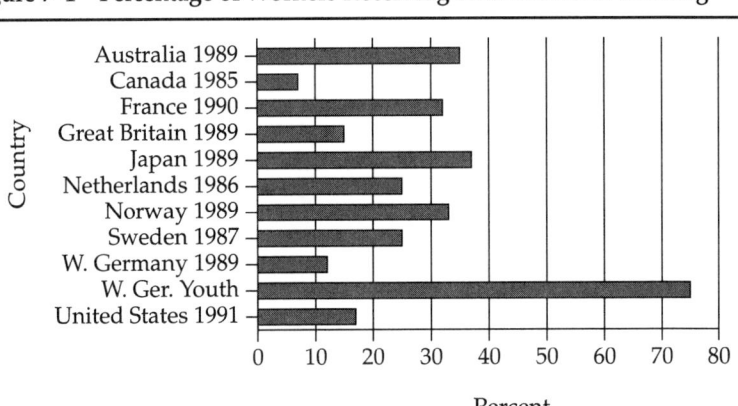

Source: Lisa M. Lynch, ed., *Training and the Private Sector: International Comparisons* (Chicago: University of Chicago Press, 1994).

The question then arises: Why has the relative supply of skilled workers not risen faster in the United States? Could it be that the wage premium and productivity gains associated with education and training in the United States are too low to make them a reasonable investment for workers and firms? The answer for the United States is a resounding no. More-educated workers earn more in the United States, and the gap is increasing. In 1979 the average full-time male (female) worker with a college degree earned 49 (44) percent more than the average full-time male (female) worker with only a high school degree. By 1995 the gap had widened to 89 (73) percent. As shown in Figure 7–2, those with less than a high school degree saw their mean family income, in inflation-adjusted terms, decline by 14 percent over the period 1979 to 1995. At the same time, those with a college degree or more saw their mean family income rise 14.2 percent over this same period. Recent evidence indicates that the returns to schooling occur because more-educated students are more productive as employees, not because higher education screens out low-ability individuals. Kane and Rouse find a year of post–high school education increases earnings by 5 to 10 percent after controlling for family background and test scores in high school.[5] Work by Ashenfelter and Krueger on identical twins found that each year of additional schooling raised later earnings of the more educated twin by 13 percent.[6]

Figure 7–2 Growth in Mean Family Income by Educational Attainment, 1979–1995

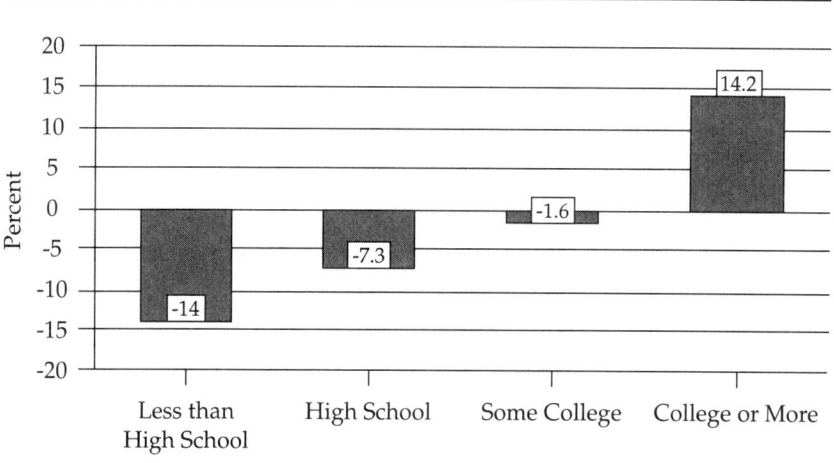

Source: Bureau of the Census, Current Population Survey, 1979 data adjusted by the CPI-U.

Table 7-2 The Impact of Private Sector Training

Study	Impact
Outcome Measure—Wages	
Lynch (1992): US non-college bound	A year of formal on-the-job training raises wages as much as a year of college
Mincer (1991): United States	Rates of return associated with an additional year of training: 4.4 to 11 percent
Blanchflower and Lynch (1994): United Kingdom	Apprenticeship training increased earnings 9 to 12 percent
Tan et al. (1993): Australia	Apprenticeships increased earnings 8 percent
Groot, Hartog, and Oosterbeek (1994): Netherlands	On-the-job training increases wages 4 to 16 percent
Westergard-Nielsen and Rasmussen (1997): Denmark	Apprenticeships raise earnings 10 percent
Outcome Measure—Productivity	
Bartel (1991): United States all industries	Productivity gains of 19 percent or more over three years in firms that train
Bartel (1989): United States all industries	Training investment increases productivity by 16 percent
Bishop (1994): United States all industries	Formal training increases an index of performance by 10 to 16 percent
Holzer et al. (1993): Michigan manufacturing	Doubling training investments results in scrap rates declining by 7 percent
Black and Lynch (1996): United States nonmanufacturing	Computer training increases labor productivity by more than 20 percent
Black and Lynch (1996): United States manufacturing	Providing a higher proportion of workers who train off-the job increases productivity
Ichniowski, Shaw, and Prennushi (1995): Steel	Where training is linked with progressive systems of HRM practices uptime is 7 percent higher
Groot (1993): Netherlands	Company rates of return to training: 11 to 20 percent

Sources: Lisa M. Lynch, "Private Sector Training and the Earnings of Young Workers," *American Economic Review* 82, no. 1 (March 1992), pp. 229–312; Jacob Mincer, "Job Training: Costs, Returns, and Wages Profiles," in J. Ritzen and David Stern, eds., *Market Failure in Job Training?* (Berlin and New York: Springer Verlag, 1991); David Blanchflower and Lisa M. Lynch, "Training at Work: A Comparison of U.S. and British Youths," pp. 233–260; Wim Groot, Joop Hartog and Hessel Oosterbeek, "Returns to Within-Company Schooling of Employees: The Case of the Netherlands," pp. 299–308; and John Bishop, "The Impact of Training on Productivity and Wages," pp. 161–200, all in Lisa M. Lynch, ed., *Training and the Private Sector: International Comparisons* (Chicago: University of Chicago Press, 1994); Hong Tan, Bruce Chapman, Chris Peterson, and Alison Booth, "Youth Training in the U.S., Great Britain, and Australia," *Research in Labor Economics* 13 (1992), pp. 63–99; N. Wester-

Continued on next page

But some have argued that even though educational attainment has increased over the past 20 years, it has had no impact on productivity, since the average annual growth of productivity has remained virtually constant in the United States since 1974. One way of solving this apparent paradox of increasing wages associated with education but constant productivity growth is to remember that at the aggregate level, the growth rate of output per hour (labor productivity) is the sum of the growth rates of multifactor productivity and the effects of capital intensity (defined as capital services per hour weighted by capital's share of total costs). Multifactor productivity measures the effects of changes in new technology, enhanced worker motivation, economies of scale of production, improved managerial skills (which result in the better use of resources), increased worker skills (which result in the better use of the available technology and capital), and other sources. What if the effect of improving worker skills could be isolated in multifactor productivity? Researchers at the Bureau of Labor Statistics (BLS) present evidence on the contribution of changing educational attainment and work experience over time on U.S. labor productivity.[7] They find that changes in the skill (as proxied by education and work experience) accounted for slightly more than 5 percent of the annual growth in labor productivity over the period 1948 to 1973 and 25 percent or more (depending on the time period chosen) since 1979. So, without the expansion of education, the country would have experienced much lower productivity growth over the last 20 years.

While it may not be all that transparent to tease out the impact of education and training on aggregate productivity, microlevel studies of establishments show significant gains in productivity associated with human capital investments. Recent research by Black and Lynch finds that increasing the average educational level of workers in a firm by one year raises productivity as much as 8 percent in manufacturing and 13 percent in nonmanufacturing.[8] In addition, Table 7-2 summarizes evidence on the significant impact that private sector training has on wages and productivity of firms. Lynch has found that a year of formal

---

gard-Nielsen and A. Rasmussen, "Apprenticeship Training in Denmark: The Impact of Subsidies," *Center for Labor Market Survey Research (Aarhus, Denmark) Working Paper* no. 97-07 (1997); Ann Bartel, "Productivity Gains from the Implementation of Employee Training Programs," *NBER Working Paper* no. 3893 (1991); H. Holzer et al., "Are Training Subsidies for Firms Effective? The Michigan Experience," *Industrial and Labor Relations Review* 47, no. 1 (1993), pp. 625–36; Sandra Black and Lisa M. Lynch, "Human Capital Investments and Productivity," *American Economic Review* 82 no. 1 (March 1992), pp. 299–312; Casey Ichniowski, K. Shaw, and G. Prennushi, "The Effects of Human Resource Management Practices on Productivity," *NBER Working Paper* no. 5333 (November 1995); Wim Groot, "Company Schooling and Productivity," mimeo., University of Leiden, the Netherlands, 1993; Ann Bartel, "Formal Employee Training Programs and Their Impact on Labor Productivity: Evidence from a Human Resource Survey," *NBER Working Paper* no. 3026 (1989).

on-the-job training raises wages for noncollege youths as much as a year of college.[9] Work by Ann Bartel and John Bishop also suggests that increased company-provided training can raise productivity of a business by 16 percent or more.[10] These gains in productivity and wages are similar to what has been found in studies on the British, Danish, and Dutch labor markets.

All of these studies suggest that investments in education and training offer substantial gains to workers and to firms. The fact that the college/high school differential has risen certainly has had some impact on the college enrollment rates. But if trends in annual earnings for full-time, year-round workers over the age of 25 are examined, it can be seen that in 1996, real median household earnings for college graduates had not grown much since the mid-1980s. However, as shown in Figure 7–3, there still remains a substantial difference in income by educational attainment.

So, if training and education are so good, why do people not get more? Part of the explanation, as recent work by Kane has shown, lies in the fact that the rising cost of tuition in the face of imperfect capital markets has

Figure 7–3 Real Median Household Annual Earnings by Educational Attainment, 1979–1996

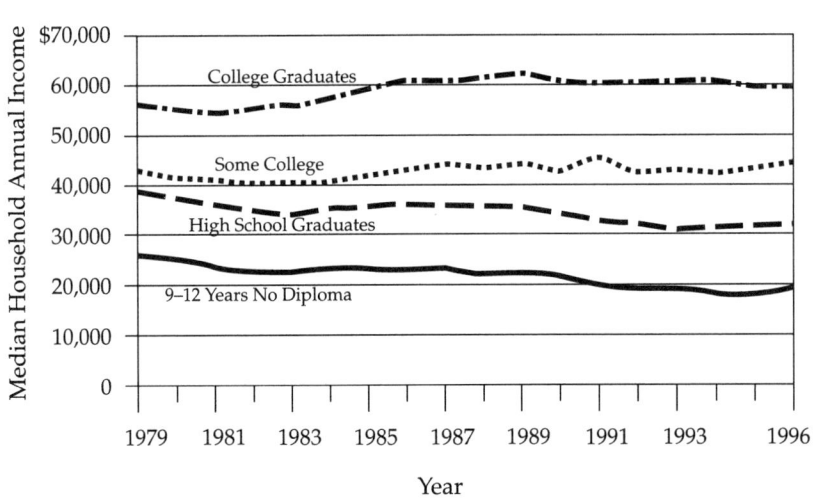

Notes: Households with householder 25 years old and over, 1996 dollars. Data from 1991 onward are not strictly comparable to previous years due to a change in the definition of educational attainment. Data from 1993 onward are not strictly comparable with previous years due to a change in earnings top-coding.
Source: Census Bureau, *Current Population Survey,* Historical Income Tables, H-13 and H-14.

had an adverse effect on college completion.[11] A recent study by the General Accounting Office shows how tuition at four-year public colleges and universities rose three times faster than the median household income between 1980 and 1995.[12] Student aid has not kept pace with tuition levels, so students and their families are relying more heavily on loans and personal finances to go to college. Given these rising costs, some are forced not to enter college, to delay entry, or to drop out of school in spite of the wage premium associated with acquiring more education.

Another disturbing trend is that poor families tend to be disproportionately concentrated in central cities, a concentration of poverty that has being rising over time. As Chris Mayer has documented, the share of the poor living in census tracts with a poverty rate more than 40 percent increased from 16 to 28 percent between 1970 and 1990, while the percentage living in tracts with a poverty rate exceeding 20 percent rose from 55 to 69 percent.[13] This increasing concentration of the poor in inner cities leads to social and economic isolation that may have a profound impact on the quantity and quality of human capital investments provided to some segments of our society.

Even though employer-provided training results in large returns, there may still be a problem of underinvestment. A firm's decision to invest in training, especially more general training, may be influenced in part by the characteristics of the workers it employs. Employees who are perceived to have higher turnover rates are less likely to receive employer-provided training. In addition, training itself may contribute to employee turnover: If new skills are of value to other employers, then firms risk having their trained employee hired away (the poaching or "cherry-picking" problem). Therefore, investments in nonportable firm-specific training are more attractive to firms than are investments in general training unless employers can find some ways to "capture" the latter investments. If firms invest in general skills of workers and workers then leave a firm, employers may end up investing in a suboptimal level of training.

In addition, smaller firms may have higher training costs per employee than larger firms because they cannot spread fixed costs of training over a large group of employees. The loss in production from having one additional worker in off-site training is probably much higher for a small firm than for a larger one. Smaller firms are also less likely to have developed extensive internal labor markets that allow them to better retain and promote employees within a firm.

Other factors besides size may influence the amount of training provided by an employer and who actually receives it. As human capital theory argues, employees who have already shown an aptitude to learn new skills by having completed more years of schooling are more likely to be provided with additional human capital investments by an employer. Various studies show that more educated employees are much more likely to obtain firm-provided training.[14] This results in the creation of both a "virtuous" and a "vicious" circle of human capital accumulation. Individuals who acquire more schooling are also more likely to receive postschool employer-provided training, while those with minimal education find it extremely difficult to make up this deficiency in human capital once they enter the labor market.

None of these issues would necessarily result in underinvestment in training as long as capital markets were perfect so that workers could borrow to finance more general training, if the government subsidized general training, or if workers accepted lower wages during training periods. However, capital markets are far from perfect, and workers differ from employers in their attitudes toward risk and time horizons. As a result, there may be a market failure in the provision of general training and the proportion of workers trained in more general skills.

But as discussed in Lynch, Japan and Germany have created institutional systems that appear to overcome the potential market failure inherent in firm-based general training.[15] There is substantial coinvestment in training in Germany, since apprentices work at substantially lower wages during their apprenticeship. At the same time, employers' contribute large sums to apprenticeship programs and the government funds extensive classroom training. The content of apprenticeship programs in Germany is codetermined with unions, employers' groups, and the government to ensure relevance and generality of skills. Finally, the certification of skills makes it worthwhile for young workers to accept lower wages, maintains uniform quality standards, and makes identifying skills much easier for employers. Traditionally in Japan, the seniority-based pay structure and lifetime employment guarantees reduce turnover, which in turn increases the probability of employers' providing general training. But this payment structure also means that employees coinvest in training by accepting lower initial starting wages while employers pay by providing more general training and lifetime employment. In addition, both Germany and Japan create incentives for youths who do not obtain a university degree to perform well in secondary school by linking their ensuing progress in the job market to their school or apprenticeship record.

This discussion on the rising premium associated with human capital and possible reasons why there may be underinvestment in human capital does not provide much insight into the empirical finding that a great deal of widening inequality in the United States (and in some other countries) is due to increases in within-group inequality. In other words, within the college-educated group, inequality has increased; within occupations, inequality has increased; and within industries, inequality has increased. What could be a possible explanation for this "other" source of inequality growth?

One possible explanation is related to the strategic choices made by firms. Lindbeck and Snower, building on a large industrial relations and human resource management literature, argue that reorganization of firms from Tayloristic task-oriented production processes to customer-oriented teams has resulted in a breakdown of occupational barriers within companies.[16] The differences of people within given occupational/educational/job tenure groups in their ability to adapt to more flexible and versatile work organizations may explain some of the widening wage inequality within groups of workers. Lindbeck and Snower predict that the movement to more horizontal work organizations with greater emphasis on cross-training will result in a labor market that is segmented into three parts: an expanding flexible, "high-performance workplace" where wages are rising; a contracting Tayloristic sector where wages are stagnant; and an expanding pool of jobless with longer durations of unemployment and lower reemployment wages. These three segments will not be necessarily industry or occupation specific. One of the implications of this model is that when researchers talk about a relative demand shift away from unskilled to skilled labor, "skill" may now also include the ability to be versatile and "learn how to learn." A worker could be "higher" skilled in the sense that he or she can do several semiskilled jobs rather than a single more specialized skill. This "versatility" skill is presumably positively correlated with education, but there will certainly be variation within education groups in the ability of individuals to adapt to change. To look at this issue empirically, matched employer and employee data and more detailed information on the skills of workers are needed. Unfortunately, there is no such data set for the United States as a whole. However, recent empirical work by Burgess, Lane, and Stevens, using the universe of workers and employers in Maryland from 1985 to 1994, suggests that the changing allocation of workers across employers played a significant role in explaining movements in the dispersion of earnings within groups of similar workers over this period.[17]

The question then becomes, Why have some firms reorganized their work organization to be more versatile in the allocation of workers across tasks, while others have not, especially in light of new findings of the impact these practices have on productivity?[18] A growing human resource management literature has attempted to shed some light on why certain firms adopt high-performance work (HPW) systems and others do not.[19] More specifically, Kochan, Levine, Olson, and Strauss argue that the structure and short-term focus of financial markets in the United States and traditional U.S. corporate governance structures make it more difficult for advocates of workplace innovations in this country to attract the resources and support needed to sustain the changes involved in moving to HPW systems long enough to achieve their full potential.[20] As a result, U.S. firms may be slower to adopt some of these new workplace practices than their European and Japanese counterparts. Finally, trade and institutions such as minimum wages and unions may have an impact on the choices firms make regarding the competitive strategy they wish to follow.

While there appears to be an emerging consensus within the human resource management field that moving to HPW systems increases productivity, there is much less information on how this affects profitability. The fact that a particular set of practices increases productivity does not necessarily mean that, in the short run, only those firms adopting those practices will be more profitable. If the costs associated with switching production processes are very high or if the higher wages that are paid to workers in these reengineered firms offset in part the monetary gains in productivity, a multiple equilibrium of practices could easily result—Tayloristic lower wage/stagnant wage firms competing against reengineered, higher-value-added, HPW systems with higher wages. In nontradeable sectors, a low-wage/low-productivity strategy may be sustainable from the point of view of employers, but it is hard to imagine how this would be a winning strategy in tradeable sectors in the medium or longer run. If the decisions firms make about work reorganization are the major reason for the increasing inequality within groups, then public policy solutions to reducing inequality become more challenging.

What We Can Do

In Chapter 3 Blanchflower and Slaughter argue that in terms of policy responses to increasing inequality, it does not matter why inequality has risen. They believe there should be short-term solutions, such as the Earned Income Tax Credit, and (perhaps) long-term solutions, such as education loan subsidies that aim to ease the acquisition of skills. This seems to be a pretty clear-cut policy solution. However, let us consider the analogy of how to solve the relatively "simple" problem of raising the temperature of a tub of tepid water to the boiling point. One strategy is simply to add boiling water to the tub. The problem with this strategy, especially for a very large tub, is that the temperature of the tub will rise very slowly, even though the new water being added is boiling. A second strategy is to build a fire under the tub to raise the temperature of the existing water. But will this be the fastest way to raise the temperature? Once the temperature is raised, how is that level maintained? To solve this problem, we need to be able to measure the temperature of the water at the starting point, monitor the temperature as the water is being added, determine the most cost-effective way of changing the temperature of the water in the tub, and, finally, figure out a way to monitor and maintain the temperature once the water in the tub is boiling.

Unfortunately, the policy debate surrounding the role of human capital investments or other strategies in reducing income inequality is much more complicated than the problem of changing the temperature of a tub of water. If we succeed in raising the temperature of the bath but have not figured out why the temperature dropped in the first place, how do we know where to look to when we are establishing a maintenance strategy for the bathtub temperature? We can fix inequality by a variety of methods in the short term, but these may not be the same policies we would keep in place in the long term to keep the inequality under control. For example, we could just use a combination of wage subsidies and tax credits to redistribute the gains the haves have made to the have-nots. But this will not contribute to overall economic growth in the same way as investments in education and training can.

Nevertheless, some of the sentiment behind Blanchflower and Slaughter's statement that the causes of rising inequality are not so important in formulating a public policy response are valid. A variety of factors have contributed to increasing inequality. Therefore, without getting bogged down in the percentage of increasing inequality due to trade, technological change, fall in the real value of the minimum wage, immigration, and shifts in product demand, what role could education and training play in narrowing the gap? Using the bathtub analogy, we might ask, How would education and training policy differ depending on whether we were trying to change the temperature of the water in the tub by adding hot water or by heating up the existing water?

A focus on the former strategy would lead to targeting the skill development of new entrants into the workplace. As mentioned earlier, the costs of obtaining higher education have been rising much faster than household income, so expansion of financial assistance to encourage young adults to stay on in school would be a worthwhile investment. Early interventions such as Head Start and dropout prevention programs also have shown returns that would warrant further resources. School-to-work programs educate and expose youths to the world of work and help motivate young people in the learning process through real applications of the concepts they are learning in the classroom. Establishing and raising national norms for standards in school, especially for those in the bottom half of the ability distribution, may go a long way to improving the high variance in basic literacy and numeracy skills found in the United States in international comparisons of literacy.

But a change in the skill level of new entrants into the labor market will take a long time to show up in average earnings of workers since most workers have long since left school. So how can education, training, and other strategies improve the skills of current workers (i.e., raise the temperature of the existing water in the tub)? Even if trade has not had a large effect on the overall rise in inequality in the United States, until now workers and businesses in certain sectors (e.g., textiles, apparel, auto, metals) do seem to be affected by trade. In these sectors, enhanced skills training that increases labor productivity would greatly assist workers and employers to compete successfully by choosing high-value-added and more versatile production processes rather than trying to compete just on cost with low-wage labor from other countries. There has been success in this area in the auto sector (e.g., Saturn) with leaner production systems and in steel with more companies pursuing a market niche strategy (e.g., minimills). The change in production strategy in these and other industries has increased the demand for extensive cross-training of workers in combination with enhanced communication and problem-solving skills. A higher-"skilled" worker is not just someone who has advanced specialist knowledge; it also can be someone with a broader range of somewhat less technical training who is more capable of moving from job to job.

Trade and technological change will inevitably result in some workers' being permanently displaced from their jobs. As shown in Figure 7-4, the percentage of people who lose their jobs and are not laid off has become a larger share of the unemployed (relative to the unemployment rate) since the mid-1980s. Many of these job losers will include those who have permanently lost their jobs due to a plant shutdown or position abolished. Data from the BLS Displaced Workers Survey shown in Figure 7-5 indicates that the percentage of all workers who were permanently displaced in the period of 1993 to 1995 remains relatively high when compared to similar points in the business cycle in the 1980s.[21] Job loss due to position/shift abolished, a category that may be linked with corporate restructuring and downsizing, has been increasing in recent years, largely among older, white-collar, and more educated workers. The costs of job loss are large and enduring. For workers who lost their jobs between January 1993 and December 1994, almost a quarter were either still unemployed or out of the labor force by February 1996. For the

Figure 7-4 Job Losers Not on Layoff as a Percentage of Unemployed and the Unemployment Rate, 1967–1996

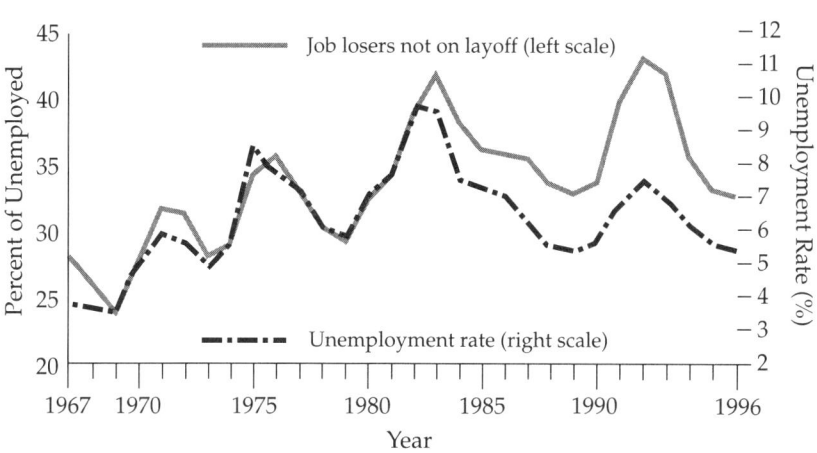

Source: Bureau of Labor Statistics annual data, *Current Population Survey*.

Figure 7-5 Permanent Job Loss: Displacement Rates of Workers, 1981–1995

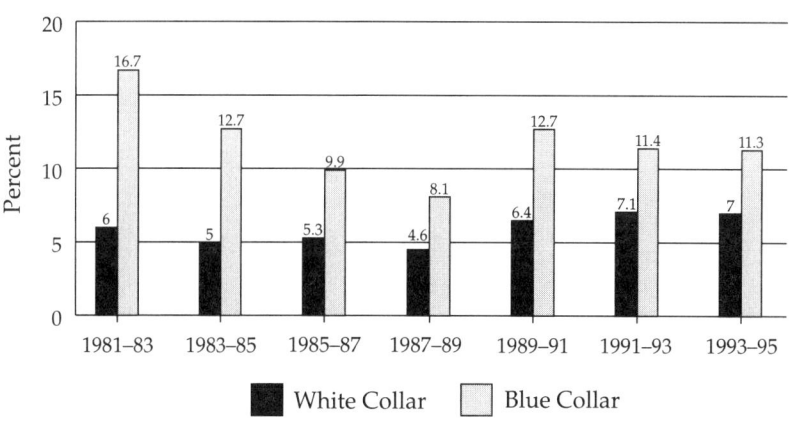

Notes: Data are for workers at least 20 years old. White collar is the sum of managerial and professional specialty and technical, sales, and administrative support occupations. Blue collar is the sum of precision production, craft, and repair occupations.
Source: Bureau of Labor Statistics, *1996 Displaced Workers Survey*, revised.

remaining three-quarters who were successful in finding a new job, slightly more than half were in jobs paying less than their previous employment. The wage costs of job displacement appear to be enduring. Recent work by Ann Huff Stevens finds that even six years after job displacement, earnings and wages remain reduced by approximately 9 percent after adjusting for work experience.[22]

In addition, in spite of achieving the lowest unemployment rate in nearly a quarter of a century, there are signs that some of the problems of long-term and structural unemployment in Europe exist even in the dynamic and flexible U.S. labor market. If trends in the unemployment rate and the percentage of the unemployed who are out of work for 27 or more weeks are compared (see Figure 7–6), it is clear that there has been a widening gap since the recession in the early 1990s that has not narrowed during the current recovery. The percent of the unemployed who are out of work for more than six months is still considerably lower than in many European countries, but it is worrying that this gap has emerged during this recovery.[23]

All of these trends suggest that reform of the nation's unemployment insurance system is needed. Historically the system has been geared to the provision of short-term temporary assistance for workers (typically in manufacturing) who would return to the same employer who laid them off. An increasing proportion of the unemployed are now permanently displaced workers, more of them are white collar, and an increas-

Figure 7–6 The Unemployment Rate and the Long-term Unemployed, 1970–1997

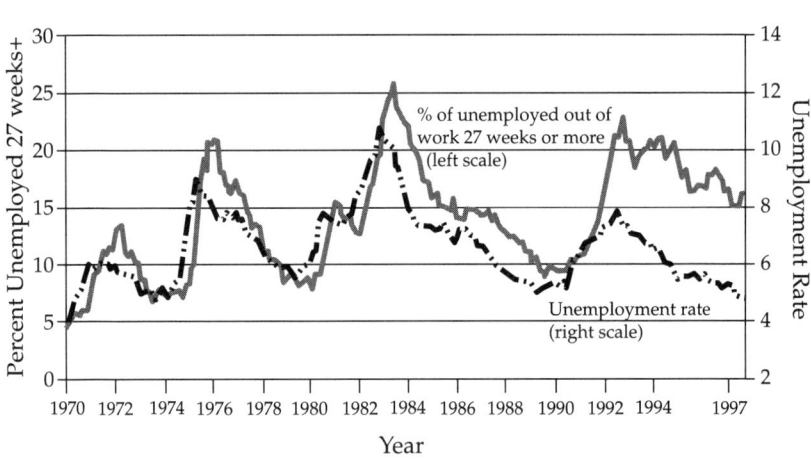

Source: Bureau of Labor Statistics monthly data, *Current Population Survey*.

ing minority are experiencing relatively long spells of unemployment even in economic expansions, which suggests an emerging problem of mismatching in the labor market.

The recently passed Workforce Investment Act of 1998 represents a potentially radical reform of our government-funded training and unemployment insurance systems and should generate more re-employment opportunities for permanently displaced workers and the long-term unemployed. The new unified system will be based on a "One-Stop" concept where employed and unemployed individuals can go to a single neighborhood location and obtain information and counseling about job training, education, and employment services (including job listings, help to file unemployment insurance claims, and evaluation of eligibility for job training and education programs). Key features of this revamped system include enhanced job search assistance plus retraining that is better linked to existing employment opportunities.

What role might government training programs play in reducing inequality? Some have argued that current expenditures for government training should be cut since they do not work or even have a negative impact on the wages and earnings of displaced or disadvantaged youths and adults. However, a recent review of the evidence on the effectiveness of such programs suggests that at least some types of government-funded training and employment programs have been successful for every population examined.[24] Table 7–3 summarizes some of this evidence. Government training programs such as some Job Training Partnership Act (JTPA) programs for disadvantaged adults, residential programs for at-risk youths, the San Jose Center for Employment and Training, some welfare-to-work programs, and job search assistance for displaced workers have shown returns to society of $1.40 or more for each dollar invested. But, as noted by Heckman, while conventional employment and training programs are often cost effective, especially for disadvantaged women, the amounts spent on these programs tend to be quite modest.[25] As a result, they are unlikely to be sufficient to lift most participants out of poverty.

Recent experimental evaluations of the U.S. JTPA program for disadvantaged male youths found negative effects of training on their earnings and no effect on the earnings of disadvantaged female youths. Policymakers assigned great weight to this empirical analysis because of its more "scientific" basis, since it was an experiment using "controls" and "treatments" rather than a statistical analysis that only a handful of economists could understand.[26] It was cited as the justification for cutting funding of training programs for youth by 80 percent. However, as new work by Heckman and Smith argues, even these experimental impact estimates are quite sensitive to the con-

Table 7–3 Examples of U.S. Government Training Programs Outcomes

Target Group	Program	Outcomes
In-School Youth	Summer Youth Employment	This program represents a large share of summer employment in high-poverty, densely populated areas and includes many youth who have never worked before. The Inspector General's report on the 1992 summer program found, "with few exceptions the [Service Delivery Areas] managed successful programs.... Participants were productive, interested, closely supervised, learned new skills they could apply to their schoolwork and took pride in their employment."
Out-of-School Youth	Center for Employment and Training, San Jose, CA	This vocational training and job placement program resulted in 33 percent higher earnings. This highly successful program is being replicated in other U.S. cities.
Out-of-School Youth	Job Corps	This residential program increased earnings by 15 percent, raised employment, reduced serious felony crime, and doubled college enrollment.
Disadvantaged Youth	JTPA	About 50 percent of youth in JTPA Title II-C are still in high school but are at risk of dropping out. A number of dropout prevention programs have cut the dropout rate in half and increased college enrollment. Classroom training for female youth raised earnings 9 percent.
Disadvantaged Adults	JTPA	This cost-effective program of classroom training, job search assistance, and on-the-job training raised earnings of female participants 15 percent higher than a control group, and men's earnings by 10 percent more than a control group.
Dislocated Workers	Various Programs	A recent study examining Pennsylvania's Displaced Worker Employment and Training Program, which pays tuition and supply costs for attending a community college, found earnings gains of 6 to 7 percent per year of education received.

struction of the experiment and as a result are quite fragile.[27] In particular, after adjusting for the fact that "controls" undertook training as well as "treatments" and that many "treatments" dropped out of the experiment before the training began, the returns to classroom training for "treatments" are potentially much more positive than previously reported.

The Workforce Investment Act of 1998 consolidates the well over 100 different types of government training programs into a voucher system to allow unemployed workers to purchase training programs of their choice. While in principal this is a good idea, workers will still need assistance in identifying the right match of training to job opportunities. In addition, as in the past some rogue institutions were created to take advantage of student loan and grant monies, some type of "consumer affairs" watchdog is needed to ensure that workers' training vouchers are not wasted. The nationwide implementation of the One-Stop Centers with responsibility for assisting workers with their training vouchers could go some ways to ensuring that this reform of the training system is a step forward.

But James Heckman argues that the costs of raising the educational levels of those at the bottom of the income distribution to get them back to the relative wages of the late 1970s would be prohibitively expensive.[28] Assuming a 10 percent rate of return to investing in human capital, Heckman calculates that it would cost $426 billion to restore earnings of male high school dropouts and graduates to their 1979 real earnings level. At first blush this sounds like an extraordinarily large sum of money. But to put this sum in some context, the government (federal, state, and local) currently spends well over $500 billion a year on education—$211 billion in higher education alone. New estimates by the American Society of Training and Development (and the author's own calculations) using data from the recent BLS survey of employer training practices suggest that U.S. employers are spending $55 to $80 billion on formal training a year. This figure would more than double if informal training were included. Firms in 1995 spent $534 billion on durable equipment. Certainly $426 billion is a lot of money, but relative to the other investments in physical and human capital currently being made every year in the U.S. economy, it is not so extraordinary.

The estimate of $426 billion includes the forgone earnings of not working and being a student. But why should the government pay all of that amount? Forgone earnings could represent as much as 80 percent of the costs of education. Finally, why spend all this money in one year? As Gary Burtless and others have argued, something like a correctly targeted 10 percent increase in education and training investment

Figure 7–7 Outlay Categories as a Percentage of the Federal Budget, 1970–1997

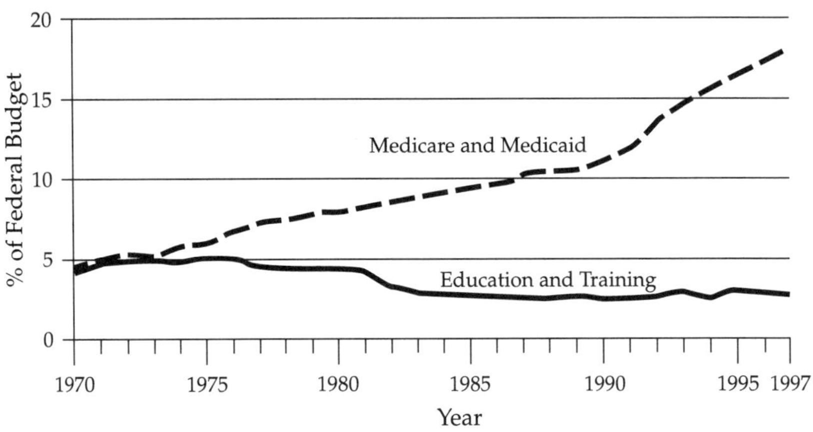

[Figure: Line graph showing Medicare and Medicaid rising from about 4% in 1970 to about 18% in 1997, and Education and Training declining from about 5% to about 2.8%.]

per year for the next ten years could go quite a long way in bringing up the earnings of those with a high school education or less.

But Figure 7–7 highlights a key issue in the federal financing of education and training programs. The percentage of the federal budget spent on education and training has fallen over the past 20 years, from a peak of 5 percent to around 2.8 percent in 1997. This pattern is similar even when federal outlays in education and training are considered as a percent of gross domestic product. This ratio peaked in 1977 at just over 1 percent and has fallen since to just under 0.6 percent in 1997. Per capita spending on education and training has fallen, and real annual spending as a percentage of the population aged 5 to 24 has fallen from more than $4,700 in the 1970s to less than $3,500 in the 1990s. At the same time, expenditures on Medicare and Medicaid have accelerated rapidly, especially in the 1990s. In the current budget atmosphere, it is increasingly difficult to allocate additional resources to education and training.

One solution might be to look to the private sector to help make up the skills gap. But as discussed earlier, employers are understandably reluctant to make general skills investments in workers that might end up being poached away. In addition, small firms may face higher per-employee training costs than larger firms. As a result, a market failure exists in the provision of general training for incumbent workers.

A possible response to this problem is to give employers, especially small and medium-size employers who hire many low-wage workers, additional tax credits for formal training expenditures. Another way is to reward suppliers of training to businesses (e.g., community colleges) with additional resources for setting up training programs for employees with less education. A third strategy is to impose a training tax that would set a standard minimum (say 1.5 to 2.5 percent) that employers would have to spend on training or else they would have to pay a tax into a general training fund. This is similar to the employer training tax in France. It has the benefit of creating a level playing field across employers and potentially solves the poaching problem. But the experience of countries like Australia, which recently adopted and abandoned such as tax, suggests that, in practice, the training levy can be relatively easy to game (i.e., to manipulate without actually providing new training).

Finally, some have argued that companies should be required to capitalize training costs and treat as assets to the firm the skills of its workers.[29] Currently training costs are expensed just like payroll, which means that training investments are not treated as an investment (pay now, benefit over time). By treating training costs like other types of investments, it is argued that enterprises "would have a more transparent justification for pursuing human resource management strategies aimed at protecting those assets from being poached away."[30] While this has some appeal, the concern is that taking away the ability to fully expense training expenses raises the costs of training at the very moment we are trying to find ways of lowering the costs to employers of providing training—especially more general training.

But if a large part of increasing within-group inequality is from the choices firms make to adapt new workplace practices, what can public policy do to encourage greater movement to firms with higher-value-added, more versatile, and higher-paid workers? If firms find it expensive to move to a different equilibrium because they do not know what the productivity gains actually might be, then one simple public policy might be to fund more research on the nature of the practices and their impact on productivity. In particular, more studies are needed on the nonmanufacturing sector, where most low-wage workers are employed. Second, policymakers should recognize the large fixed costs associated with switching production systems. For example, team training means that large numbers of workers simultaneously need to be moved off the production line for training and as a result no output is produced. Perhaps a more favorable tax treatment that helps firms fund these large up-front costs of switching systems, especially for small and medium-size firms, should be considered.

Conclusions

Table 7–4 presents a menu of possible policy options that could be considered to help return the United States to a country in which the "rising

Table 7–4 Remedies for Reducing Wage Inequality

- *Adjustment assistance* to reduce structural and long-term unemployment
    - Trade and technology adjustment assistance
    - Database for job matching linked to education and training opportunities (building on the U.S. Department of Labor National JobsBank)
    - Job placement, child care, portable health insurance
- *Skill upgrading* to increase the relative supply of skilled workers
    - *Education*
        - Head Start
        - Raise the standards in K–12 for the bottom half of the ability distribution
        - Increased expenditures on education
        - School-to-work programs
        - Tuition assistance/Pell grants
    - *Training*
        - Tax credits for formal on-the-job training (OJT) for small and medium-size establishments (SMEs)
        - Resources to help SMEs to band together to purchase training
        - Expansion of Pell grants to include nondegree courses for dislocated workers
        - Tax credits for companies that switch to HPW systems
        - Evaluate and disseminate research on effectiveness of OJT and HPW
        - Consolidate government training programs
- *Income security* to cushion the effects of job displacement and provide a safety net for those who choose work over welfare
    - Index minimum wages
    - Expansion of the Earned Income Tax Credit
    - Reinvent the unemployment insurance system into a re-employment system
    - Develop saturation policies targeted at poor communities to promote investments in housing, businesses, schools, training, and job creation to reduce social and economic isolation

tide raises all the boats," not just the yachts. More generally, in the public policy debate on education and training, we need to move away from a belief that all expenditures on education and training are just part of a fixed pot. Too often the debate on education and training falls down to one of reallocation from one program to another, or weighing the relative merits of funding Head Start or giving displaced workers training vouchers. All these programs are complements. Not recognizing synergies between education and training investments means that we end up not taking advantage of all the possible returns these programs could give individuals, firms, and society as a whole.

The moment for addressing the issue of widening inequality is now. We have an economy that is booming, job growth that is the envy of western Europe, low unemployment, real wages finally beginning to rise, the highest employment rate ever, and shrinking welfare rolls. The costs of raising the temperature of the "bathtub" now are a lot lower than they will be the next time we enter a downturn.

But training and education are not magic elixirs that will solve all of the problems associated with rising wage inequality. Reform of our training and education system for new entrants into the labor market will affect relative wages only after a long lag since new entrants represent such a small proportion of the overall workforce. But to begin to narrow wage inequality permanently, we need to consider investments in incumbent workers. However, funding training for such workers requires substantial financial and institutional support. Even if we are successful in raising the skill levels of new entrants and incumbent workers and reducing the wage gap to its pre-1980s level, the demand for increased training and education will not stop. International trade and technological change will continue to put pressure on our economy to raise the level of human capital investment to maintain and improve living standards and productivity.

Notes

1. See Gary Burtless, *A Future of Lousy Jobs? The Changing Structure of U.S. Wages* (Washington, DC: Brookings Institution, 1990); Richard Freeman, ed., *Working under Different Rules* (New York: Russell Sage, 1994); Frank Levy and Richard Murnane, "U.S. Earnings Levels and Earnings Inequality: A Review of Recent Trends and Proposed Explanations," *Journal of Economic Literature* 30, no. 3 (1992), 1333–81.
2. Stephen Nickell and Brian Bell, "Changes in the Distribution of Wages and Unemployment in OECD Countries," *American Economic Review* 86, no. 2 (May 1996), 302–8.
3. Christoff Buechtemann, Johann Schupp, and D. Soloff, "Roads to Work: School-to-Work Transition Patterns in Germany and the U.S.," *Industrial Relations Journal* 1 (June 1993), 97–111.
4. Nickell and Bell, "Changes in the Distribution of Wages."
5. Thomas Kane and Cecilia Rouse, "Labor Market Returns to Two- and Four-Year College: Is a Credit a Credit and Do Degrees Matter?" *American Economic Review* 85, no. 3 (June 1995) 600–614.
6. Orley Ashenfelter and Alan Krueger, "Estimates of the Economic Returns to Schooling from a Sample of Twins," *American Economic Review* 84, no. 5 (December 1994), 1157–73.

7. Bureau of Labor Statistics, U.S. Department of Labor, "Labor Composition and U.S. Productivity Growth, 1948–90," Bulletin 2426, December 1993.
8. Sandra Black and Lisa Lynch, "Human Capital Investments and Productivity," *American Economic Review* 86, no. 2 (May 1996), 263–67.
9. Lisa M. Lynch, "Private Sector Training and the Earnings of Young Workers," *American Economic Review* 82, no. 1 (March 1992), 299–312.
10. Ann Bartel, "Productivity Gains from the Implementation of Employee Training Programs," *NBER Working Paper* no. 3893; John Bishop, "The Impact of Previous Training on Productivity and Wages," in Lisa Lynch, ed., *Training and the Private Sector: International Comparisons* (Chicago: University of Chicago Press, 1994), 161–200.
11. Thomas Kane, "College Cost, Borrowing Constraints and Timing of College Entry," *Eastern Economic Journal* 22, no. 2 (Spring 1996), 181–94.
12. U.S. General Accounting Office, "Higher Education: Tuition Increasing Faster Than Household Income and Public College Costs," August 1996.
13. Chris Mayer, "Does Location Matter?" Paper prepared for the Federal Reserve Bank of Boston Conference, 1996.
14. John Barron, Dan Black and Mark Loewenstein, "Employer Size: The Implications for Search, Training, Capital Investment, Starting Wages, and Wage Growth," *Journal of Labor Economics* 5, no. 1 (January 1987), 76–89; Bishop, "Impact of Previous Training"; James Brown, "Why Do Wages Increase with Tenure?" *American Economic Review* 79, no. 5 (December 1989), 971–999; Lynch, "Private Sector Training"; Lee Lillard and Hong Tan, "Private Sector Training: Who Gets It and What Are Its Effects?" RAND monograph R-3331-DOL/RC (Santa Monica, CA: RAND Corporation, 1986); Jacob Mincer, "Job Training: Costs, Returns and Wages Profiles," in J. Ritzen and David Stern, eds., *Market Failure in Job Training?* (Berlin and New York: Springer Verlag, 1991).
15. Lynch, ed., *Training and the Private Sector*, 1–24.
16. A. Lindbeck and D. Snower, "Reorganization of Firms and Labor Market Inequality," *American Economic Review* 82, no. 2 (May 1992), 299–312.
17. Simon Burgess, Julia Lane, and David Stevens, "Jobs, Workers and Changes in Earnings Dispersion," *Centre for Economic Policy Research Working Paper* no. 1714, October 1997.
18. See Black and Lynch, "Human Capital Investments"; Mark Huselid, "The Impact of Human Resource Management Practices on Turnover, Productivity, and Corporate Financial Performance," *Academy of Management Journal* 38, no. 3 (June 1995), 635–72; and C. Ichniowski, K. Shaw, and G. Prennushi, "The Effects of Human Resource Management Practices on Productivity," *NBER Working Paper* no. 5333, November 1995.
19. See Casey Ichniowski, Thomas Kochan, David Levine, Craig Olson, and George Strauss, "What Works at Work: A Critical Review," *Industrial Relations* 35, no. 3 (Summer 1996).

20. Ibid.

21. Displaced workers are persons 20 years and older who lost or left jobs because their plant or company closed or moved, there was insufficient work for them to do, or their position or shift was abolished.

22. Ann Huff Stevens, "Persistent Effects of Job Displacement," *Journal of Labor Economics* 15, no. 1 (January 1997), 165–88.

23. Given the low current unemployment rate, workers who are unemployed for more than six months are not eligible to receive any unemployment insurance.

24. U.S. Department of Labor, *What's Working (and What's Not)*, Office of the Chief Economist, January 1995.

25. James J. Heckman, "What Should Our Human Capital Investment Policy Be?" *Jobs and Capital*, Milken Institute for Job and Capital Formation (Spring 1996), 3–10.

26. "Treatments" are those individuals who by random assignment were deemed eligible to participate in a government training program and "controls" are those who by random assignment were designated as ineligible to participate in government training.

27. James J. Heckman and Jeffrey A. Smith, "The Sensitivity of Experimental Impact Estimates: Evidence from the National JTPA Study," *NBER Working Paper* no. 6105, 1997.

28. Heckman, "What Should Our Human Capital Investment Policy Be?"

29. OECD, *The OECD Jobs Study: Facts, Analysis, Strategies* (Paris: OECD Publications, 1994).

30. OECD, *Measuring What People Know: Human Capital Accounting for the Knowledge Economy* (Paris: OECD, 1996).

Index

A
American Society of Training and Development, 209
Apartheid economy, defined, 54
Autor, David H., 75, 79

B
Baldwin, Robert E., 76
Bell, Brian, 193–94
Benefits
 hourly pay and, 26
 low-skilled workers and, 26
 union negotiations for, 26
Berman, Eli, 75, 77, 79, 123–24
Bernard and Jensen, 137, 140–41
Bhagwati, Jagdish, 76
Black, Sandra, 197
Blanchflower, David G., 3, 80, 193, 202–3
Blau, Francine D., 84
Blomstrom, Magnus, 103
Border control, 182
Borjas, Georges J., 78, 81, 87, 123, 162, 165–67
Bound, John, 75, 77, 79, 123–24
Buchanan, Patrick, 1, 102
Buechtemann, Christoff, 194
Bureau of Economic Analysis, 126
Burtless, Gary, 209

C
Cain, Glen C., 76
Camarota, Steven, 3
Card, David, 80

Center for Immigration Studies, 166
Choate, Pat, 102
Clinton, President Bill
 EITC increases and, 57
 fast-track authority for, 2
 health care plan, proposal of, 59
 technology as source of inequality and, 47
College graduates, 47–48
Company-based training
 benefits of, 197–98
 countries using, 194, 200
 education synergies with, 212
 financing for, 210–11
 German system and, 193–94
 impact of, 196
 inequality and, 194
 problems from, 199–200
 reforms, 213
 worker skill improvements and, 204
Council of Economic Advisers, income-contingent student loans, 57
Crime
 causes of, 50–51
 costs of, 50
Current Population Survey, 166

D
Davis, Steve, 123, 141
"Deindustrialization" Hypothesis, 104

DiNardo, John E., 79
Diversity immigration, 153–54
  lottery elimination and, 181
Doms, Mark E., 110, 140
Dunne, Timothy, 123, 132, 139–40
Dynarski, Susan, 71

E
Earned Income Tax Credit (EITC)
  disadvantages of, 179–80
  hardship mitigation with, 56–57
  short-term solution for, 202
Earnings distributions
  changes with, 24–25
  gender in, 23
  skilled workers and, 23–24
  statistics for, 22–23
Earnings falls
  foreign countries and, 29–30
  job market history with, 28
  "new inequality" and, 27–28
  U.S. changes in, 29
  wage growth and, 28
Education
  attainment versus productivity with, 197
  benefits of, 197–98
  company-based synergies with, 212
  employer-provided training problems and, 199–200
  German system for, 193–94
  immigrant earnings and, 157
  immigrant labor market and, 156–57
  poverty concentration and, 199
  reforms in, 213
  tuition costs for, 198–99
  worker skill improvements from, 204
  See also Human capital investment policies

Emergency Committee for American Trade (ECAT)
  comparison characteristics in, 99–100
  research findings from, 98–99
Employment
  between industries, 122
  U.S. job growth and, 40–41
  within manufacturing plants, 121
  See also Trade and technology
Employment Outlook, 38
Employment stability, 34
Employment-based immigration, 153
  changes for, 180–81
Encarnation, Dennis, 103
European monetary unit (EMU), 2
European Union, 102
Exporting, research findings, 133

F
Factor price equalization, 165
Factor-proportions approach, 165
Family incomes
  changes in, 34–36
Family structure and wage inequality, 51
Family-based immigration, 152–53
  restructuring of, 181
Fast-track authority, 2
Federal Reserve Bank, 29
Feenstra, Robert C., 87, 106
Filer, Randall K., 165
Foreign direct investment (FDI), 11
Foreign investment
  adjustment costs from, 112
  debates about, 96–107
  domestic job structures and, 107–11

Foreign investment (*continued*)
  globalization's social contract and, 111–13
  income distribution and, 95
  policy designs for, 112
  positive impacts from, 111–12
  social contract issues and, 112–13
  taxation and trade and, 112
Foreign trade
  employment changes from, 121–22
  wage dispersion and, 120
Fortin, Nicole, 84
Freeman, Richard B., 3, 78, 81, 84, 111, 123, 162, 166–67
Friedman, Milton, 58

G
General Accounting Office (GAO), 17
General Agreement on Tariffs and Trade (GATT), 88
Germany
  educational system in, 193–94
  firm-based training in, 200
Glickman, Norman J., 108, 111
Globalization
  commercial disputes arising from, 2
  financial flows and, 3
  income distribution and, 1
  support for, 2–3
  U.S. trade deficit and, 3–4
Goldsmith, James, 45
Government training programs
  federal budget and, 210
  funding for, 207–9
Graham, Edward, 109–10
  deindustrialization hypothesis and, 104
  import changes and, 105

"Gravity model," 103–4
Great sucking sound. *See* Outward investments
Griliches, Zvi, 75, 77, 79, 123–24
Gross domestic product (GDP), 5, 35–36
Gruber, Jonathan, 71

H
Haltiwanger, John, 77, 123, 128, 139, 141
Hanson, Gordon, 87, 106
Hardship mitigation
  benefits from, 57
  as inequality strategy, 56
Head Start, 203
  wage inequality reducing, 212
Health insurance, 26–27
Heckman, James, 209
High performance work systems, inequality and, 202, 206
Homelessness
  characteristics of, 51
  national response to, 54
Horst, Thomas
  exports versus foreign direct investment and, 102
  import levels and, 105
  research approaches of, 100
  "threshold effect" and, 100–1
Hours of work
  consequences of, 44
  United States versus other countries in, 43
Human capital investment policies
  education strategies and, 204
  federal budget training expenditures and, 210
  financing company-based training with, 210–11
  government training outcomes and, 208

government-funded training and, 207–9
skill development and, 203–4
solutions for, 202–3
structural unemployment and, 206
technological changes and, 204–6
training cost investments for, 211
unemployment insurance reforms in, 206–7
Humanitarian immigration, 153

I
Illegal immigration
 quantity of, 149
 reduction of, 181–82
Illegal Immigration Reform and Immigrant Responsibility Act (1996), impact of, 152
Immigration, 168–76
 capital stocks effects from, 155
 earnings of, 157
 economic effects of, 160
 foreign countries and, 82
 high school dropouts and, 45
 impact of, 45–46
 income inequity and, 80–81
 labor market issues and, 154–61
 legal quantity of, 149
 literature on, 161–66
 model for, 161–64
 policy recommendations for, 176–84
 socioeconomic characteristics of, 159
 U.S. policy on, 150–54
 workforce size from, 158–60
Immigration Act (1990), impact of, 152, 154
Immigration literature problems
 migration patterns and, 164–65
 occupation versus city comparisons in, 166
Immigration literature review
 focus of, 161
 income inequality and, 163
 labor supply and, 162–63
 minorities wages and, 163–64
Immigration and Nationality Act (1965), 151–52
Immigration and Naturalization Service (INS), 149
Immigration non-policy actions, 179–80
Immigration policy, 1
 border controlling and, 182
 disadvantages of, 183–84
 family immigration restructuring and, 181
 immigrants numbers with, 150–52
 legislation effects from, 151–52
 recommendations for, 176–84
 selection criteria for, 180
 visa categories and, 152–54
Immigration Reform and Control Act (1986), 152–54
Immigration research findings
 approach advantages in, 176
 high-skilled immigrants impacts in, 173–74
 illegal alien calculating in, 166
 immigrant and wage relationships in, 171
 individual-level variables in, 167
 low-skilled occupations analysis in, 172–73
Imports, 121
Income inequality
 ameliorating policies for, 22

Income inequality (*continued*)
  causes of, 45–48, 74–75
  conclusions of, 84
  family incomes and, 34–36
  goals of, 67–68
  growth of, 37–40
  historical levels, 36
  impact of, 48–54
  political consensus for, 89
  public policy responses to, 88–90
  real earnings falling, 27–30
  reconciling, 85–86
  social consequences of, 21–22
  solutions for, 60–61
  strategies for, 54–60
  United States and, 21, 36–45
  women and, 41–43
  See also United States inequality
Inequality problems
  college educated and, 201
  company-provided training problems and, 199–200
  educational benefits for, 197–98
  foreign countries and, 192–94
  high-performance work systems and, 202
  training benefits and, 196–98
  U.S. skilled worker supply and, 195
Inequality remedies, 202–13
Inequality world wide, 37–40
International trade
  Stolper-Samuelson testing and, 76–77
  trade flows analysis and, 77–78
  unskilled labor and, 75–76
  See also Trade

J
Jaeger, David A., 165
Jail populations, 51

Jensen, J. Bradford, 3, 102, 110, 133, 137, 140–41
Job Training Partnership Act (JTPA), 19, 51, 207–9
  jail populations and, 51
Jobs Corps, 51

K
Kahn, Lawrence M., 84
Katz, Lawrence, 75, 78–81, 123, 162, 166–67
Kletzer, L. G., 77
Kochan, Thomas, 202
Kposowa, Augustine J., 163
Krikorian, Mark, 3
Krueger, Alan B., 75–76, 79
Krugman, Paul R., 77, 109
Kuznets, Simon, 164

L
Labor economists, versus trade economists, 85–86
Labor market functions, 54–55
Lawrence, Robert Z., 75–76, 105–6, 124
Leamer, Edward E., 76
Lemieux, Thomas, 84
Less skilled workers
  hours worked and, 30–31
  opportunities for, 43
  outward investment and, 105–7
  versus immigration, 45–46
  versus skilled workers wages, 68–73
  versus women's employment, 41–43
Levernier, William, 163
Levine, David, 202
Lindbeck, A., 201
Lipsey, Robert, 102–3, 110
Loveman, G., 80

Low-paid workers
  benefits for, 26
  earnings of, 30
Low-skilled immigration, reduction disadvantages, 183–84
Lynch, Lisa, 3, 197, 200

M
Machin, Steve, 79
Macroeconomic expansion, 55
Manufacturing technology measuring
  capital types for, 126
  difficulty in, 125
  organizational capitalism and, 127
Manufacturing trade effects
  "between and within" components and, 124–25
  hypothesis investigation and, 123
Manufacturing wage dispersion
  conclusions for, 119–20, 141–44
  cross-sectional evidence of, 134–40
  framework for, 120–22
  hypotheses for, 118
  methodologies of, 122–27
  microdata for, 127–31
Mayer, Chris, 199
Men
  earnings falling of, 28–29
  hourly earnings of, 39
  versus women's salaries, 47
  women's employment and, 41–43
Microdata
  assumptions of, 127
  plant differences in, 128–30
  shortcomings of, 127–28
Minimum wages
  foreign countries and, 84
  real value of, 82–84
Mobility
  inequality and, 31, 33
  lifetime income and, 33
  probability estimating, 31–32
  United States versus other countries and, 44–45
Moran, Theodore, 3
Murphy, Kevin, 75, 123
Musick, Nathan, 133

N
Nickell, Stephen, 193–94
North American Free Trade Agreement (NAFTA), 98

O
Olson, Craig, 202
Organization for Economic Cooperation and Development (OECD), 69
  hours of work and, 43
  unemployment rates and, 40
  wage deflation and increases for, 29
Outward investments
  absence of, 106–7
  benefits of, 97
  central bank monetary authorities and, 98
  comparison elements of, 100
  defined, 95
  ECAT research, 98–100
  "gravity model" and, 103–4
  home-country labor and, 101–2
  Horst and, 100–1
  jobs versus product exporting, 96–97
  less skilled worker impacts and, 105
  pro-labor proponents and, 102
  stay-at-home viability, 102

Outward investments (*continued*)
  technological changes, 105–6
  unskilled worker changes, 105
  versus exports, 102–3

P
Partridge, Mark D., 163
Pearce, R. D., 103
Perot, Ross, 45, 102
Pischke, Jorn-Steffen, 79
Productivity
  research on, 211
  versus educational attainment, 197

R
Ramey, Valerie A., 87
Real earnings
  growth of, 70–71
  versus unemployment rates, 70
Refugee Act (1980), 152
Revenga, Ana, 124
Rickman, Dan S., 163
Roberts, Mark, 140

S
Sachs, Jeffrey, 76, 124
Schmitz, James, 132
Schuh, Scott, 77
Schupp, Johann, 194
Sclof, D., 194
Shatz, Howard, 76, 124
Siphoning-off-the-Good-job hypothesis
  aggregate job loss studies and, 108–9
  compensation differences and, 109–10
  competitiveness versus operational streamlining, 108
  defined, 95
  focus of, 107–8
  foreign investor nationality and, 110
  imperfect competition and, 109
  national security and, 111
  perfect competition conditions of, 108–9
  research conclusions, 110–11
  union activity and, 111
Skill investments
  higher education subsidies, 57
  job training programs, 58
Skilled workers
  earnings distributions, 23–24
  supply of, 195
  technology and, 139–40
  versus less skilled worker wages, 68–73
  wages and, 121
Slaughter, Matthew J., 3, 75–76, 87, 105–6, 124, 193, 202–3
Snower, D., 201
Social contract, foreign investment and, 112–13
Social Science Quarterly, 149
Social Security system, 9, 49
Standard Industrial Classification (SIC), 13
Stobaugh, Robert, 106
Stolper-Samuelson theorem
  international trade and, 75–76
  testing of, 76–77
Strauss, George, 202
Structural wage programs
  employment subsidies and, 59
  goal of, 58
  health insurance mandates and, 59
  minimum wage impacts and, 58–59
Swedenborg, Birgitta, 103

T

Technological changes
  direct evidence of, 79
  educated worker and, 79–80
  problems of, 79
  productivity growth and, 121
  skilled worker wages and, 121
Technology
  employment patterns and, 132–33
  versus trade, 133, 141
  wage inequality and, 47
  wage structure changes and, 134–39
Technology cross-sectional evidences
  exporting and, 133
  production based changes, 140
  skilled worker changes, 139–40
  sources of, 131–32
"Threshold effect"
  rationale for, 101
  results of, 100
Time-series approach, 165
Tinbergen, Jan, 47
Topel, Robert H., 163
Total factor productivity (TFP), technology measuring, 125
Trade
  deficit, 3
  impact of, 45
  international influences and, 75–78
  restrictions toward, 59–60
  See also International trade
Trade economists, versus labor economists, 85–86
Trade restrictions
  benefits of, 59
  cost of, 59–60
Trade role, 141

Training programs
  benefits of, 197–98
  See also Company-based training; Government training
Troske, Kenneth R., 3, 102, 123, 139–40

U

Unemployment
  country comparisons in, 70
  insurance system reforms for, 206–7
  macroeconomic expansion and, 55
  rates of, 206
Unemployment insurance, system reforms, 206–7
Unions
  benefits negotiations by, 26
  decline of, 82
  development problems of, 55–56
  foreign countries and, 82–83
  independent sector organizations and, 56
  inequality reductions by, 46
  as inequality strategy, 55
  minimum wages impact and, 82–84
  wage inequality and, 46, 82
United States
  democracy basis for, 53
  earnings changes in, 29
  inequality and, 37–40
  real earnings attitudes and, 27
  trade deficit and, 3
  versus employment, 40–41
  versus European mobility, 44–45
  women employment in, 41–43
  work hours in, 43–44

United States Commission on Immigration Reform, policy suggestions, 180–81
United States labor market
　changes in, 68–73
　job growth and, 40–41
　versus other countries, 69–70
Unskilled workers
　imports and, 121
　outward investment and, 107

V

Visa
　categories for, 152–54
　economic benefits from, 154
　employment-based immigration and, 153
　ethnic basis for, 151–52
　illegal aliens amnesty and, 154
Vredeling, Hans, 102

W

Wage inequality
　labor market changes and, 68–73
　principal conclusions for, 4–19
　remedies for, 18–19, 212
　within-group wages and, 72
Wage structure changes
　nonproduction change reasons for, 137–39
　nonproduction labor calculating and, 135–36
　nonproduction labor changes and, 136–37
　skill-intensive plants and, 134–35
　within-plant changes and, 139
　worker wage falling and, 134
Weiss, Herle Yahr, 102–3
Welch, Finis, 123
Williamson, Jeffrey, 5
Women
　benefits changes for, 26–27
　earnings distributions and, 23
　earnings shifting and, 24–25
　employment stability for, 34
　family income and, 35–36
　low-paid workers and, 30
　trade impact and, 45
　versus less skilled workers, 41–43
　versus men's salaries, 47
　wage increases in, 42–43
　wage inequality and, 46–47, 72
Woodward, Douglas P., 108, 111
Worker supply changes
　immigration and, 80–82
　impact of, 80
Workforce Investment Act (1998), 207, 209

About the Authors

DAVID G. BLANCHFLOWER is a labor economist and Chair of the Department of Economics at Dartmouth College. He is a research associate at the National Bureau of Economic Research (NBER) in the United States, the Center for Economic Performance (CEP) in the United Kingdom, and the Canadian International Labor Network (CILN).

STEVEN A. CAMAROTA is a resident scholar at the Center for Immigration Studies in Washington, D.C. He holds a master's degree in political science from the University of Pennsylvania and a Ph.D. in Policy Analysis from the University of Virginia. Dr. Camarota has testified before Congress on the effect of low-skilled immigration on American workers. His articles on the impact of immigration on the labor market have appeared in both academic publications and the popular press, including *Social Science Quarterly,* the *Washington Post,* the *Chicago Tribune,* and *Public Interest.*

ALBERT FISHLOW was the Paul A. Volcker Senior Fellow for International Economics at the Council on Foreign Relations until June 1999. He is now a Senior Economist at Violy, Byorum & Partners Holdings LLC, and a Visiting Professor at the Yale School of Management. He had been professor of economics at the University of California at Berkeley until June 1994, where he was also the first dean of International and Area Studies from January 1990 until July 1993. He joined the Berkeley faculty in 1961 upon completion of Ph.D. studies at Harvard. From 1978 to 1983 he was professor of economics and director of the Center for International and Area Studies at Yale University. He returned to Berkeley as professor in 1983, and became chair of the department in 1985. He served as deputy assistant secretary of state for Inter-American Affairs from 1975 to 1976 and has been a member of many public task forces related to Latin American affairs. He is on the board of the Social Science Research Council and serves as chair of its executive committee.

His research has addressed issues in economic history, Brazilian and Latin American development strategy, economic relations between industrialized and developing countries, and the problem of foreign debt. Among his recent publications are "Future Sustainable Latin American Growth: A Need for Savings," *Review of Black Political Economy* (Summer 1996); "Is the *Real* Plan for Real?" in Susan Kaufman Purcell et al., *Brazil under Cardoso* (Boulder, 1997); and "Contending with Capital Flows: What Is Different about the 1990s?" with Barry Eichengreen, in Miles Kahler, ed., *Capital Flows and Financial Crises* (Ithaca, 1998).

RICHARD B. FREEMAN holds the Ascherman chair of Economics at Harvard University. He is currently serving as faculty co-chair of the Harvard University Trade Union Program and is program director of the National Bureau of Economic Research's Program in Labor Studies. He is also co-director of the Centre for Economic Performance at the London School of Economics and visiting professor at the London School of Economics.

He is a member of the American Academy of Arts and Sciences. He has served on five panels of the United States National Academy of Science: High Risk Youth; Post Secondary Education and Training in the Workplace; Employment and Technical Change; Demographic and Economic Impacts of Immigration; and National Needs for Biomedical and Behavioral Sciences. His research has focused on youth labor markets, economic discrimination, social mobility, income distribution, and equity in the marketplace. Some of his recent books include *What Workers Want?* with Joel Rogers (New York, 1999); *The Welfare State in Transition: Reforming the Swedish Model*, with Robert Topel and Birgitta Swedenborg (Chicago, 1997); *Differences and Changes in Wage Structure*, edited with Lawrence F. Katz (Chicago, 1995); and *Working under Different Rules*, edited, (New York, 1994).

J. BRADFORD JENSEN is a senior research scientist at the H. John Heinz III School of Public Policy and Management at Carnegie Mellon University and is the executive director of the Carnegie Mellon Census Research Data Center.

His recent research focuses on issues of international trade, competitiveness and productivity growth, and wage inequality. He has publications in academic journals, including the *Journal of International Economics*, the *Journal of Economic Behavior and Organization*, and the *Brookings Paper on Economic Activity: Microeconomics*. His research has been cited in popular press publications including the *Wall Street Journal, Fortune*, and *Business Week*.

Prior to joining the Heinz School, he was an economist at the Center for Economic Studies at the U.S. Bureau of the Census. He received his Ph.D. in Economics from Stanford University. Prior to attending Stanford, he was a consultant with Arthur Andersen & Co. He received his B.A. in Mathematics and Economics from Kalamazoo College.

MARK KRIKORIAN is executive director of the Center for Immigration Studies in Washington, D.C. He frequently testifies before Congress and has published articles in the *New York Times,* the *Washington Post,* the *Chicago Tribune,* the *Christian Science Monitor, Commentary, National Review,* and elsewhere, and has appeared on the *NewsHour with Jim Lehrer,* CNN, C-SPAN, Fox News Network, MSNBC, National Public Radio, and many other television and radio programs. He holds a master's degree from the Fletcher School of Law and Diplomacy, Tufts University, and a bachelor's degree from Georgetown University. Before joining the center in February 1995, he was an editor at the *Winchester* (Va.) *Star* as well as editor of a publication on marketing via electronic media.

LISA M. LYNCH is the William L. Clayton Professor of International Economic Affairs at the Fletcher School of Law and Diplomacy, Tufts University. She is a coeditor of the *Journal of Labor Economics,* a research associate at the National Bureau of Economic Research, and she was the chief economist at the U.S. Department of Labor from 1995 to 1997. She graduated with honors from Wellesley College (1983) and received a Master of Science (1979) and Ph.D. in Economics (1983) from the London School of Economics. She has also taught at the University of Bristol, Ohio State University, and the Sloan School of Management at MIT. She has published over 50 articles and books on youth labor markets, international comparisons of private sector training, and the impact of human resource management practices on productivity and compensation.

THEODORE H. MORAN holds the Karl F. Landegger Chair in the School of Foreign Service, Georgetown University, where he teaches and conducts research at the intersection of international economics, business, foreign affairs, and public policy. Dr. Moran is founder of the Landegger Program in International Business Diplomacy, and serves simultaneously as director of the Pew Economic Freedom Fellows Program and the Georgetown Leadership Seminar. His most recent books include *Foreign Investment and Development* (Institute for International Economics, 1998); and *Managing International Political Risk: New Tools, Strategies, and Techniques* (Blackwells, under the auspices of the World Bank Group, 1998). From 1993 to 1994, he served as senior adviser for economics on the Policy Planning Staff of the Department of State, where he had responsibility for trade, finance, technology, energy, and environmental issues. He is consultant to the World Bank Group, the United Nations, various governments in Asia and Latin America, and the international business and financial communities.

KAREN PARKER directs the currency research group at the Chase Manhattan Bank. An economist by training, she works closely with the foreign exchange group, devising currency risk management strategies for external and internal clients. Before joining Chase in 1997, she was on the staff of the International Monetary Fund, where she was the principal economist assigned to India. The focus of her research was monetary policy and financial sector reform; she also developed a macroeconomic model to assess the consequences of alternative fiscal strategies.

In 1995 Ms. Parker coauthored the Whittome report, a critical assessment of IMF surveillance of Mexico in the period leading up to the 1994 peso crisis. That report formed the basis for a number of initiatives endorsed by the fund's Interim Committee to improve program design and monitoring. From 1995 to 1997 Parker took a leave of absence from the fund to teach at the Woodrow Wilson School of Public and International Affairs at Princeton. She also served as a fellow at the Council on Foreign Relations, where she researched the sequencing of economic policy reform in emerging markets. While at the council, Parker directed a study group on globalization and the distribution of wages in the United States, chaired by John Lipsky, Chase's chief economist.

Parker earned a doctoral degree from Stanford University, where she wrote her dissertation on the role of expectations in the Mexican foreign exchange market. She lived in Mexico as a Fulbright scholar in 1989–90 while carrying out research for her dissertation in conjunction with economists at the Bank of Mexico. Parker graduated summa cum laude from Princeton University, and has traveled extensively abroad in the course of her work.

MATTHEW J. SLAUGHTER is an assistant professor of economics at Dartmouth College, a faculty research fellow at the National Bureau of Economic Research, and a visiting fellow at the Institute for International Economics. He has also served as a visiting scholar at the International Monetary Fund and the Federal Reserve Bank of Minneapolis, and as a consultant to the World Bank. He received his Ph.D. from the Massachusetts Institute of Technology in 1994.

KENNETH R. TROSKE is currently an assistant professor of economics at the University of Missouri-Columbia. He received his Ph.D. from the University of Chicago in 1992. His primary field is labor economics. Prior to moving to the University of Missouri, he spent seven years as a research economist at the U.S. Census Bureau, where he created the Worker-Establishment Characteristics Database, which is the largest employer-employee matched data set available containing information on U.S. workers and their employers. He has used these data to examine issues such as the effect of technology on worker wages and wage dispersion, and labor market discrimination.

Troske's publications include "Workers, Wages and Technology," *Quarterly Journal of Economics,* 1997 (with Mark Doms and Timothy Dunne); "Inter-Firm Racial Segregation," *Journal of Labor Economics,* 1998 (with William J. Carrington); "Sex Segregation in U.S. Manufacturing," *Industrial and Labor Relations Review,* 1998 (with William J. Carrington); "Further Evidence on the Employer Size-Wage Premium from Worker-Establishment Matched Data," *Review of Economics and Statistics,* 1999; and "Worker Wages, Characteristics and Productivity: Evidence from Employer-Employee Match Data," *Journal of Labor Economics,* 1999 (with Judith Hellerstein and David Neumark).